To both my families

and

the staff and students of Kiraeni

# KING ALFRED'S COLLEGE
# WINCHESTER
Library: 01962 827306

To be returned on or before the day
marked below, subject to recall

# WRITING "INDEPENDENT" HISTORY

# WRITING "INDEPENDENT" HISTORY

African Historiography,
1960–1980

**Caroline Neale**

CONTRIBUTIONS IN AFRO-AMERICAN AND
AFRICAN STUDIES, NUMBER 85

**Greenwood Press**
WESTPORT, CONNECTICUT · LONDON, ENGLAND

**Copyright Acknowledgments**

Permission to reprint portions of the following works is gratefully acknowledged.

Material from *Beware, Soul Brother; Poems* by Chinua Achebe. Copyright © 1971, published by Heinemann Educational Books Ltd. Permission is for world excluding Nigeria.

Material from *An Introduction to the History of West Africa* by John Fage. Copyright © 1957, and copyright © 1969, published by Cambridge University Press.

Extracted from RETURN TO MY NATIVE LAND, trans; A. Berger & Bostock (Harmondsdworth, Penguin Books Ltd., 1969). Originally published in CAHIER D'UN RETOUR AU PAYS NATAL (definitive edition, Présence Africaine, Paris, 1956).

**Library of Congress Cataloging in Publication Data**

Neale, Caroline.
  Writing "independent" history.

  (Contributions in Afro-American and African studies, ISSN 0069-9624 ; no. 85)
  Bibliography: p.
  Includes index.
  1. Africa—Historiography.  I. Title.  II. Series.
DT19.N43   1985        960'.072        84-15756
ISBN 0-313-24652-1 (lib. bdg.)

Library of Congress Catalog Card Number: 84-15756
ISBN: 0-313-24652-1
ISSN: 0069-9624

First published in 1985

Greenwood Press
A division of Congressional Information Service, Inc.
88 Post Road West
Westport, Connecticut 06881

Printed in the United States of America

10 9 8 7 6 5 4 3 2 1

# CONTENTS

# ACKNOWLEDGMENTS

I should like to thank Martin Chanock for every kind of help; Christopher Wrigley for the unfailing tact and judgement, not easy to combine, with which he supervised the thesis on which this book is based; David Henige, for his generous encouragement and good advice; Richard Stuart, David Dorward, Margaret Killingray, and Lorne Larson, for help with sources; for editorial comment and help in producing the manuscript, Barbara Neale, Walter Neale, Jonathan Neale, Irene Savage, and Hilary Kahn; and Richard Brown and Anne Caley.

# WRITING
# "INDEPENDENT"
# HISTORY

# 1

# INTRODUCTION

> "Political independence could only have meaning if it was accompanied by *historical independence.*"
>
> B. Ogot, "Towards a History of Kenya",
> *Kenya Historical Review*, vol. 4 (1976), p. 1.

In the decade following the political decolonisation of Africa, the mainspring of new historical writing was a desire to achieve intellectual decolonisation through a revision of African history. The coming of independence was no ordinary change of government; it was a change in the relationship of black nations to white nations, and of black to white in Africa. It called for a new representation of the relationship that had obtained up to that point. There had been a political statement that black and white were to treat each other as equals; now there was needed a cultural demonstration that such a thing was possible. The new version produced in the sixties did provide a basis for pride in past achievements, but the idea that it was, thereby, helping Africans to throw off the domination of European ideas was illusory. "Achievements" were still defined in Western terms, in the context of an evolution from more primitive political forms toward the modern nation-state, which was seen as the culmination of mankind's progress to date. The creation of African self-respect was felt to rest upon repeated demonstrations that Africans, too, had participated in and contributed to this development. Where colonial writing had tried to show that Africans stood outside of the "mainstream" of progress, post-independence writing sought to portray them as active within it; the mainstream, however, is a Western idea, and one which scarcely anyone thought to question.[1] The priority was "to get the black man back into the wonderful 'birth of civilisation' story . . . to prove that [he] lived not only in pre-literate tribal societies, but was right there in all the major events of 'world history' ".[2] The result was a decade of history which focused on the triumph of African nationalism, and on those aspects of the African past which were seen as contributing to its evolution.

The purpose of this study is to raise a number of historiographical questions about the "liberation" of a history. I want to compare the version of African history produced in the sixties with the colonial version, to look at the assumptions and purposes, the ideas about progress, worth, pride, and shame which they entailed, and whether they differed essentially. I look at the ways in which the assumptions and purposes of the new version circumscribed the production of history, and at how the writing of African history changed in the subsequent decade when disillusionment with the performance of African national governments brought about a change of purpose. The new history sought to turn colonial history on its head, and, to simplify somewhat, that is what it did. It was the older version upside down, with many of its faults intact. The contemptuous treatment of Africans was gone, of course, but the ethnocentric views of what history is about lived on in the design of "independent" history, nor have they disappeared with the recent rejection of nationalist history by the "political economy" school.

By way of introduction, then, let us highlight the Western ideas about the nature of history, whose dominance will be traced throughout this study.

To say that the assumptions of Western historians are ethnocentric is not to accuse them of some sort of academic crime. Ethnocentrism is not a position which is taken up at university; it is, rather, an element of culture which is given up rarely, with difficulty, and incompletely. The form it takes in the writing of African history by whites and also, to some extent, by Africans educated in the European tradition,[3] is a combination, therefore, of attitudes learned in childhood which have nothing to do with the discipline of history; of a particular orientation to the history of the world which *is* taught in schools and universities; and of the unique development of African history as a reaction to a body of white racist propaganda.

As children we Europeans and Americans learn that our lives are better than those of our grandparents, and that it has always been so; progress has been steady from generation to generation. We look back upon the rough lives of peasants or pioneers and are glad to forego the romance we associate with them. The further back we go in time, the more comical, painful, disgusting, and superstitious do people's lives appear, until we reach that cartoon character, Stone Age man. There is the counter-theme of "old-fashioned virtues", but the force of the idea of progress is stronger: with the passage of time there are always, through the efforts of individuals, gains for everybody in material wellbeing, in cultural stimulation, in behavioural choice and freedom, in political power, sophistication, and participation, in creativity, in religious enlightenment, personal and social relations, and even in sensitivity. All these things come to mind when we think of "progress" and most of them when we think of "civilisation". A related idea is that each of us has more all-around competence than our ancestors, as if everyone who swallowed a medicine were a doctor, or everyone who pressed a light switch could wire a house. The technology to which we have access, in industrialised society, is thought of as a skill which each of us possesses, so that, contrasting myself, the purchaser of a stainless steel carving knife, with a primitive forger of unwieldy iron blades, I think I am more competent than he at solving the problem of cutting up my chicken.

This picture of progress which fills us with confidence as children is based on dramatic contrast with a stereotype; the savages from whom we all progressed live almost like animals, with the most primitive of tools and of cultural ideas, and with virtually no sense of past or future, so that they do not ask themselves that most natural of questions for people in a literate society with its ongoing record of achievement: what can we contribute to the great March of Mankind? For progress is seen as a kind of fund-raising effort, to which each person, or each culture, gives what it can and gives it consciously, with a vision of what is to be built in future.

Primitives who do no more than feed themselves, we learn as children, existed in our homelands a very long time ago, and are still to be found in the deserts, the jungles, and the very high places of the world. These people would prefer to live in a society like ours if they could, assuming that irrational traditionalism did not blind them to its advantages, and they would be right to prefer it; furthermore, they could gain such a life by borrowing materially, culturally, intellectually, and sometimes morally from us willing donors, as our ancestors borrowed from Greece, Rome, China, and Arabia. They would then cease to exist as living fossils and join the twentieth century, the model for which, in most people's minds, is not the Kalahari nor Calcutta, but New York, excluding Harlem. This is, of course, a model, and not the reality. New York City contains Harlem as well as Fifth Avenue, and the world contains Calcutta as well as New York. The fact that we accept the model as a description of reality, and are prepared to regard Calcutta as an imperfect approximation to New York, is connected with the identification, in our intellectual system, of the idea of progress in history with the idea of evolution in biology.

The idea of physical evolution organises all the forms of life which exist, fully functioning, at present, as well as those which have died out, into a hierarchy stretching simultaneously from low to high and from past to future. Man is the highest form of life, and his evolution is traced in terms of functional improvements, as well as over time. Other primates are at once lower and earlier forms of life. Organisms which have persisted over millions of years, although better versions of the same thing have continued to develop, are thought of as living fossils, creatures whose way of life has been made obsolete by conditions in most places but which survive in isolated pockets where their environment has not changed to hasten their destruction. Similarly, many human ways of living are thought of as earlier stages on the way to New York, survivals of a lower form of culture whose days are numbered, and rightly so, for although they might have many virtues, they are not the best there is. In fact, changes in culture *do* often come about in a way comparable to the mechanism of physical evolution; something new is tried, preferred, and adopted, and replaces the old way altogether. But if we accept the analogy with evolution, five assumptions are implied:

1. That whatever is new is likely to be an improvement.
2. That any widespread change is for the better.
3. That a development which benefits some will cause increased suffering to others, that this is natural and "can't be helped".

4. That older ways are likely to die out.

5. That the process is inevitable, and that those who are left behind lack something which, to belong fully to the contemporary form of their kind, they ought to have.

For Western man, imbued with evolutionary ideas in the area of science, such a view of history is natural. Many of us do not even know that other views are possible.

To call an historian an evolutionist, therefore, because of his assumptions about the nature of progress, or a liberal, because of his global optimism regarding political process and advance, is little more than to say that he partakes of his culture. But it is not only in popular culture that historical evolutionism is taken for granted. In academic history, too, we find the distinction between societies whose achievements qualify them as participants in history, belonging to the time in which they live rather than some other era, and those which fail the test. We hear of people "living in the Stone Age", suddenly "catapulted into the twentieth century". We talk of people being "ahead of" or "behind" "their time", "still" or "not yet" doing this or that. The bumptious self-congratulation with which this evolutionism used to be expressed has become muted, to be sure, in the last few decades. Early in this century, the writing of history was very much bound up with demonstrating the development of superior *national* cultures, German, British, or whatever. While the two World Wars cast doubt on the wholesomeness of nationalistic fervour, which declined in historical writing as the century wore on, a general belief in progress was not snuffed out. In 1961, the British historian E. H. Carr put it forward as the only meaningful reason to study history:

History properly so-called can be written only by those who find and accept a sense of direction in history itself. The belief that we have come from somewhere is closely linked with the belief that we are going somewhere. A society which has lost belief in its capacity to progress in the future will quickly cease to concern itself with its progress in the past.[4]

Now let us see how this idea of progress was carried over into African history.

For historians writing in the colonial period, civilisation, with its seeds in the Near East and its springtime growth in the Mediterranean, had taken root in Western Europe and flourished there. Civilisation meant the domestication of agriculture and husbandry, urbanisation, the growth of trade and production, the creation of a leisured class, the accumulation of wealth and its sponsorship of art, music, and architecture, the skill of writing and the cultivation of learning, and the pursuit of scientific knowledge building on the recorded discoveries of the past. That these things had developed and continued to develop in Europe was indisputable; and it was firmly believed that they were good. That they had developed to a much lesser extent in Africa was not disputed either. There was much less evidence of these things than there is now, for people were not at that time motivated to look for it; and the evidence that there was, in the accounts of visitors to Africa and in captured artifacts, was felt to be trivial or else the result of early influences from the Mediterranean. Africans did not have the wheel; except in Ethiopia, they did not have the plough. In the colonial image of Africa, people built only in mud and straw like the two little pigs (the stone buildings of Zimbabwe were assumed to be relics of a foreign visitation); they had crafts, not arts; they did not write; no discoveries could be recorded so scientific progress could only be of the slowest; and their wealth was barely exploited by the Africans themselves. They were not organised for civilisation, because they were not capable of starting the ball rolling by themselves. And once Europeans had done it for them, they still had several hundred years of social evolution to make up without being temperamentally suited to it, so that not a great deal could be expected all at once. There was a path of progress, which proceeded by stages. This was exemplified by the European past and all that it contained.

The African past, by contrast, was nothing more than the "unrewarding gyrations of barbarous tribes in picturesque but irrelevant corners of the globe", to quote (as every Africanist did) Trevor-Roper's memorable phrase. "History", he continues, "is essentially a form of movement, and purposive movement too. . . . Perhaps, in the future, there will be some African history . . . but at present there is none: there is only the history of the Europeans in Africa."[5] Even in 1960 an historian of Africa, A.J. Hanna, could write:

On the whole, the picture was one of brutality, callousness, suffering and futility, and . . . the situation did not include any factors which offered hope of improvement in the future. . . . If it had not been for the coming of the

British . . . the tribes of the Rhodesias and Nyasaland would have remained, for centuries or perhaps millennia, sparsely scattered over a vast area, dominated by . . . the capriciousness of nature, without the art of writing or the use of numbers . . . with no ideals higher than the pride of bloodshed, with their whole environment and conditions of life promoting an attitude of apathy, improvidence and fatalism.[6]

It was this picture of failure then, that African historians had to deal with when, in the sixties, the political position of Africans was reversed and colonial history, which had rationalised their subjection, was rejected. The new nations needed a new history, and it must refute the old, because the old was both wrong and damaging to African pride. As Ali Mazrui writes:

[If] there [are] aspects of Africa's past which deserve to be described as savage, . . . these aspects are already fairly extensively documented. It now becomes important that the mere accumulation of extra information does not perpetuate the Trevor-Roper myth. Only a process of counter-selection can correct this, and African historians have to concentrate on those aspects which were ignored by the disparaging mythologies.
So commitment to the correction of human error in this case might involve purposive discrimination in terms of what is emphasised and what is augmented in the pool of human information. And yet to correct error is as respectable an aim as to increase knowledge.[7]

The error Mazrui referred to was not the idea that there are low and high places in human development (the low places exemplified by small-scale organisation and simple arrangements for production and exchange, the high by industrial capitalist societies), nor the idea that the latter have a right to hold the former in contempt. The error was in supposing that the course of African history tended more towards the first situation than the second. The idea of social and political evolution went unchallenged, as did the idea that it was meritorious to evolve as quickly and directly as possible (an idea which does *not* attach to biological evolution!) and that a people should be proud if they had, and ashamed if they had not, been in the forefront of this movement.

What was challenged, instead, was the picture of stagnation in pre-colonial Africa, and of subsequent African lack of initiative. Historians set out to show, not that whatever Africa had had was somehow humanly worthwhile, but that Africans deserved the respect of others, and could respect themselves, because they had had in their past the things that Europeans valued. As Bethwell Ogot writes:

We demonstrated that African societies had well-organised states, practised democracy, socialism, family planning and engaged in long distance trade with properly organised markets. We proved to our satisfaction that Africans had religions, philosophies, military organisations, legal systems, medicines and technologies. In short, we tried to demonstrate that Africa . . . had a rich and significant history.[8]

Its development was presented as just as good as Europe's, because it was the same; and also because it was (sometimes) contemporaneous. This is important because, as Chanock points out, evolutionary history is competitive —"As there is but one path of human development, history can be looked upon as an inter-societal race for progress."[9] This point of view is exemplified by E.R. Sanders, who wrote: "[Historians] began to discover that Africa was not a *tabula rasa*, but that it had a past, a history which could be reconstructed; that it was a continent which knew empire builders at a time when large areas of Europe stagnated in the Dark Ages; that it knew art and commerce".[10]

The British and French pasts had seen a move from local communities with relatively little internal differentiation to feudalism with an ever more centralised focus of power, and later to monarchies which had broadened into empire, until at last power devolved upon parliaments, which ruled nations of mixed peoples under one law, one economic system, and one allegiance. All right then, we were told, the African past was like that too. In some ways, in some places, so it was. But what is interesting is the way in which historians went overboard for those ways, those places.

They took the great variety of ways of living and thinking which exist and have existed side by side in Africa, where herders have drifted through the capitals of kings for hundreds of years and are camping now on the pavements of cities, and assigned each one to its place in the different phases of man's development laid down by the scheme of Western history, so that some belonged to the past and some to the future, with which the present was identified. The key to understanding the model with which historians approached this phasing of African history is the idea of nationalism, for it was the success of nationalism which called forth the revision of history. History, says Basil

Davidson, should provide "a meaningful approach to the largest cultural phenomenon of twentieth century Africa—the advent and advance, one may even say the overwhelming victory, of nationalism and all its implications".[11] That this is the "largest cultural phenomenon" is an extraordinary assertion, but even scholars who would not go that far gave it great importance in Africa's history because it was particularly important to them, bringing African countries into line with others as it did. And as the successful management of nation-states was seen as the test of equality with whites, it seemed important to try to establish that this form of government was not a wholly alien one, handed down by the imperial powers, but that it was in some sense the natural culmination of an indigenous development. From this comes the idea that there was a natural course of African history which would have produced something like the modern nations all by itself, even if their growth had not been forced and their particular forms determined by colonial rule.[12] It is in this sense that Davidson refers to "the restarting of the processes of African history after the long episode of colonial alienation",[13] as if African history were some independent force which had spent the colonial period behind bars, restrained, but biding its time.

That African nationalism has been for many a moving and courageous struggle is in no way disputed; what is of interest here is the reason for scholars' situating its origins as far back into the past as possible, and further still, and the distorting effect this had on the representation of African history.[14] As a political movement, nationalism took its force from the colonial situation; but as an historical idea, it derived its mysterious domination over centuries of African history from the evolutionism which placed Europeans and their political works at the pinnacle of man's development.

What happened was that historians constructed a sort of "Whig Interpretation"[15] of African history, taking the triumph of nationalism as the culmination of Africa's socio-political development. Each period had its focus, some aspect which could be seen, in retrospect, to contribute towards this end, and its progress would be charted, its contribution assessed. Let us first sketch the outline of Africa's progress discerned by historians in the sixties, and then look at the distortions that such a view of history produced.

Imagine national sovereignty as a dye injected into the plant of African history; at once certain trends, certain sequences, stand out like the veins of a leaf. Cities, kings, conquests, migrations, and mixing of peoples; caravans of gold and slaves; African businessmen, bishops, and lawyers; boys on their way to school, students in exile; freedom fighters, party secretaries, congresses, ballots, and presidents. The Nuer and the Dinka, the Bushmen and the Pygmies, are a pale wash of background where the dye is not absorbed. History deals with those who advanced or retarded progress towards national sovereignty, and those who had nothing to do with it are not the historian's concern.

The major themes of the period before European contact were perceived as "centralisation", the strengthening of a single political authority, and "enlargement of scale", that is, territorial expansion, usually by conquest. Efforts which increased centralisation were presented in a positive light, with little regard for their significance in their own time and place. Of the strengthening of the Ganda monarchy, for example, remembered in oral tradition as a time of "bad and bloody tyran[ny]", Roland Oliver wrote in warmly congratulatory terms, because "Without doubt . . . strong government was an aid to expansion . . . [enabling Buganda to move] from a feudal to a bureaucratic system, in which subordinate administrators held office during the king's reign". He reserved fainter praise for Rwanda, which although it "developed a political and cultural coherence never reached by . . . the other main states of the region . . . never reached either the administrative efficiency of the Ganda concept of officialdom, or Buganda's alertness to the outside world and readiness to respond to its challenge".[16]

It is apparently not the process but the direction of change which is important here, and Buganda was going in the right direction. What it was the right direction for, however, none of Buganda's past rulers could have been expected to know; how, then, does a congratulatory overview help to illuminate the process of centralisation?

An air of disappointment, by contrast, surrounds those communities which missed their chance, like Ogots's " 'stateless societies', the Dinka and the Nuer . . . [who] have lived more or less in one region for several centuries, and yet they have not even evolved a *Rwotship*".[17] Ogot in fact put contemporaneous types of social organisation on a continuum to correspond with different phases of historical development, stating for example that "One of the major results of the intrusion of the Bantu into East Africa was the gradual replacement of the hunter by the cultivator—that is their arrival marked the transition from the hunting to the cultivating stage of civilisation''.[18] The effect of this kind of writing was to lend an air of inevitability to something which did not always happen, and to give the impression that societies which did not change were ''anachronisms or survivals''.[19]

Within this evolutionary view of history, the many stateless societies of Africa were written about comparatively little, and then often in the context of speculations as to how they developed central authority. Oliver and Atmore write, for example.

By about A.D. 1400 much even of the back country of Africa was in a state of active development. Stateless societies there were, exhibiting a quality of passivity and relative changelessness, but these were rare. Throughout much of the southern two-thirds of Africa it would seem that populations were growing and that societies and economies were alike becoming more complex.[20]

Small chiefdoms, like the *ntemi* of East-Central Africa, were chronicled in the process of becoming bigger; kingdoms and empires occupied the latter end of the continuum along which polities moved, or ought to have done. ''The whole meaning of progress'', as Wrigley puts it, ''is the transition from tribe to state, from segmentary to centralised political system''.[21]

Reaching back to the earliest times which we can reconstruct, then, the ''mainstream'' for historians was occupied by societies which grew into states, and the heroes were the rulers who pushed or pulled them into shape.

In the period of trade with Europeans, before the conquest, the heroes of this version were those who succeeded in using the trade to their advantage, whose kingdoms did not become impoverished or disintegrate under the pressures of the slave trade. Indeed Fage at one point characterised the slave trade as ''purposive'' because, while it ''tended . . . to weaken or destroy more segmentary societies'', it speeded up the process of centralisation in the stronger kingdoms.[22] (This article of Fage's did in fact spark criticism, particularly from Wrigley, not because it was atypical but because the extreme expression of political evolutionism drew attention to the implications of the viewpoint as a whole.)[23]

Next came the conquest, and who were the heroes then? Not the leaders of the ''romantic, reactionary struggles against the facts, the passionate protest of societies which were shocked by the new age of change and would not be comforted".[24] No, the heroes were the new men, those, again, who made a "successful adaptation"—like Oliver's Buganda whose "readiness to respond to . . . challenge . . . [would] be the secret of Buganda's triumphant adaptation to the coming of Europe in the late nineteenth century".[25]

Once European rule was consolidated, the leaders of resistance became the forces of progress, as long as the sort of resistance they led looked "forward"—to nationalism—not "back"—to tribalism; as long as, in Oliver and Atmore's words, they "were thinking in modern terms—not in terms of a reversion to tribal beliefs and tribal organisations, but in terms of Christian churches under African leadership, and of African successor states based on the existing colonial territories and governed along Western rather than traditional African lines".[26] Resistance of any sort was about sovereignty, of course—but to get onto the side of progress it had to contain features which were developed by later nationalist movements into successful techniques. Looking at a wide range of efforts involved in religious resistance movements—spirit possession, oracles, prophecy, bullets-to-water magic, cattle killing, witchcraft eradication—all equally plausible to participants in the sense that all of them relied upon supernatural aid—historians dismissed those which did nothing to undermine colonial domination as escapes into fantasy, and wrote up the others as aspects of organisation or propaganda.[27] The distinction was a Western one, and the opportunity to understand what people in such movements thought they were doing was lost or postponed until such time as the preoccupation with nationalism weakened.

As the century wore on, the focus was the nationalist struggle, the leadership, platform, and organisation of political parties, and the form of government with which each nation embarked on independence.

In the selection of material, therefore, and in the differing emphasis placed upon events, nationalism and the evolutionist ideas behind it dominated the writing of African history from independence until well into the seventies. This produced three main kinds of distortions in our appreciation of the African past. First, an historicism was introduced, assigning various communities to stages of development, thus obscuring their role in their own time and place. Second, and related to this, the subject was narrowed to the evolutionary areas of focus and to those aspects of them which historians saw as functioning to propel or retard the progress of the designated craft down the mainstream. Where historians found evidence of forms of organisation which resembled those of the European past, they extrapolated firm evolutionary trends, treating the rest as peripheral to history. Material which might have given a truer picture of the time appeared extraneous, or anomalous, or did not appear at all. Third, values were allowed very much to dictate what could appear in the new history books and how it would be represented. In the face of the needs of new nations in Africa, objectivity looked like cynicism. The role of sheer embarrassment in the revision of African history should not be underestimated. It is honest of Mazrui to articulate the danger that the "mere accumulation of extra information [might] . . . perpetuate the Trevor-Roper myth". Many historians, however, did not announce their intentions in this way but simply dropped from their agenda material which was felt to reflect badly on African societies, or transformed it, so that slavery became a family affair; conquest an offer of law, order, and wider markets; cannibalism a social cement; and authoritarian terror a means of introducing new grounds of loyalty to the state. One example must suffice, but it is one which reveals a good deal about the new historians' understanding of their role in representing material. With the revised version of Shaka's wars it is evident how the goal of history was allowed to dominate the contemporary reality. Whatever horrors they may have involved at the time and for whatever reason they may have been undertaken, we were urged to regard wars of conquest as "positive" because of their "effects" on the enlargement of scale. Shula Marks, for example, wrote that although:

It was the destructive aspects of the *Mfecane* which were almost immediately felt . . . out of this maelstrom new peoples, even new nations, were being born. . . . Shaka's achievement in welding a multi-tribal nation out of the numerous tribes of Nguniland in the short span of twelve years, a nation which has long outlasted the military power on which its greatness was based, was in itself outstanding. . . . And further north, in the Transvaal, Zambia, and Tanzania, previously disorganised people were also to profit from the Nguni example. It was often those people who were either Nguni offshoots or who had responded positively to the Nguni challenge, who were able to withstand the vicissitudes of the nineteenth century and to resist new invaders—whether Voortrekkers, Arab slave traders or even the colonial regimes at the turn of the century.[28]

Omer-Cooper, too, found the *Mfecane* encouraging:

All the Zulu-type kingdoms could be said to constitute experiments in multi-tribal nation-building. One of the most striking features of the *Mfecane* is indeed the very general success which attended the numerous and different attempts at forming political units out of originally separate peoples. It suggests that the task of instilling a sense of political unity into peoples of different language and culture in a limited time, the task which faces every political leader in the newly independent countries, is not so difficult as pessimists tend to maintain.[29]

Here was a clear statement of what the new history had to offer, and to whom; as Wrigley said, "the tendency of recent African historiography to celebrate the rise of states is evidence that it is being written almost exclusively from the point of view of Africa's present ruling class".[30] This might seem odd, when we are accustomed to think of the new history as radical, and radical thinking is not usually associated with ruling-class interests. But as Chanock put it,

African history . . . must serve those who want to change. This has been called a transition from colonial to radical history, but change can be a ruling class interest as much as conservation can be. . . . The desire of the radicals to give their modernising ideology indigenous roots is all the more comprehensible since the transformation they desire involves to a large degree a continuation and intensification of the alien pressures introduced by European domination.[31]

Thus, the evolutionist framework lent itself to the kind of history which was most useful to the leaders of new African nations, and this circumstance contributed to the production of an easily accepted version of the past with a smooth surface appearance. An element of inconsistency, however, a curious double standard, was characteristic of nationalist history, for there was a racial bias as well as an evolutionist one, and frequently these pulled against each other. European activity might or might not be judged progressive, but the same criteria were not used in evaluating it. Europeans did not get on to the side of progress by doing the things Africans were praised for doing. European initiatives in cash-cropping, small businesses, let alone nationalism, were reactionary because they got in the way of African ones. In particular, European contributions to the enlargement of scale were usually anathema to the African historian. But if Sunni Ali and Shaka were praiseworthy as enlargers of scale, why not Cecil Rhodes? Historians apparently put white and black activities into different mental compartments to preserve the integrity of the sides in the race for progress.

The men who carved up Africa at the Congress of Berlin were blamed for splitting ethnic groups and forcing them to live under alien governments—what else were the African empire-builders doing?—yet it was called unification!

Generations of divided loyalties, frustration, and isolation were called "taking the best of what the new world had to offer while retaining what was best from the old ways". Wars of genocide were called "forging new loyalties which cut across tribal barriers". Only by refusing to enter into the experience of the past at all could historians coin such phrases; only by refusing to think about famine, to return to the best example, could they offer the new invigorating *Mfecane*. They flinched from the kind of empathy that history demands, lest it lead to remarks that would be seen as "negative" or disrespectful. But was it really respectful to require that Africa's past be forced into line with Europe's if it was to have a respectable place in the march of civilisation? On the contrary, true respect required that we look at what had actually been going on in Africa—at country as well as town, subjects as well as kings, followers as well as leaders, dissent as well as unity, and treat it *all* with the same respect, and the same critical eye, as we would any white nation's past. To admire an African king as much as an English one is not the same thing at all.

All these areas were not, in fact, accorded equal attention. This was not because kings, cities, international trade, and centralisation were so prominent that other areas of interest did not readily present themselves. As Martin Chanock pointed out, writing about Malawi:

We focus on the role of the educated elite in a peasant dominated country; on the influence of industrialisation in the most rural part of Central Africa. The same kind of historical writing has been evident in the large body of literature on Nigeria and Ghana which failed to give due weight to the social forces whose values were not the same as those of the historians.[32]

It was, as he said, a matter of values, which governed the use of language and image, light and heavy emphasis, and speculation in the many areas where evidence was sparse. The inaccuracy of the post-independence version of history was not a matter of fact or detail, but of the whole picture conjured up by historians of the African past, of jungles and savannas thick with bureaucracy, laced with trade, ponderous with wisdom, at the same time smugly at peace and heroically at war, a picture which was simply the product of a particular selection of material inspired by the two biases picked out above. How could we possibly know such things? And what reality could be thus described? It was inspirational, but it was not informative. "African historiography has been important in Africa for reasons of pride", says Terence Ranger, *"because it could not possibly have been useful for anything else."* [33]

Thus we are brought to a point of reassessment, fifteen to twenty years after the first concerted efforts simply to "[demonstrate] the . . . viability of the field".[34] Occasionally, evolutionary history of a congratulatory flavour still comes off the presses, particularly in histories such as surveys and textbooks which attempt to capture an audience assumed to be prejudiced to some degree, and to present them with a synthesis of the historiographical Story So Far. For many historians, however, from the generation which produced it as well as from the automatically critical one that followed, the decade of nationalism now represents a phase which a "mature" African history has left behind.[35] To some it now seems regrettable, both from a political point of view, in that it served the interests of new regimes which in hindsight were not what historians hoped they would be, and from an intellectual point of view, in that historians concentrated on narrowly political themes at the expense of social and economic ones. To others, it seems to have been a necessary phase, in that the racism against which nationalist history reacted was crippling to proper endeavours in any direction. Only when the ghost of colonialist history had been laid to rest was it possible, in this view, to proceed with a history in which some Africans, as well as Europeans, would be seen as exploiters, oppressors, collaborators, or even, simply, people who made mistakes. The chief thru﹐ ' of this new history has come from people applying Marxist ideas more, or less, systematically, and the debates of recent years have been largely between these and unlike-minded scholars, or among Marxists who feel that other Marxists are not Marxist enough. One gets the impression from these debates that, while nationalist history was a phase, political economy is the truth; the clouds of mystification have been broken through, and now real light can get in. It is as well to remember that it was precisely in this way that nationalist historians once viewed their own endeavours. Each intellectual generation has seen what The Times called for, and believed that they called for the truth, and has gone out to look for it. The key historiographical question, therefore, is how an historian sees The Times. In the sixties, The Times were Independence; in the seventies, they were Continuing Poverty.[36] Both were features of both decades, of course, so The Times must be in the mind of the historian, and this is where an intellectual history of African history must focus. Let me say that there is nothing nihilist in this examination. Each reformulation of questions may well be an improvement on the one before, and my own feeling is that Marxist enquiry can reveal more than nationalist elegy. The question of how a line of enquiry eludes or occurs to an historian is a valid question, however, whatever the case.

In the past two decades, African history has moved, on the face of it, from a position of supporting new elites which slotted into an imperial system of capitalist appropriation from the Third World, both in terms of their class position and in terms of their model of future development, to supporting the poor of Africa by exposing the workings of that system with the tools of political economy. If, however, we try to see in the broadest terms what the two positions have in common and where they differ, at least three observations can be made. Both are characterised by a view of history which is evolutionary, unilineal, and unidirectional, and assumes a progressive option to be available. Whether nationalist or Marxist, this is a cultural view, not a universal truth, and in this respect Marxism continues the domination of Western ideas over African history. The models of both schools of thought are Western ones, their adoption by African academics notwithstanding. Secondly, both points of view have been experienced, in their time, as support for the underdog. Finally, many of the same people have supported both points of view.

They are different models, to be sure, and in terms of the new one the heroes of the previous model ought never to have been seen as underdogs at all. They were protagonists in a different contest, one which occupies only a minor arena in the present analysis of oppositions. And it would be easy to suppose that the shift in analysis is a case of scales falling from eyes, were it not for the embarrassment that still occurs when fresh regimes, even self-consciously socialist ones forged in the experience of wars of liberation, separate themselves from the interests of their poor on attaining office.

A thread of continuity is discernible through the last two decades of historical writing, as Western scholars go into the study of Africa with certain principled expectations of Africans derived from their views of Western history, and it is disappointment with their performance in terms of these expectations which opens the way for changes in historical analysis.

There can be no doubt that many historians who emerged in the countries of origin of colonial Africa's ruling class felt that they *were* doing something radical in offering the new nations an anti-colonial history, paying the new leadership the compliment of identifying its interests with those of the "country as a whole". The challenge of Marxist history, and the scholarly climate in which it was welcomed, grew out of the growing recognition of the disparity of interests that had been obscured, for a time, by the popularity, and the promise, of nationalism. Many historians were disappointed both by the cynicism of African leadership and by the success of neo-colonialism. "Westernisation" had been misunderstood by historians, and the evolutionary model could not explain the anomalies: The persistence of magic in politics, of religious solutions to social ills, of tribal organisation, and of official terror.[37] The experience of independence revealed the weakness of a model of history in which Europe and America led the world in a common progression. An important change in perspective was found in "development of underdevelopment" theory, according to which the West did not so much lead as gain an unmatchable advantage by taking from the colonised world the means to progress. These, being economic, were not restored with political independence.[38] This model provided an alternative to the strategy of the sixties, when historians picked out Africa's historical similarities with Europe as a basis for confidence in its future, and made it possible to look at Africa as part of the Third World, sharing the disadvantages imposed by its historical relationship with Europe, and needing a new strategy. It was, moreover, a theory in which Marxist and nationalist ideas could be (if uneasily) combined, and as such it provided a transition to the large body of writing in the tradition of political economy which followed.

The next six chapters discuss these developments in African history from a number of angles. Chapter two examines nationalist history as a reaction to colonial history, looking at books written for students or a general audience, in which values and purposes are most clearly expressed. Chapter three illustrates the limitations of nationalist history more specifically, by showing how it distorted scholarly understanding of African religious movements. Chapter four considers the belief that history written by Africans must be different from that written by whites, and finds more contrasts between East and West African historians than between African and European ones. Chapter five looks at other attempts to foster pride through the creation of a group identity—in Indian history, feminism, and African literature—to see what they have in common and compare the changes they go through. Chapter six sets out differences between Marxist and nationalist history, and looks at attempts in the sixties to combine the two. In every chapter the issue with which we began remains central: Can and should history be used to foster pride? With the concluding chapter we take this question to a study of oral traditions, to see to what extent the need for pride is apparent, and is met, in "indigenous" African history, and compare some of the historical ideas expressed in traditional histories with some of our own.

## NOTES

1. Two writers who did were C.C. Wrigley, "Historicism in Africa: Slavery and State Formation", *African Affairs*, vol. 70, no. 279 (1971) and M. Chanock, "Development and Change in the History of Malawi" in ed. B. Pachai, *The Early History of Malawi* (London, Longman, 1972).

2. O. Patterson, "Rethinking Black History", *Harvard Educational Review*, vol. 41, no. 3 (1971), p. 305.

3. The extent to which Africans writing African history share assumptions with Americans and Europeans is the subject of Chapter four.

4. E.H. Carr, *What Is History?* (Harmondsworth, Penguin Books, 1961), p. 132.

5. Broadcast lecture by Hugh Trevor-Roper, reprinted in *The Listener* (London, November 28, 1963), p. 871.

6. A.J. Hanna, *The Story of the Rhodesias and Nyasaland* (London, Faber and Faber, 1960), p. 40; quoted in B. Ogot, "Three Decades of Historical Studies in East Africa, 1949–1977", *Kenya Historical Review*, vol. 6, nos. 1/2 (1978), p. 25.

7. A. Mazrui, in his "Epilogue" to Okot p'Bitek's *African Religions in Western Scholarship* (Nairobi, East African Literature Bureau, 1970), p. 123. Mazrui is here describing an approach to African history, rather than endorsing it.

8. Ogot, "Three Decades", p. 29.

9. Chanock, "Development and Change", p. 431.

10. E.R. Sanders, "The Hamitic Hypothesis", *Journal of African History*, vol. 10 (1967), p. 531.

11. B. Davidson, "Questions about Nationalism", *African Affairs*, vol. 76, no. 302 (Jan. 1977), p. 39.

12. The "natural course" of African history is discussed further, and illustrated in Chapter 2.

13. Davidson, "Questions", p. 46.

14. For example, see A. Temu, "The Rise and Triumph of Nationalism" in eds. I. Kimambo and A. Temu, *A History of Tanzania* (Nairobi, East African Publishing House, 1969).

15. The term originated with H. Butterfield, *The Whig Interpretation of History* (Harmondsworth, Penguin Books, 1931).

16. R. Oliver, "Discernible Developments in the Interior c. 1500–1840" in eds. R. Oliver and G. Matthews, *History of East Africa* (London, Oxford University Press, 1963), p. 190.

17. B. Ogot, "Kingship and Statelessness among the Nilotes" in eds. J. Vansina, R. Mauny, and L.V. Thomas, *The Historian in Tropical Africa* (London, Oxford University Press, 1964), p. 300.

18. B. Ogot, "The Role of the Pastoralist and the Agriculturalist in African History" in ed. T. Ranger, *Emerging Themes of African History* (Nairobi, East African Publishing House, 1968), p. 127.

19. W. MacGaffey, "African Ideology and Belief: A Survey", *African Studies Review*, vol. 24, nos. 2/3 (June/Sept. 1981), p. 234.

20. R. Oliver and A. Atmore, *The African Middle Ages, 1400–1800* (Cambridge, Cambridge University Press, 1981), p. 29.

21. Wrigley, "Historicism", p. 120.

22. J. Fage, "Slavery and the Slave Trade in the Context of West African History", *Journal of African History*, vol. 10, no. 3 (1969), p. 402.

23. See Wrigley, "Historicism".

24. R. Robinson and J. Gallagher, "The Partition of Africa" in ed. F.H. Hinsley, *The New Cambridge Modern History* (Cambridge, Cambridge University Press, 1962), vol. 11, pp. 639–40.

25. R. Oliver, "Discernible Developments", p. 190.

26. R. Oliver and A. Atmore, *Africa Since 1800* (Cambridge, Cambridge University Press, 1967), p. 158.

27. See, e.g., C. Young, *Politics in the Congo* (Princeton, Princeton University Press, 1965), pp. 281–88; for a critical survey, see D. Parkin, "Medicines and Men of Influence", *Man* N.S., vol. 3 (1968).

28. S. Marks, "The Rise of the Zulu Kingdom" in ed. R. Oliver, *The Middle Age of African History* (London, Oxford University Press, 1967), pp. 90–91.

29. J.D. Omer-Cooper, *The Zulu Aftermath: A Nineteenth Century Revo-

*lution in Bantu Africa* (London, Longmans, 1966), pp. 173 ff.; quoted in Wrigley, "Historicism", p. 120.

30. Wrigley, "Historicism", p. 123.

31. Chanock, "Development and Change", p. 433. Also see C. Ake, "The Congruence of Political Economies and Ideologies in Africa", in eds. P. Gutkind and I. Wallerstein, *The Political Economy of Contemporary Africa* (Beverly Hills and London, Sage, 1976), pp. 204–11.

32. Chanock, "Development and Change", p. 434.

33. T.O. Ranger, "Towards a Usable African Past" in ed. C. Fyfe, *African Studies Since 1945* (London, Longman, 1976), p. 23.

34. Ibid., p. 18. "State of the art" writing includes Fyfe, *African Studies*; J. Lonsdale, "States and Social Processes in Africa: A Historiographical Survey", *African Studies Review*, vol. 24, nos. 2/3 (June/Sept. 1981); MacGaffey, "Ideology"; A. Temu and B. Swai, *Historians and Africanist History: A Critique* (London, Zed Press, 1981); B. Ogot, "Three Decades"; I. Wallerstein, "The Evolving Role of the Africa Scholar in African Studies", *Canadian Journal of African Studies*, vol. 17, no. 1 (1983).

35. See, e.g., Lonsdale, "States and Social Processes"; Temu and Swai, *Africanist History*.

36. Ranger, "Usable Past".

37. For an interesting discussion of Western misunderstanding of certain modern Zairean ideas, see W. MacGaffey, "African History, Anthropology, and the Rationality of Natives", *History in Africa*, vol. 5 (1978), especially pp. 112–16.

38. In developing this approach, Africanists borrowed from the ideas of André Gunder Frank, who has written several pieces on underdevelopment in Latin America. Chapter six discusses this, and other aspects of Marxist writing on Africa, in some detail.

# 2

# WRITING FOR STUDENTS

HINDRANCES TO DEVELOPMENT

The great empires of the ancient world such as Egypt, China, India and Babylon spread along and from great river valleys. These empires had not the same kind of civilisation as ours, but have a right to be regarded as civilised; some arts, e.g., those of writing and building appear to have begun in them. Western and Southern Europe are the parts of the world in which our complex modern civilisation was born—with its distinctive "freedoms"—and from which it has spread over much of the world. The Negro peoples of Africa had tribal cultures rather than great empires; they had not invented the art of writing or even the wheel. The latter is one of the first steps in progress because it increases communications.

This paragraph comes from a book written for African primary schools[1] by Ernest Loftus, O.B.E., M.A., B.Sc. (Econ.), F.R.G.S., in 1954. Interestingly enough, it was reprinted in 1969; but it represents a kind of textbook we are not likely to see again in Africa.[2] With the end of the colonial period, colonial history came under violent attack, and rightly so. How dare the conquerors imply the conquered were not civilised?[3] How could the writer refer to "the slow development of the human race south of the Sahara and Ethiopia?" The response from black and white historians alike was, Africans *were* civilised. But how to prove it? And they proved it by showing that Africa had had in its pre-colonial past (and sometimes *before* England did) the things which made the West civilised—well, perhaps not the wheel, but there was writing, there were great empires, big buildings. The defenders of African civilisation never challenged the definition of civilisation, the values of the conquerors, but conducted the defense in terms of these values. "It is to whites", as Orlando Patterson says, "that the historically-conscious blacks seek to measure up."[4]

One way to begin a critique of history written shortly after the colonial period is to look at the literature produced for schools and for university students. In this kind of writing, historians' assumptions become particularly transparent. When they have to cover a lot of ground in a short survey, their selection must be fairly rigorous and the principles by which they make it are easily identified. One can see what they consider most important over the whole span of African history, or what they consider most important for students to know (for party functionaries, these may be very different things, but for scholars they are supposed, at least, to coincide). By looking at the language they use, moreover, one can see what value judgments they wish to convey to students: the feeling, as well as the information about their past, that they would like them to absorb.

As well as being revealing in these ways, the history written for African schools is an unusually important part of African history as a whole. The main drive of historical writing in the sixties was towards the "decolonisation" of history. Now, for whom was this? It was not aimed at a European reading public, but at an African one, and that public is largely composed of students and others who read the same sort of things that students read. There is neither a significant public for very specialised studies nor a significant popular literature for people casually interested in history. The importance of school histories is the greater, moreover, because the opportunities of carrying on with the study of history at a higher level are so limited. We are not, therefore, dealing with a minor branch of historical writing in this case, but with one in which scholars at the highest levels should and do take an active interest.

It may be objected that it is not legitimate to identify school histories with academic history in this way. For one thing, the process by which they are produced is often as much political as academic. As Cornevin puts it:

In this decolonisation of history . . . there is a temptation of an emotional
nature, that is to represent the Colonial period as ''an iron age between two
golden ages'', . . . a golden age before the whites, the golden age of independence. . . . At governmental level, this desire is apparent in the national
commissions set up to reform history syllabuses in an attempt to set out the
African point of view.[5]


But who actually advises on these reforms and supplies the material
they require?

In Western countries, books for schools are often written by schoolteachers and others who cannot easily keep up with the most recent
work in their field. But in African history this is not the case. Some
books are written by schoolteachers and other non-academic writers,
but many are by people who are currently lecturing in universities: Oliver
and Fage, Curtin, Burke, Webster, Boahen, Omer-Cooper, Afigbo,
Ayandele, Gavin, Fyfe, Ikime, Igbafe, and Darkwah, to name a few.[6]
A glance at the authorship of *Tarikh*, a periodical published by Longmans for the Historical Society of Nigeria and intended for use in
schools, will yield more academic names.

Whether the assumptions that permeate these schoolbooks are also
to be found in academic works is a problem for another chapter. I shall
argue that they are. For the moment, let us look at what the schoolbooks tell an African student about his past.

We can begin with the problem with which this chapter began, the
need to respond to the general message of histories written in the colonial period, that Africans had no very significant history before they
were stimulated and/or instructed by visitors from the outside world,
Hamites or Europeans. Many of the points of reaction in post-colonial
history, and a good deal of its fervour, are quite understandable if we
look at what was implied in textbooks of the colonial period. It is perhaps because a reaction was so badly needed, and because it took the
form of attacking particular areas of insult rather than rethinking the
historical attitude to Africa as a whole, that the various illogicalities of
the new history went unnoticed for a number of years. It is equally
important, however, that the new history, being a mirror image of the
old, fitted right in with the Western historian's picture of what history,
and progress, are about, so that Fage, for example, was able to produce either version with equal conviction.[7] Both these factors have

contributed to the new picture of Africa's past, then—the first providing the motivation for a new version, the second making it appear coherent—and it will be helpful to look first at the background of colonial textbook history.

In general, the textbooks stressed the differences between Europeans and Africans in history. In the first place, the educationists really believed there was a fundamental contrast to be made. In 1936 Coupland wrote that "whereas England's experience has been active (at any rate in recent centuries), that of Africa has been passive",[8] so that the nearest thing possible to an African-centred history must be one which dealt with the interaction between Africa and Europe; and Elliot, who thought of the old and the new in Europe developing continuously like the "chrysalis and the butterfly", saw the old and new in Africa as "two butterflies of different species".[9] But in any case, this was also a matter of deliberate educational policy. The reasons for stressing difference varied with time and place. We often think that colonial history was designed to convince Africans they were intrinsically inferior, and there was certainly an element of this. Governor-General Roume, for example, recommended that African pupils be led to compare "the unstable and bloody past of their country with the peaceful, tranquil and fecund present", as a way "to attenuate the native vanity".[10] English educationists, however, often had something a little more inspirational in mind: the progress of Europe was to serve as a model of what Africans might accomplish if they fell in willingly with the colonial course of development. W.E. Ward, who taught history at Achimota College in Ghana from 1925 to 1940 and later advised the Colonial Office on education and wrote several widely used textbooks, wrote that history for the African pupil must try to answer "the great question that is always at the back of his mind: why is the European so much 'wiser' and stronger than himself, and can the secret of his wisdom and strength be acquired?"[11] The feeling was that it could be, if the African could be brought to make the "universalist heritage" of Western history his own. The phrase is Murray's, who wrote that a "primary aim of history teaching in Africa is to put the African into the stream of history from which he has been absent so long".[12]

In answer to this kind of remark, then, it became important for the new historians to assert that the African had never been absent from the stream of history. The oft-repeated statement that Africans had no history might technically mean nothing more than that they recorded none, but clearly more was implied: they had done nothing important enough to merit recording, either. When historians now affirm that Africa has indeed got a history, it is the latter claim that they mean to contradict. Similarly, the idea that there was a natural course[13] of African history which was interrupted by the colonial period makes sense (if at all) in opposition to the "two butterflies" theme. Development by stages towards centralisation, it is held, *was* the natural course, and did not depend upon Africans' willingness to take up an alien heritage. This theme appears in articles by Ogot[14] and Horton[15] which deal with stateless societies, and Basil Davidson was still developing it as recently as 1976:

However one may care to label it, this African model of community has been undoubtedly one of the begetters of African nationalism. It is possible to argue that this would have emerged very clearly if there had been no colonial intrusion. There is much to suggest that the modes of self-organisation of a significant number of African peoples in the nineteenth century had reached a point of growth where forms of large organisational change were in course, or at least in prospect. Kings in some polities acquired more power than before. Peoples without kings developed new forms of central authority. Groups of neighbouring communities were perhaps on the verge of forming new constellations of multi-ethnic composition. As it was, there came instead the colonial intrusion; and the history of the Africans became, for a while, much more the history of the Europeans than the history of themselves.[16]

A further element in colonial educational policy may be partially responsible for the preference given in the sixties to drum-and-trumpet history: this was the feeling that an emphasis on local and/or mass history, as opposed to the history of leaders and states, would assert a conservative influence on African pupils. On the one hand, the strengthening of tradition would act against the tendency of education to increase individualism among Africans, which led to a disintegration of society and was felt to threaten colonial rule; on the other, pupils would be taught that progress was a matter of slow improvement by the mass of people, not of agitation and sweeping change by the few. The history of political change in Europe was a tricky subject, therefore, as was the history of states in Africa. In the late 1920s, in fact, teachers noticed a reluctance on the part of their pupils to learn about African culture; they were suspicious that this educational offering was an attempt to retard their progress, and apparently they were right.[17] The post-independence enthusiasm for movement and change in African history, and the embarrassment where there seems to have been none, may owe something, therefore, to the opposite emphasis in early colonial teaching. Writers in *Tarikh* and elsewhere stress the point that the societies they write about were "not static",[18] as if to be static were an obvious disgrace. A similar disgrace accompanies small-scale political organisation. Batten, whose series of textbooks was standard reading in colonial schools, wrote that Africans were "living mostly in uncivilised tribes when found by Europeans. But even in Africa, all the tribes were not completely uncivilised". In the sixteenth century the Shona had had "some form of central government", and in the nineteenth century the Ndebele had "set up an empire"; apart from these scattered achievements, the empires of the Western Sudan had reached a "higher stage" than the rest of Africa.[19] Perhaps it was natural, then, for the new history to seek to magnify the role of states and to play down other forms of organisation or represent them as stages in the development of statehood, while virtually hounding the word "tribe" from the language.

They were not concerned to question the value which imperialist historians had placed on empires, but to put to rest any doubts about the empire-building capabilities of Africans. For even where pre-colonial states were recognised in colonial history, they were never put on a par with the British Empire. The latter was represented as being based upon an identity of interests between rulers and ruled which had never prevailed before.[20] Discussing the history of the Western Sudan from the fourth to the nineteenth centuries, in the 1957 edition of his *An Introduction to the History of West Africa*, Fage wrote:

At their peak these empires were often of considerable extent, but their fall was apt to be as swift as their rise. The conquered peoples each retained their distinctive customs and language; they had little in common with each other except the fact of their subjection to the same conquering people. None of the great empires succeeded in constituting such diverse elements into a united nation, and their political relations with the subject people were for the most part determined by the maintenance of military rule and the levying of tribute.[21]

Compare John Hatch's assertion, in a book significantly entitled *Africa: The Rebirth of Self-Rule* (published in 1967), that "Ghana, Mali,

Kanem, Songhai, and a number of Hausa states . . . all demonstrated that their rulers had learnt how to organise large numbers of people into one society".[22]

A contributing factor to the decline of these empires, according to Fage, was the low calibre of their rulers:

Administration of the large areas of territory comprised in most of the Sudanese empires, even if (as was often the case) it did not go much further than the organisation of the collection of tribute, was only possible so long as the military machine was capable of backing it up. . . . The longer an empire lasted, the more corrupt and inefficient its administration was apt to become, and the more its rulers tended to concentrate on ensuring their own wealth and pleasure, so that provincial governors and subject peoples had both more incentive and more opportunity to rebel or to co-operate with the new invader.[23]

Other states to the south experienced similar problems at a later date: "Eventually, of all the greatness of Benin, all that survived was the unchecked and self-destructive lust of its rulers for power and human booty".[24]

This way of speaking of pre-colonial rulers has, of course, been reversed in post-colonial history. No longer do we find the sort of idiom Jean Rouch used in 1953 to sum up Sonni Ali: "His disturbing and terrible personality dominates the history of the Songhay, for whom he is the great and cruel hero. The twenty-seven years of the reign of the *Si*, conqueror, engineer, organiser, master-magician, represent the brief peak of Songhay civilisation".[25] Today, the peak is a plateau, and is dominated by Askia Muhammed, who followed Sonni Ali's contribution in the military field with a more balanced statesmanship; and there are no more "master-magicians", but, rather, religious leaders. We often find, in fact, the rehabilitation in later histories of characters whom it is such a strain to admire that nobody used to make the effort. Shaka has been mentioned already, and Kabalega appears in a new light in the 1970 volume of *Tarikh*. In an article called "Kabalega and the Making of the New Kitara", Uzoigwe writes:

There are two sides to [Kabalega's] character; on the one hand, he was a difficult and complex personality; on the other, he was a man who genuinely loved his people. Certainly, he was ruthless towards the rebellions. But he displayed a remarkable kindness and liberality towards his *abarusura* (army) as well as towards all others whose loyalties were not in doubt. He was deeply interested in guns and in all things military. In actual combat he was imaginative and brave.

This picture hardly matches up to either the whimpering, drunken coward of Baker's description or the bloodthirsty savage who indulged in barbaric orgies that Casati portrayed in his book. . . .

The reign of Kabalega, indeed, may fairly be described as the era of the common man's monarchy. It was a new, exciting, revolutionary era which was cut short by British intervention. Kabalega must be seen as one of the most tragic casualties of British imperialism.[26]

Character assessment, then, is another area in which the judgement of colonial history certainly required balancing; and a look at the colonial version shows us where the new one had its inspiration. But, instead of righting the balance of truth, or, where truth cannot be determined, at least of historical sympathy, the new history often produced a mirror image as false and extravagant as the colonial one it sought to displace.

The limited recognition of African political achievement in the European mould is further attenuated in colonial histories by the fact that, even where points were given for statehood, some were taken away again for barbarism. The African part in the slave trade was stressed, along with the human sacrifices of Benin.[27] Lugard's description of the bloodbath that was Kano prison before British rule[28] was often quoted, and the pointless waste of "tribal warfare" deplored. This kind of thing was usually part of a comparison between "then" and "now": with British conquest, "inter-tribal war, human sacrifices, cannibalism, and slave raiding were soon to become things of the past".[29] Life under British rule was seen as a liberation from oppression, and the conquest was represented as having been quick and easy for this reason, with little more than token, and far from unanimous, resistance. Batten wrote, for example, that "The common people had suffered many evils at the hands of their Fulani rulers, and welcomed the British occupation as a distinct change for the better."[30] Fage—who in the 1960s characterised the slave trade as "purposive" because it contributed to the centralisation of the strongest African kingdoms[31]—was at one with other colonial historians in seeing it, in the fifties, as leading to a degradation which only the British could redeem:

It would be wrong to suppose that the disintegration of the Yoruba empire was due solely to the European demand for slaves. But one of the principal reasons why the provincial chiefs broke away from Oyo control was that they wanted a larger share of the profits of the slave trade than the Alafin and the court officials were prepared to allow them. . . . [Once civil strife began, the ready market in slaves and guns] made it virtually impossible for the Yorubas to return to a more peaceable way of life unaided. . . . The social canker which had beset Yorubaland was only finally checked by the imposition of external authority and the introduction of new social doctrines in the form of British rule and Christian missions.[32]

Following this Africa-wide deliverance, what we now call resistance was characterised as "rebellion", as in the sentence, "The peaceful progress of the country was suddenly broken in 1905 by the 'Maji-Maji' rebellion".[33] (This was written as late as 1960, in Clarke's *A Short History of Tanganyika*, which was reprinted in 1962 [with corrections], 1963, 1965 [again corrected], and in 1971!)

Here, then, is the background against which developed the emphasis in the 1960s and 1970s on resistance at every stage of the colonial encounter. The resisters were no longer characterised as thugs, nor did the rulers who had fought against the conquering British appear as bloody tyrants. Human sacrifice disappeared from the accounts of Benin, Kano prison was no longer mentioned, the nature of traditional slavery in Africa was sharply differentiated from the slavery of the trade with Europe, and the wars which used to be thought so destructive of progress, and so pointless, were justified or, better, celebrated. Fyfe's school history of Sierra Leone contains the following extraordinary "Notes for Teachers": "Some history books say that the wars fought in West Africa were just 'tribal wars' fought for no reason. Show your pupils how the wars mentioned in this chapter . . . were all fought for reasons that the people who fought them could justify rationally".[34]

The classic example of destructive war, of course, was the *Mfecane* in Southern Africa, and Gideon Were now wrote: "In spite of the misery and destruction it caused, it would be wrong to conclude that the effects of the *Mfecane* were wholly or even largely negative. Its constructive effects were profound and long-lasting and it is for these that it should be remembered". He mentioned the incorporation of refugees into "new, powerful and united states"; the defensive response of other societies, like the Nyamwezi and Hehe, to these; the "growth of national cohesion and unity" resulting from the adoption of Zulu military techniques and political organisation by other peoples; and a new type of leadership based on survival of the fittest. ''Hence the emergence of bigger, stronger and better-organised nations, in which law and order were effectively maintained and severe discipline enforced'', and in which the army, rather than relations of kinship, was the basis of power.[35]

The last we shall examine of the burdens which colonial historians placed on later ones is that most all-embracing one, the outright racism of the colonial version of African development. Progress in early centuries was attributed to the influence of visitors and migrants from the north, either Phoenicians or Hamites, an ethnic category which was then regarded as white. Later editions of Fage's book have dropped this idea, of course, but in 1957 he hammered in the whiteness of the Hamites again and again. ''Before the life of these various Negro peoples was modified by the influence of white peoples'', he wrote, they lived in self-sufficient, politically autonomous descent groups. He granted that it was ''difficult and dangerous'' to generalise, ''but it would seem that in West Africa the original impulse for the change from small descent-groups to territorial states was military conquest by white peoples from North Africa''. The history of the Sudan from the fourth to the nineteenth century was ''largely one of a succession of great territorial empires'' established by white invaders or Negroes who acquired techniques and weapons by contact with whites; and ''The dominant theme in the history of West Africa for the last 2,000 years has in fact been the contact and conflict of its black peoples with white intruders and the effect of the expansive activities of the white peoples on the development of the Negroes''.[36] It is interesting to compare his statement, only seven years later, that ''There seems no question in fact that the empires of Ghana, Mali and Songhai rank among the highest achievements of Negro Africans in history''![37]

On the other side of the continent, the southward spread of the Bahima in the fourteenth and fifteenth centuries, which is the historical counterpart of the influence of Hamites on West Africa, is described by Clarke in *A Short History of Tanganyika*:

Soon the whole of Bukoba district became a copy of civilisation in Uganda, which was far better than anything that existed in Tanganyika. . . . The indigenous people accepted the rule of the invaders willingly and peacefully because they saw that the invaders were more advanced and better organisers than themselves. The invaders brought a more civilised way of life with them.

In judging cases and quarrels, the invaders did not favour one clan more than another; they were strangers and judged with fairness to both sides. . . . Wherever they went, the Bahima spread their better system of government which led to the building up of stronger tribes. They were the most important group of people civilising other peoples in the larger part of Tanganyika before the arrival of Europeans in the nineteenth century.[38]

We have already seen how, from that point on, European tutelage was considered crucial to further African development. Equally racist in its implications, though understandable in terms of the readily available sources, was the emphasis on European, rather than African, activities in Africa. In this connection, it is interesting to look at the table of contents of a book (published in 1962) called *Some Famous Names in Africa*. The names are: Father Goncalos da Silveira, Moshesh, Paul Kruger, Cecil Rhodes, Jan Smuts, Ferdinand de Lesseps, Leon Faidherbe, Marshal Lyautey, Sir William Mackinnon, Lord Lugard, Dr. Aggrey, and Dr. Albert Schweitzer. Only two are black Africans.[39]

Racism of this kind died hard, even when it went out of fashion with independence. An unconscious expression of it is found in the illustrations of "modern man" (contrasted with *homo habilis*) in Johnston's *Early Man in Zambia*, published in 1970,[40] and of Old and New Stone Age people in Sharman's *Africa Through the Ages*, published in 1964.[41] Although the books are about Africa, the people shown are white.

These examples show some of the faults that writers of school books in the sixties and seventies tried to correct. It was implied that Africans were far behind Europeans in political and technological development by the time whites first came to Africa, and that their development since then (by no means up to the level of Europeans) had been due to efforts by whites in various roles to create an environment in which it was possible to be civilised, and then to civilise them. It followed from this that accounts of African history would be unbalanced in a number of ways. First, the period of white contact usually got much more space than all the time preceding it. Second, events in Europe were given a disproportionate amount of space. Third, within Africa, events in which Europeans were involved were considered more important than ones which purely concerned Africans. Fourth, Africans were cast in a passive role, receiving various kinds of benefits and blows, the decisions affecting them being made very largely by Europeans.

What was done to correct this? There was a shift of focus, geo-graphically speaking, from Europe to Africa, and in time from the pe-riod of European contact to the centuries before whites were known in Africa. There is not actually more writing on this early period than on the later one, because of the vast amounts of material available on the period of white involvement, and the comparatively scanty sources for the time before. But every effort has been made to enlarge our knowl-edge of pre-colonial times, including the recording of oral traditions, and the development of techniques for interpreting them. We are in-terested now in things that Africans did, with or without Europeans being involved; as well as pushing the reconstruction of African his-tory back before the European period, this means that we try to write something about places which are as yet very little known to the aca-demic world. In outline histories we write about "the interior" as well as the coasts, even if this means extrapolating, perhaps misleadingly, from very scanty or non-contemporary sources.[42]

Along with this interest in the African role in events has come a different kind of presentation of Africans. They are actors, innovators, people whose responses matter.

So far so good. Given this focus on Africa and her people, post-independence historians could have written from almost any point of view. But as far as studies of the pre-colonial past were concerned, nearly all wrote the same kind of history, their thinking dominated by the need to explode the myth of African inferiority. Thus, African progress was compared with that of Europe in the centuries before the two races ever met. This could only be done, of course, if it was as-sumed that human history was a one-way evolution. Not only was this assumption clear in what was written about the African past, but it was also evident that historians, black and white alike, thought that the most recent and therefore the best stage of this evolution to date was rep-resented by the Western world. It was this assumption which made it possible to write about a people "failing" to develop a particular form of government or economy;[43] or being catapulted into "the twentieth century" or "the modern world". It is language like this which lends an air of inevitability to the nation state and the capitalist system, not just for the peoples who actually have them now, but for those who have not, and therefore, though they are alive in 1984, for example, are said to be living in another century. This also enabled historians not to think about the great variety of ways of living that there are *now*, so they need not try to explain them. Anthropologists no longer describe surprising aspects of culture as "survivals", but historians got away with this kind of thinking easily. A student reading African history should find it very interesting to note the context and meaning of such words as backward, primitive, advanced, modern, success, failure, necessary, strength, weakness, achievement, development, progress—he will find that they usually make sense only in terms of this supposed evolution towards the ways of the West.

This has a bearing, too, on the last point made above, that Africans were now regarded as people whose responses matter. The reader of African histories will notice that only some kinds of responses mattered. The Bushmen and the Dinka get up every day and about their business, but it seemed to be of very little interest to historians.

It is because of this that I say the new version was only partially explicable in terms of necessary reactions to the old. The previous section showed a number of areas in which reaction was both necessary and predictable. But the form the reaction took depended not only upon the insults themselves but upon the assumptions of the new historians with regard to what history was for—i.e., to create a particular set of values—and what was to be valued. Because history was conceived as a tool of socialisation more than as a branch of knowledge, material had to be removed from the presentation of the past which gave an unfavourable impression, and favourable material had to be exaggerated. In the transition from colonial to post-colonial history, the values dictating what was favourable did not change; all that happened was that the historians changed sides, backing the black race instead of the white. But they saw no reason to question the nature of the contest in which they took sides; they were backing Africans now in what was still an effort to prove that blacks could be as good as whites at the things whites thought worth doing. The real difference is that in the colonial period history was brought as evidence that Africans had no European kinds of achievement in their past, so if they were to prove that they were as worthy of admiration as Europeans they must do it in the present and future by adopting alien ways. After independence, history was brought as evidence that European kinds of achievement had always existed in the African past, that, in fact, they were African kinds of achievement as much as European. My objection to this is not that it is not true, but that these kinds of activity were given a positive value which, in the first place, I do not think they deserved, but which, leaving value judgement of any kind aside, led to a particular kind of falsification of the African past by dictating the exaggeration of some aspects of it, the minimisation of others, and hence a degree of mis-understanding of all. At the bottom of it was an evolutionism which is a feature of Western thought and should not be mistaken either for a universal truth or for a universal way of thinking. The rest of this chapter looks at this evolutionism in books written for students after 1960.

First, if history was an evolution, it was also a race, in the eyes of our historians. "In the early Middle Ages", Colin Nicholson wrote, "there were states in the Western Sudan which were equal to those in contemporary Europe".[44] Equal how? He cites Al Bekri's visit to Ghana "In 1067, only a year after William of Normandy conquered England"[45] and his descriptions of the wealth and elaborate ceremonial of the court, the king's dress and regalia, and the two hundred thousand warriors the king of Ghana could put in the field. So impressive was all this, in fact, that Nicholson reassessed the position a few pages further on. The travellers' reports, he felt, "clearly show that some states in Af-rica were possibly more advanced than those of medieval Europe. The rulers of Ghana, Mali, and Songhai . . . controlled wealthy, ordered societies, in which trade flourished and men could lead peaceful lives within the walls of fine cities like Timbuctu and Kimbu".[46] Thus Af-rican power was just as powerful, African pomp just as pompous, in the Middle Ages, as in Europe. "Europe had its Charlemagne, its Charles the Great", wrote C.H. Wesley, "and Africa has its Askia the Great".[47] Ronald Segal, editor of the Penguin African Library, as-sured us that African culture was also just as good:

And while the centres of European culture flourished, decayed, and sprouted in their turn, empires in Africa rose, ruled, resisted, and succumbed. Scholars studied and disputed in Timbuctu as in Paris, and what the Italians accom-plished in pigment, the artists of Benin achieved with bronze. The cultures were different, but only on the horizontal. The vertical, the separation into superior and inferior, was a product of conquest.[48]

George Pollock, too, drew attention to the Benin bronzes, which he said were "far more than folk art"; moreover, "the impressive stone ruins of Great Zimbabwe in Rhodesia prove that African architectural ability did not halt at the thatched hut".[49] Akinola wrote, "Portuguese records indicate that Mombasa was a prosperous city bustling with commercial activity. Her stone buildings and her standard of civilisation compared favourably with that of medieval Portugal".[50] Burke wrote:

Today the peoples of Africa are discovering that the accomplishments of their ancestors compare favourably with those of the European peoples who formerly ruled them.[51] . . . When we note that Kush, Axum, and Ghana had attained high levels of culture well before the Normans invaded England in 1066, we realise how old African civilisations are.[52]

Nelson Kasfir commented that Muhammed Ture of Songhai "created a standing army based on regular conscription perhaps two hundred years before European states were sufficiently organised to do the same thing";[53] and Hatch remarked similarly that "the kingdom of Ghana existed during the period of European feudalism; it was certainly better ordered than many European states of its time".[54]

Now we can see why the study of the African past became the study of kingdoms. We in the West did violence to our own history by focussing on rulers, and tracing through them the development of Western society. (By "rulers" I mean ruling classes, as well as kings.) Since the Second World War there has been disillusionment with nationalist and elitist history in Europe, and more recently an upsurge of interest in the lives of ordinary people. But African history was stuck with the traditional Western view of what was important in the past. Thus, to show that Africans might be as proud of their past as we were of ours, we dug up their capital cities and wove the story around them. Pollock wrote, "Nor did African history begin with the civilising mission of Europeans. It evolved independently, colourfully, over many centuries. It involved great leaders, great armies, great bureaucracies, and impressive works of art."[55] Where are the followers, the bureaucratised? It was Pollock who characterised the Benin bronzes as "far more than folk art". What does this say about folk art, then? And Great Zimbabwe proved, for him, that "African architectural ability did not halt at the thatched hut".[56] There are a few Zimbabwes, an Engaruka, and a Bigo; but there are millions of thatched huts in Africa.

The obsession with kingdoms is reflected in the tables of contents of book after book. Apart from the many books which are written specifically about kingdoms,[57] and biographies of rulers,[58] there are those which purport to be histories of the whole continent, or the whole of

West Africa. Time and again, their coverage follows the same general plan: Ancient Egypt, Empires of the Sudan, States of the Forest, and, more briefly, East and Central Africa. Here stateless societies do normally get a mention, although in Chijioke's *Ancient Africa*, containing thirteen chapters about West Africa, one on Ethiopia, and one on "The Lands of East and Central Africa", even the last is no more than a tour of kingdoms. There is one paragraph on "The Coastlands of East Africa", one on "Zimbabwe", one on "The Kingdom of the Monomotapa", and one on "The Rozwi, the Later Rulers of Zimbabwe".[59]

Both Oliver and Ogot comment on the preference historians show for states, Oliver attributing it to the fact that they "create and preserve" their traditions more efficiently than stateless societies, and leave more monuments; moreover, they simplify the historian's task by "[reducing] to manageable numbers the population units he has to describe".[60]

But, apart from the problems of using royal traditions as historical sources,[61] the paucity of information on stateless societies was partly a reflection of the paucity of research on them (Lamphear's work on the Jie, for example, reveals a greater depth and chronological accuracy of tradition than herding societies are supposed to possess),[62] and partly a reflection of what historians consider noteworthy. We still have to ask *why* more people were not interested in investigating the history of stateless societies?

As for monuments, the ones to which Oliver refers are monuments for archaeologists. Ian Cunnison shows that on the Luapula any rock or tree or hill may be a monument for oral tradition.[63]

Ogot, however, condemns "the Royal approach" outright. He takes for his example a history syllabus of "one of the important Teacher Training Colleges in Kenya", the major headings of which were as follows:

   i. Kingdoms along the Nile Valley
  ii. Kingdoms of North-East Africa
 iii. Early Kingdoms and Empires of Western Sudan
 iv. Later Kingdoms and Empires of Western Sudan
  v. States of Guinea Forest
 vi. States and Kingdoms of East Africa

vii. Kingdoms and Empires of Central Africa
viii. States and Kingdoms of South Africa.

There is no need here to comment [he comments], on the impression given by such a syllabus that those African peoples who developed forms of centralised states are the only ones worthy of attention, and that the many others who did not are insignificant: current research on the pre-European history of Africa has effectively disposed of it.[64]

If this is the case, then the decision to teach history in terms of kingdoms must have been dictated by something other than the lack of knowledge of stateless societies. It is suggested that this something else was a positive enthusiasm for empires. Chanock derived the same impression from his reading of Central African history. He quoted Burton, who wrote:

"It is always a pleasure . . . after travelling through the semi-republican tribes of Africa, to arrive at the headquarters of a strong and sanguinary despotism. Only those who have lived in Africa can understand how it is so". Many historians [Chanock remarks] have obviously shared Burton's pleasure. Conquest states, military states, or trading states, based upon a ruling warrior class or an elite whose power grows through control of trade are all, it seems, on the side of progress, and the oppression or exploitation which their activities involved, though not ignored, is of secondary importance to their "achievements".[65]

Indeed, once we see what short shrift was accorded the subjects of precolonial empires, it is not surprising that people living outside them received so little mention in textbooks.

We have seen already how the study of pre-colonial African states was used in African history. Their existence, their splendour, their very comparability with contemporary European states was taken to explode the myth that Africa was a dark continent before the arrival of the white man, in what Orlando Patterson calls the "three P's approach—Black history as the rediscovery of princes, pyramids, and pageantry".[66] In what did this "splendour" consist? In book after book we read the descriptions of the Western Sudan by Al Bekri, Al Omari, and Ibn Battuta, as well as the latter's experience of the East African coast. The various Arab travellers and historians are the only contemporary sources, so no writer could leave them out.[67] And just because they admired gold, fancy clothes, and displays of wealth and power, does not mean that the reader must. But in fact the admiration of these writers was used to build up a whole romantic picture that these books invited *us* to admire. Again it is not the use of these sources that is objectionable but the *way* they were used.

Nicholson, for example, wrote:

As our knowledge of Africa expands, it is clear that far from being a "Dark Continent" sunk in simplicity and savagery, Africa had a long and complex history. . . . While Europeans were plunged in medieval feuds and religious wars, the kingdoms of Ghana, Mali, and Songhai were enjoying prosperity and peace, and the ships of the Zenj pursued a trade which spanned the Indian Ocean and touched the Pacific.[68]

We could take this passage as a starting point for looking at the intellectual dishonesty involved in much of post-colonial African history. Simplicity was bad, complexity was good. War was bad, peace was good. Poverty was bad, prosperity was good. It is hard to quarrel with this, when it is put (as it nearly always is) at the level of generalisations which cover each society as a homogeneous whole.

But how were these things achieved? There was peace—for whom? There was prosperity—for whom? There was peace, at the end of a war, or at the price of independence. These empires were not built without repeated wars against rivals and against those within the empire who aspired to power or dissented from the system under which they lived. (Strangely enough, the writers who celebrated peace where they found it, celebrated war as well, the multitude of soldiers, the battle dress, the thunder of hooves, the courage of the commanders— as long as the more civilised side won.) And what about the prosperity of these kingdoms, where the king of Ghana's horses slept on carpets provided by the taxes of the conquered, where the court of Songhai was supported by the labour of slave estates? Aigbokhai wrote:

Askia Mohammed Ture reformed and put the economy of Songhai on a firm basis. . . . His reforms increased the yield of state revenue from slave-worked estates, regular contributions from the provinces, tributes from vassal states and proceeds from state-controlled commerce, particularly the trans-Saharan trade. The resultant prosperity helped, among other things, in the establishment of a standing professional army vital to the strength and stability of Songhai. . . . Mohammed Ture's political astuteness and administrative genius helped to make him one of the great rulers of Songhai.[69]

These wars, these taxes, the many forms of forced labour[70] and the inequalities of wealth were not hidden by the history books. They were, on the contrary, brought forward as evidence of what Africans could accomplish when they tried!

Time and time again we are told that figures of the past were great because they "added" large areas of territory to their empires,[71] because they "united" many different peoples under one system of law, order, and administration,[72] and because they "strengthened" the central power of the state. Zimbabwe is remarkable not only for its beauty but for the evidence it provides that a central power was able to mobilise an enormous labour force on its behalf.

Who built Zimbabwe? Much time and emotion have been devoted to the argument about whether Phoenicians or Africans built it, which is certainly crucial if one thinks that people live in mud huts because they are stupid, or that if Africans did not build Zimbabwe it is proved that they could have done it if they had tried. What ought to be of interest is, which Africans built it and why? To what sorts of political relations among *Africans* does it attest?

And what about unification? This theme runs from the beginnings of the Sudanic kingdoms to the current politics of African nations, but while there may be different views about unification in the latter context, it is always presented as a good thing in the pre-colonial period. Thus people like Mirambo and even Shaka became heroes. Without observing this enthusiasm for unification, moreover, it is difficult to understand Kofi Darkwah's use of the word "solved" in the following sentence: "However, by formally ceding Eritrea to the Italians, Menelik created a problem for Ethiopia, which was not solved until 1952, when Eritrea was re-united with the rest of Ethiopia".[73] Certainly Eritreans did not regard the problem as solved!

If proof were needed that the attitudes outlined above were not inescapably imposed by the sources for the period, it is provided by the rare school books which described African kingdoms without celebrating them too. There are two books on Benin, for example (one by Kit Elliot, the other by Elizabeth McClelland), which convey a great deal of information, chiefly from the Portuguese sources, without endorsing their value judgments or adding many of the author's own, and without suppressing the oppressive aspects of the Oba's rule (except for McClelland's unique omission of the subject of human sacrifice!).[74]

The authors of these books did not purport to offer an historical approach different from the mainstream one, but they *were* different, inasmuch as they treated Benin with historical imagination rather than trying to make it a one-dimensional symbol of African achievement. Their books were more realistic, and gave the reader credit for being able to think about more than one facet of history. And by giving such a lot of space to describing the things of the common people, they avoided giving the impression that only rulers mattered.

Basil Davidson, however, deserves to be discussed on his own, for he self-consciously attempts to provide African children with a socialist view of their history. His books are particularly interesting for us, because he alone takes up the idea of people's control over their own lives, but cannot bring himself to follow it very far because he feels an apparently conflicting obligation, that of inspiring young Africans with pride in their past. This would not be a conflict, of course, if he were not stuck with the traditional Western view of what constitutes an historical achievement.

Once whites appear on the scene he is all right, because he can write in terms of the conflict between black and white in the economic systems of African countries and of the world, of the political fight for independence, and of the dangers of neo-colonialism and the need for a further struggle for economic independence. But his treatment of the pre-colonial past can only be described as schizophrenic. He dwells on the greatness of the old kingdoms of Africa, but says that stateless systems were just as good, each being a political solution to a particular set of problems in organising social life and relations with other groups. And sometimes—briefly—he discusses the problems of inequality, of "unfreedom" and exploitation involved in the growth of larger units with power and wealth increasingly centralised.[75] But for the most part he would like to believe that these kingdoms were developed by their populations as a whole and served their interests. The difficulty of reconstructing such a development is reflected in the confusion of such passages as: "Being able to feed its people well made it possible for Egypt to build one of the greatest civilisations of all time",[76] or:

These activities on Ghana's part [i.e., more efficient farming and warfare due to the use of iron] made its people realise that they needed a new and better kind of government. The old, simple tribal government would no longer do. A strong, growing nation needed a government with a regular army and many workers. In short, Ghana was ready to become a state with a king at its head.[77]

This process is described in a book for older readers, again:

With the growth of states like Ghana, the people of West Africa were invent- ing new methods of living together, of governing themselves, of raising money to pay for government, and of producing wealth. These ways needed a single strong authority or government which could rule over many lesser authorities or governments. This central authority or government could only, in the thought and customs of the times, be a king. In states like Ancient Ghana, the power of government increased still further. Important kings became kings over lesser kings. They became what we call emperors.[78]

This is meaningless. What is meant by words like "inventing" or "became"? How did this actually happen? Davidson does not say, be- cause he does not know. This is acceptable. What is not acceptable is the description of the "becoming" of emperors as some sort of deci- sion of the people. In the effort to present Africans as making their own history, Davidson confuses the people with the state. The situa- tion in which the people are the state is certainly desirable, but it does not follow that it existed in the empires of the African past. Nor is it likely to accord with any student's experience of politics. So why should students have to learn it? Because it seems good to Davidson to de- scribe pre-colonial Africa as a scene of independence, which, in the case of some of these empires, is not easy. Their rulers were indepen- dent of Europeans, of course, but that is a truism as there were no Europeans about. He seems to want to use the word, because of its positive emotional charge, where it can have no application except possibly to imply that allegiance to the old empires was voluntary and enthusiastic, unlike allegiance to the European empires in Africa. As there is no way of knowing such a thing, he can only imply it by the use of language, and hope that in the climate of enthusiasm for the new nations his characterisation of the old ones will be welcomed un- questioningly:

In the old days, through the long centuries of the rise and ripeness of their iron age, Africans built political, social and economic systems of their own. . . . They gave birth to the states and empires of West Africa, to those of Monomotapa and the Changamir and many others. Then Africa, or part of Africa, went into trading partnership with the nations of Western Europe. This ended badly for Africa, as we have also seen: it ended in the one-sided partnership of the slave trade. And the slave trade opened the door to the colonial system. But the colonial system reduced Africa to servitude.

So the greatest task of the present and the future must be to find ways of *re-building* African independence on a thoroughly modern, efficient and united basis.[79]

Davidson's difficulties illustrate the nature of the inconsistency which was always just beneath the surface of the new history. That it *had* a surface was due to the appearance of consistency provided by the virtual unanimity of historians in presenting Africans as competent, wise, well-intentioned, and noble (a presentation they felt was necessary to refute the earlier picture of Africans as incompetent, foolish, cruel, and venal). This could seem to work, at a simple level, for the period of confrontation with Europeans, who provide a foil for these qualities. But, for times when all the parties involved in conflict, cruelties, or disasters were African, the need for a more complex and realistic view becomes apparent. It is racism to make a special case of the African character, either way; it is also inadequate to the writing of history.

Why then did the new history take the line it did?

One reason is that this kind of history met many of the needs of the elites who took over the governments of African nations at independence. The glorification of the centralised, hierarchical polities of the past served as a useful form of indoctrination in obedience to present regimes. Revolts against white rulers were quite properly presented as natural and brave. But revolts against the black rulers of the past were presented as among the problems they had to combat in unifying their peoples and strengthening their governments, just as, already, the independent governments were having to do. As Kasfir puts it, "Ancient African empires are important today precisely because modern African leaders say they are", and "The most important political heritage of ancient empires is the unifying role of the myths they left behind".[80]

This is an aspect of the new history of which the student should be aware. It is not suggested, however, that it was the conscious intention of all the historians we have been looking at. What they tried to do was to instill in Africans a pride in their pre-colonial past which would in turn give them confidence in their ability to manage their post-colonial present and future. Introducing the collection *Africa from Early Times to 1800*, McEwan said, ''African history provides a context of man's development into which many of the problems and aspirations of the present can be meaningfully placed, thus stimulating a broader sense of tradition and a deeper pride of achievement which lend natural and legitimate support to the growth of nationhood''.[81] The message was that Africans used to be powerful like Europeans, so why should they not be again? But the other side of this message is that in each kingdom some Africans were powerful while others were not. The contradiction involved in holding up ancient African independence as a basis for pride and strength in the world of today is hidden by the identification of subjects with kings, but it is there, nonetheless. If there were relatively independent Africans, they were precisely the ones ignored by the history books because their decentralised ways of life did not lead to the preservation of records or lasting remains. The ones who do feature in the books were those over whom the domination of kings was most thoroughgoing and successful, and it is the success, rather than the failure, of this kind of domination which is brought as evidence of African independence. If these are the models with which students are asked to identify, why should they derive confidence from their past? Why not rather a feeling that only the rulers are important, not the ruled, and that the way to be important is to get to the top? It is not surprising that this is the real message of African school history. It is also the message of Western school history. It is the message that adults communicate to children, that people in authority communicate to people whose lives are in their hands. This is not a conscious conspiracy. This is the way we think.

And it is not conducive to confident, egalitarian relations between people. In ''Education for Self-reliance'', Nyerere wrote:

We have said that we want to create a socialist society which is based on three principles: equality and respect for human dignity; sharing of the resources which are produced by our efforts; work by everyone and exploitation by none . . . in which progress is measured in terms of human well-being, not prestige buildings, cars, or other such things, whether privately or publicly owned.[82]

In view of this, is it appropriate to admire the rulers of Mali, and pass on? Was Zimbabwe really an appropriate symbol for the freedom fighters of Rhodesia?

But the task of rewriting African history in a way more appropriate to the aims of which Nyerere spoke is not easy, especially for European historians. Davidson's problem is a very real one. Is it right to reexamine the governments of the pre-colonial past with a more critical eye? Is it not destructive? What right have white historians to say that while African history may have been a series of success stories for some people, it was not necessarily that for most people? Does this not take us back to the colonial idea that Africans' efforts to govern themselves were pathetic?

They could only be pathetic if the comparison is with an outside world in which failures, cruelties, and disasters are felt to have been negligible. If it were not for the myth of the supremely well-run Western society, the myth of the African past moving from strength to strength would not be so necessary. Nonetheless the Western myth exists, and Kasfir writes:

Perhaps the most fundamental use of myths is to decolonise African peoples by restoring their dignity. Without the myths of great African successes people would tend to copy Europeans. This might mean the continuation of attitudes of inferiority, since copying is not creative. But with a sense of greatness in their own past, a past which belongs to Africans alone, the opportunity to strike out on new paths—develop new patterns of government and politics—will permit genuine creativity.[83]

It may be felt that nobody who has not suffered from contempt on racial grounds can understand the need black people have to prove themselves in white peoples' terms, before anything else can be accomplished, and this may be true. Certainly it is a terrible feeling to despise yourself because other people despise you. The question historians must face, then, is: which is the right solution? Must people become whatever it is that other people respect, or should other people stop despising people who are not like them in some ways? Whether the latter would meet the need of people struggling for dignity is something only those people could say; it is a psychological question, and an important one, but one which cannot be answered here. We are concerned not so much with the demand for myth as with its supply, and the question whether European historians at least, who do not need the myth, should reexamine their attitudes towards supplying it.

But even from the point of view of the demand for myth, something remains to be said. Kasfir assumed that the establishment of a new African myth would clear the way for creativity. But a major point which this chapter, and this book, try to make, is that the myth was not a liberating or creative one, but an imitative one, as success was still defined, and measured, in European terms.

It may be thought that, with the growing emphasis on lines of division in the African past replacing the demonstration of unity which occupied historians in the sixties, school history will eventually take on the lineaments of what is fashionable at a higher level. It is in this area, however, that the questions raised here remain urgent, both because of the connection of education with the state (which, whatever its rhetoric, remains of course the ruling structure) and because it is widely felt that students should be inspired with confidence, not doubt. For both these reasons, school histories persist in trying to be "positive", and we must continue to ask what this can mean.

Where can teachers of African history turn, then, for the best resources? If we look at the recent syntheses of African history aimed at the undergraduate level and above, where the factor of official ideology should not be so dominant, some interesting observations can be made. The two massive surveys begun in the seventies, the Cambridge and UNESCO histories of Africa, provide one kind of contrast, the one-volume treatments by Fage and by Curtin *et al.*, another.

One of the striking things about the multi-volume surveys is their contrasting editorial policies. The Cambridge History gives the lie to the old proverb, "Out of Africa, always something new". It has been welcomed for bringing together so much information under one roof, but the choice of authors, nearly all sometime colleagues at the School of Oriental and African Studies, makes for a presentation reminiscent in every way of the sixties. Because it is so long, and aims at such comprehensive coverage, it is very little marred by the rhetoric of progress; on the other hand, it is not much informed by recent interests, either. The continuing influence of evolutionist and nationalist ideas can be illustrated from the introduction to the middle volumes of the *Cambridge History of Africa*, published in 1975 and 1976. The ideas of centralisation, integration, African initiative, and African resistance dominate these chapters, intended to give an overview of the important developments of the periods with which these volumes deal (1600–1790 and 1790–1870, respectively). Indeed, Richard Gray finds "resistance" in the circumstance that slaving chiefs and traders did not sell more people than they did! "The fact that in the Atlantic hinterland as a whole the direct, demographic impact of the slave trade was confined to less than disastrous proportions can in some respects be considered as the most important of African achievements during this period".[84] After making the best of some very unpromising material in this way, he outlines the other major trends of the period.

African vitality, seen here in the resistance to, and large scale control of, the slave trade, was often manifest elsewhere in continued, ordered, constructive innovations. Politically these centuries were marked by many instances of consolidation, by the expansion and centralisation of political institutions, by firmer, closer-knit areas of order and security.[85]

The extension of trade is likewise seen in a wholly positive light, and "initiative" is a key word. Summing up, Gray writes, "For the most part, Africa was still arbiter of her destiny. African initiative was still supreme".[86]

The impression of orderly progress here owes everything to the use of language. The same is true of John Flint's picture of the next eighty years. He writes, for example, of the development of Ethiopian "patriotism", which "was to present the Egyptian and later Italian invaders with a unified and vibrant resistance". How can a resistance be vibrant? Still, along with "vitality", this is part of the language of African history since independence.

In Flint's estimation, "In African political history the most outstanding phenomenon of the period was the creation of states bearing many of the attributes of nationalism".[87]

The UNESCO history approaches similar ideological ends by a very different editorial route: a system of selecting authors according to their nationality, and, one suspects, their acceptability as champions of blackness too, for Diop has been invited to restate a theory which has long been regarded as belonging to the literature of Negritude rather than to African history. The book's stated aim is, in fact, the rehabilitation of African history, which "needs rewriting, for up till now it has often been masked, faked, distorted, mutilated. . . . Scholars give out its image as one of nothing but poverty, barbarism, irresponsibility, and chaos".[88]

Each of these surveys, therefore, is a monument to the scholarship and motivations of the sixties; at the same time, they are the obvious reference works for teachers in the future.

Teachers would do better, instead, to look to the one-volume work *African History*, written by Curtin, Feierman, Thompson, and Vansina, and published in 1978. Its usefulness is all the more evident when compared with Fage's offering in the same year of *A History of Africa*. This is a trade and politics book, in which "centralised" is equated with "positive",[89] town dwellers are "more advanced in almost all the arts of life" than pastoralists,[90] and slavery is somewhat rationalised because "In African conditions [only?] institutions of servitude could be used to build up societies which could offer enlarged opportunities for the achievement of wealth and security".[91] Again, the rhetoric of progress is much sparser than in the sixties, but the view of history is the same. The last section is called, unsurprisingly, "Independence Resumed".

A real alternative, however, is found in the book by Curtin *et al.*; indeed, it is the result of a conscious effort to provide an alternative, "different from the main lines of African history as they were understood in the past . . . less interested in the deeds of the great than . . . in the culture and behaviour of ordinary people", with less emphasis on political history and more on "social, economic, and intellectual trends".[92]

Ethnocentric thinking is present, certainly—there is a tendency, presumably arising from the Western tradition of constitutional social engineering, to regard political systems as the results of conscious design by the people living under them[93] and there is a statement that this design is for the benefit of all: "Scarcity of some factors of production or increasing concentrations of people required more and more sophisticated ways to harmonise their interests, such as better decision-making processes and better-defined channels for the use and devolution of power".[94] But the book is not structured in conformity with this statement, and where we might expect an air of congratulation—for example, in treating Sudanic empires, Shaka's state-building efforts, or centralisation in the Interlacustrine region—the presentation is fairly value-free or else presents the reader with contending points of view. *African History is* a history, and not a sales pitch.

## NOTES

1. *A Visual History of Africa* (London, Evans Brothers Ltd., 1969; first published 1954), p. 8. An exercise at the foot of the page sums up what is felt to be important

Put in the missing words:

1. because of . . . difficulties, the African peoples of long ago could not form a great
   . . .

2. They lived in small . . .

3. The tribes were often . . . and were always . . . each other.

2. Apart, that is, from its companions in the "Visual Histories" series, which cover single countries as well as the whole of Africa; see, e.g., J.D. Clarke, *A Visual History of Nigeria* (London, Evans Bros. Ltd., 1971; first published 1956).

3. Technically speaking of course, the word "civilised" simply means "living in cities"; but it carries many more connotations in common usage, as will be apparent, and it was to these that the new historians objected.

4. O. Patterson, "Rethinking Black History", *Harvard Educational Review*, vol. 41, no. 3 (1971), p. 308.

5. R. Cornevin, "The Problems and Character of African History" in ed. T.O. Ranger, *Emerging Themes of African History* (Nairobi, East African Publishing House, 1968), p. 76.

6. For example: P. Curtin, *Africa South of the Sahara* (Morristown, N.J., Culture Area Studies, General Learning Corporation, 1970); F. Burke, *Africa* (Boston, Houghton Mifflin Co., 1970); R. Oliver and J. Fage, *A Short History of Africa* (Harmondsworth, Penguin, 1968; first published 1962); J.B. Webster and A.A. Boahen, with H.O. Idowu, *The Revolutionary Years: West Africa since 1800* (London, Longmans, 1967); J.D. Omer-Cooper, E.A. Ayandele, A.E. Afigbo, and R.J. Gavin, *The Making of Modern Africa: vol. 1, The Nineteenth Century to the Partition* (London, Longmans, 1968); and *vol. 2, The Late Nineteenth Century to the Present Day* (London, Longmans, 1971). O. Ikime, *Nana of the Niger Delta* (London, Heinemann, 1972); P.A. Igbafe, *Obaseki of Benin* (London, Heinemann, African Historical Biographies, 1972); R.H.K. Darkwah, *Menelik of Ethiopia* (London, Heinemann, African Historical Biographies, 1972); A. Boahen, *Topics in West African History* (London, Longman Schools Edition, 1966).

7. Two different editions of his *History of West Africa* will be compared below.

8. R. Coupland, *History Textbooks for Schools in British Tropical Africa* (London, Oxford University Press, 1936), pp. 1–4. Coupland was himself a serious historian of Africa, and wrote several academic works on African history.

9. A.V.P. Elliot, "The Teaching of History in Africa: Preliminary Considerations", *Overseas Education*, vol. 5 (1933/34), p. 174.

10. Quoted by A. Moumouni, in *Education in Africa*, trans. P.N. Ott (London, Deutsch, 1968), p. 45.

11. W.E. Ward, "The Writing of History Textbooks for Africa", *Africa*, vol. 7 (1934), p. 197.

12. A.V. Murray, *The School in the Bush* (London, Frank Cass & Co., 1967; first published 1929). The quotation is from the 1967 edition, pp. 203–04.

13. E.g., "The natural course of African history was savagely halted by European conquest and centuries of the slave trade".—G.F. Pollock, *Civilisations of Africa: Historic Kingdoms, Empires, and Cultures* (Middletown, Conn., An American Education Publication Unit Book, 1970), p. 5.

14. B. Ogot, "The Role of the Pastoralist and the Agriculturalist in African History; The Case of East Africa", in Ranger, *Emerging Themes*.

15. R. Horton, "Stateless Societies in the History of West Africa", in eds. J. Ajayi and M. Crowder, *History of West Africa* (London, Longman, 1971), vol. 1.

16. B. Davidson, "Questions about Nationalism", *African Affairs*, vol. 76, no. 302 (Jan. 1977), p. 42.

17. See D. Westermann, "The Value of the African's Past", *International Review of Missions*, vol. 15, no. 59 (July, 1926), p. 428. This aspect of early colonial history is discussed by Martin Chanock in a piece of work in progress, dealing with the place of African history in colonial education. I am grateful to him for the loan of his notes and advice on this subject.

18. See *Tarikh*, vol. 4, no. 2 (1973), *Government in Pre-Colonial Africa*: E.A. Ijagbemi, "A Note on Temne Kingship in the Early Nineteenth Century", p. 29; and J.A. Atanda, "Government of Yorubaland in the Pre-Colonial Period", p. 11. The societies in these articles are described as "not static", while Pollock (*Civilisations*) celebrates "movement": "Instead of languishing in darkness and isolation, as many Westerners believed", Pollock writes, "Africa was a centre of world history for many centuries. Africans conducted a regular trade with India, Indonesia, and even China. And within the African continent itself there was a constant movement of peoples and exchange of ideas".

19. T.R. Batten, *Tropical Africa in World History, Book I: The Foundations of Modern History* (London, Oxford University Press, 1951; first published 1939), pp. 45–46.

20. Ibid., p. 91 ff.

21. J. Fage, *An Introduction to the History of West Africa* (Cambridge, Cambridge University Press, 1957), pp. 16–17.

22. J. Hatch, *Africa: The Rebirth of Self-Rule* (London, Oxford University Press, 1967), p. 16.

23. Fage, *Introduction*, pp. 17–18.

24. Ibid., p. 93.

25. J. Rouch, *Contribution à l'histoire des Songhay* (Dakar, Institut Français d'Afrique Nègre, 1953), pp. 179–86, 213–21, quoted in translation in ed.

P.J.M. McEwan, *Africa from Early Times to 1800* (London, Oxford University Press, 1968), p. 68.

26. G. Uzoigwe, "Kabalega and the Making of the New Kitara", *Tarikh*, vol. 3, no. 2 (1970), pp. 7, 13.

27. See, e.g., Sir Arthur Burns, *History of Nigeria* (London, Allen & Unwin, 1929), pp. 22, 36, 40, 166–68, 187–89. For a sample of the "city of blood" school, here is Loftus, "Nigeria", p. 31 (describing the capture of Benin by British forces in 1897): "Benin was soon captured. It was a city of blood, full of human sacrifices. Men and women were found nailed to trees and huge pits were filled with human bodies. The open space in front of the king's house was covered with corpses". The illustration on this page, titled "Scenes in Benin at the Time of its Capture", depicts bodies scattered in the street and skeletons affixed to trees. The exercises following this passage are distinctly colonial in their emphasis:

Exercises:

1. How did the Consuls of the Niger Coast Protectorate punish mis-rule?

2. What was the cause of so much oppression by the chiefs of the coast towns?

3. Who was Chief Nana and why was he banished?

4. Why was Benin captured by the British?

28. F. Lugard, *Report on Northern Nigeria 1902* (Colonial Reports: Annual no. 409), para. 45. This is quoted in T.R. Batten, *Tropical Africa in World History*, Book 3 (London, Oxford University Press, 2nd edition, 1951; first published 1939), pp. 82–83; and in Burns, *Nigeria*, p. 177.

29. Batten, *Handbook*, p. 383.

30. Ibid., p. 391.

31. J. Fage, "Slavery and the Slave Trade in the Context of West African History", *Journal of African History*, vol. 10, no. 3 (1969), p. 402.

32. Fage, *Introduction*, p. 91.

33. P.H.C. Clarke, *A Short History of Tanganyika, The Mainland of Tanzania* (Dar es Salaam, Longman Tanzania Ltd., 1960), p. 102.

34. C. Fyfe, *A Short History of Sierra Leone* (London, Longman, 1962), pp. 181–82.

35. J. Were, *A History of South Africa* (London, Evans Bros. Ltd., 1974), p. 80.

36. J. Fage, *Introduction*, pp. 7–16 passim. For a similar obsession with white and black mixtures in the Western Sudan, on the part of a French historian, see Yves Urvoy, *Histoire de l'Empire du Bornu* (Paris, Larousse, 1949), pp. 47–59, 61–66, 87–92, quoted in translation in McEwan, *Africa*.

37. J. Fage, "Some Thoughts on State Formation in the Western Sudan before the Seventeenth Century", *Boston University Papers in African History*, vol. 1, ed. J. Butler (Boston, Boston University Press, 1964), p. 20.

38. Clarke, *Tanganyika*, pp. 46, 51.

39. J. Parr, *Records of Achievement: Some Famous Names in Africa* (London, Evans Bros. Ltd., 1962).

40. S. Johnston, *Early Man in Zambia* (London, Oxford University Press, 1970), p. 17.

41. M. Sharman, *Africa through the Ages* (London, Evans Bros. Ltd., 1964), pp. 7–8.

42. See B. Davidson with F.K. Buah, *Growth of African Civilisation: History of West Africa 1000–1800* (London, Longman, 1965), p. 52, and B. Davidson, *A History of East and Central Africa to the Late Nineteenth Century* (Garden City, N.Y., Anchor Books, Doubleday and Co., 1969; first published by Longman in 1967), pp. 182–84, and C. Nicholson, *The Making of Africa* (London, Wayland Publishers, The Documentary History Series, 1973), p. 22.

43. "In any event, this hypothesis would hold that the lag in African development came at a later stage—not from the slow development of agriculture, but from the failure to move on to the urban civilisation of the bronze age, as Egypt and Mesopotamia did". —R. Curtin, *African History* (Baltimore, Service Centre for Teachers of History Publication no. 56, Waverley Press, 1964), p. 26.

44. Nicholson, *Making of Africa*, p. 11.

45. Ibid., p. 12.

46. Ibid., pp. 15–16.

47. C.H. Wesley, *Neglected History: Essays in Negro-American History by a College President* (Wilberforce, Ohio, Central State College Press, 1965), p. 155. Quoted in Patterson, "Rethinking", p. 306.

48. In his editorial foreword to Oliver and Fage, *Short History*.

49. Pollock, *Civilisations*, p. 5.

50. G. Akinola, "The Mazrui of Mombasa", *Tarikh*, vol. 2, no. 3 (1968), p. 27.

51. F. Burke, *Africa*, p. 45.

52. Ibid., p. 49.

53. N. Kasfir, *Politics in Africa: An Introduction* (Kampala, Milton Obote Foundation, Adult Education Centre, 1968), p. 18.

54. Hatch, *Self-Rule*, p. 17.

55. Pollock, *Civilisations*, p. 5.

56. Ibid., p. 5.

57. E.g., D. Chu and E. Skinner, *A Glorious Age in Africa: The Story of Three Great African Empires* (Garden City, N.Y., Zenith Books, Doubleday and Co., 1965); G.F. Pollock, *Civilisations*; and M. Shinnie, *Ancient African Kingdoms* (New York, Mentor Books, 1970; first published 1965).

58. D. Sweetman, *Queen Nzinga, The Woman Who Saved Her People* (London, Longman, Makers of African History, 1971); G.K. Osei, *Shaka the*

*Great, King of the Zulus* (London, The African Publication Society, 1971); P. Sanders, *Moshweshwe of Lesotho* (London, Heinemann, African Historical Biographies, 1971); Darkwah, *Menelik*; D. Killingray, *Samori Touré: Warrior King* (Amersham, Bucks., Round the World Histories, 30, Hulton Educational Publications, 1973). See also the various biographical articles in *Tarikh*.

59. F.A. Chijioke, *Ancient Africa* (London, Longmans Beginning History, 1966).

60. R. Oliver, "Western Historiography and its Relevance to Africa" in Ranger, *Emerging Themes*, p. 56.

61. These are discussed in Chapter 7.

62. J. Lamphear, *The Traditional History of the Jie of Uganda* (Oxford, Clarendon Press, 1976).

63. I. Cunnison, *History on the Laupula: An Essay on the Historical Notions of a Central African Tribe* (The Rhodes-Livingstone Papers no. 21, published for the Rhodes-Livingstone Institute by Geoffrey Cumberlege, Capetown, Oxford University Press, 1951). See p. 3.

64. B. Ogot, "Some Approaches to African History", in ed. Ogot, *Hadith I* (Proceedings of the Annual Conference of the Historical Association of Kenya, 1967, Nairobi, East African Publishing House, 1968), pp. 6–7.

65. M. Chanock, "Development and Change in the History of Malawi" in ed. B. Pachai, *The Early History of Malawi* (London, Longman, 1971), p. 431.

66. Patterson, "Rethinking", p. 305.

67. In addition to the travellers, like Ibn Hawqal, El Macoudi, Ibn Battuta, and Leo Africanus, there were "historicogeographic compilers", El Bekri, Ibn Said, Ibn Khaldun; see Cornevin, "Problems and Character", p. 84.

68. Nicholson, *Making of Africa*, p. 21.

69. S.A. Aigbokhai, *West African History for the Certificate Year* (London, George Allen and Unwin, 1971), p. 11.

70. See, for example, E.A. Ijagbemi, "The Mende of Sierra Leone" in *Tarikh*, vol. 5, no. 1 (1974), on pre-colonial agriculture by villages of slaves.

71. B. Davidson, *A Guide to African History* (Garden City, N.Y., Zenith Books, Doubleday and Company, 1965), p. 25; S.B. Omorogie, *Emotan and the Kings of Benin* (Singapore, Makers of African History, Longman Group Ltd., 1972), p. 44; Aigbokhai, *Certificate Year*, p. 11.

72. Darkwah, *Menelik*, pp. 21–24.

73. Ibid., p. 30.

74. K. Elliot, *Benin* (Cambridge, Cambridge University Press, 1973); E.M. McClelland, *The Kingdom of Benin in the Sixteenth Century* (London, Oxford University Press, 1971).

75. In his *West Africa*.

76. Davidson, *Guide*, p. 6.

77. Ibid., p. 22.

78. Davidson, *West Africa*, pp. 39–40.

79. B. Davidson, *A Guide to African History* (London, George Allen and Unwin, 1971), pp. 91–92.

80. Kasfir, *Politics*, pp. 16, 18.

81. McEwan, *Africa*, p. v.

82. J. Nyerere, "Education for Self-Reliance", in his *Ujamaa: Essays on Socialism* (London, Oxford University Press, 1970; first published 1968), pp. 50–52.

83. Kasfir, *Politics*, p. 20. Kasfir is using the word "myth" here to mean a false but gratifying version of history. In a later chapter on oral tradition it will be suggested that folk myths are not about success but about the insoluble conflicts and problems of life. In the present discussion, however, it is clear what Kasfir has in mind, and in the last paragraphs of this chapter, I shall use the word in the same sense in which he uses it.

84. *The Cambridge History of Africa*, general editors J.D. Fage and R. Oliver (Cambridge, Cambridge University Press, 1975- ), vol. 4 (ed. R. Gray) and vol. 5 (ed. J. Flint), p. 4.

85. Gray, *Cambridge History*, vol. 4, p. 6.

86. Ibid., p. 12.

87. Flint, *Cambridge History*, vol. 5, p. 3.

88. *UNESCO General History of Africa, vol. 1, Methodology and African Prehistory*, ed. J. Ki-Zerbo (Paris, UNESCO; London, Heinemann Educational Books; Berkeley, University of California Press, 1981), p. 2.

89. J. Fage, *A History of Africa* (London, Hutchinson, 1978), p. 298.

90. Ibid., p. 67.

91. Ibid., p. 316.

92. P. Curtin, S. Feierman, L. Thompson, and J. Vansina, *African History* (London, Longman, 1978), p. v.

93. Ibid., pp. 35, 82.

94. Ibid., p. 35.

# 3

# STILL TOO CHEATY, TOO THEFTY, TOO MOCKERY

At this point in time [the turn of the century] the Christian missionary, or, in some parts of tropical Africa, the Muslim missionary, was fortunately available to help build up again what had been broken down.

> R. Oliver and A. Atmore, *Africa since 1800*
> (Cambridge, Cambridge University Press, 1967), p. 155.

No political or religious activities have marred the even tenor of native life.

> District Commissioner, Kasama, Annual Report, Kasama, 1933;
> quoted by T.O. Ranger in ''Mchape and the Study of Witchcraft
> Eradication''
> unpublished paper to the Lusaka Conference on the History
> of Central African Religious Systems (Aug.-Sept. 1972).

The preceding chapter documented evolutionist patterns of thinking in school textbooks and related literature on the African past. We saw that many of these books were written by academic historians, rather than by professional textbook writers relying on secondary sources alone. The question remains, however, whether the same assumptions were found in books and articles written for the rest of ''the field'', rather than for students. Perhaps the evolutionist stance was simply an attitude assumed for a particular audience? Or could it be the unavoidable result of the attempt to condense such a lot of history into a few books in uncomplicated English? As Butterfield says, ''abridgements may be based more or less consciously upon some selective principle . . . [and] are often falsified by the assumption that the essentials of the story can be told, leaving out the complications".[1]

So it is natural, when condensing history, to look for "unifying themes"; without them the past would hardly make a story. But the principle of selection we are looking at here—the Western, evolutionist principle—operated not only in the abridgement of African history, but in specialised studies as well. We can see how it permeated the rewriting of African history by looking at one field of study fairly thoroughly. I have chosen the study of religious movements[2] for this demonstration, for a number of reasons:

1. It is not a field which originates from a concern with the place of independent African countries in the world, as, for example, the study of nationalism itself, or of political parties, or Westernisation, "modernisation", or industrialisation would be; it is probably more significant, therefore, to demonstrate the evolutionist bias in a field like religious movements than in one of these others, where its influence is more to be expected.

2. These movements, described as "anti-witchcraft", "millenarian", and by various other terms, span pre-colonial as well as colonial times, so they cannot be associated simply with the process of Westernisation.

3. Although they have a political dimension (and this is the one which was most emphasised in the 1960s), they do not present themselves as primarily political. If their more obvious concerns were accorded less importance by historians wishing to situate them in a line of political development, therefore, this is a good illustration of misrepresentation of a phenomenon because of the strength of the bias.

I shall argue, in fact, that throughout the 1960s the right questions were seldom asked about these movements because a particular kind of future was assumed. That is, while historians were tracing, with approval, a political evolution towards the kind of national governments that African countries adopted on independence, it was impossible to understand what religious movements were and are about.

Religious movements have been treated as a stage in political development culminating in the independence of the present nation-states, roughly as follows: "primary resistance" came first—immediate, spontaneous military efforts which failed because whites had more effective military organisations, communications, backing, etc. Then came religious movements, an intermediate stage between primary resistance and "modern" nationalist movements. The less militant movements were regarded as a substitute for politics, either pathological escapes into fantasy, or organisations people joined because they had no other way to express their desire to be somebody, to organise something away from European supervision. When political activity was suppressed, people had to turn to spiritual activities, of less interest to them intrinsically and of less importance historically, but giving them something to do. In terms of organisation and planning, the more militant movements, by contrast, were seen as improving on primary resistance, in that religious leaders could organise large numbers of people through wide-ranging networks. This gave the people the confidence of supernatural backing and traditional authority, and—where a cult attracted people from different ethnic groups—united people who otherwise regarded one another with suspicion. On the other hand, they were ineffective because they misjudged their own and their enemies' resources, and because they relied on "supernatural" aid. They were therefore superseded by political parties leading nationalist movements, which gained independence by a combination of parliamentary procedures and the threat of force, and set up representative governments modelled upon Western ones.

In this view, the features of religious movements which merited scholarly attention were their anti-European content and their usefulness to nationalist movements, either as a memory,[3] to refute the idea that Africans were passive or contented in the first half of the century, or in terms of the limited political advances they achieved before they were defeated.

This interpretation does not work. Religious movements were not just an intermediate phase, brave but misguided, between diffuse wars of resistance and organisation into parties on a national scale. Most of Africa is territorially independent; but there are still religious movements. This is because they were not about the problem of white domination alone; they were about the problem of evil, which is not solved just by getting rid of whites. The millenarians did not think it would be. They concerned themselves first of all with confessing their own wickedness, purging the community of incorrigible witches, and trying to level the inequalities of wealth and power which made ordinary people want to use witchcraft on each other. It is true that religious movements seem to have multiplied in response to white domination. This is because the whites brought new roles, jobs, rewards, and frustrations, at the same time freeing some Africans from the power of traditional sanctions. Thus inequalities among Africans increased, and they recognised the change; but they also knew that in taking up the new opportunities they did each other wrong. And they hoped that by getting rid of the evil in themselves they would gain the moral strength to get rid of the whites.

For years historians failed to see this because they saw these movements in the context of the development of nationalism, in which the central concern was the struggle between black and white for power. They seemed to be ineffective efforts to get black government and it was not brought out that they were really efforts to get a moral government (which, to them, *meant* a black government, and a good deal more).

Because of the limited context within which historians were interested in religious movements, it was not until after independence that they were forced to pay attention to all that was actually said and done in these movements. "The basic feature of both messianic cults and rational nativistic movements", wrote Linton, "is that they represent frankly irrational flights from reality. Their differences relate only to the ways in which such flights are implemented, and are, from the point of view of their functions, matters of minor importance".[4] Historians in the sixties, too, were more interested in the results than in the nature of religious movements. But when doubts set in about what their function was, scholars had to look more closely at their specific workings and their ideology. It was necessary to make detailed local studies, to understand each one in its own local context. One result of this has been the discovery that such movements go much further *back* in time than was supposed; the importance of the European "impact" is accordingly diminished. Another result has been an increased respect for the intellectual efforts discovered in the movements: the reinterpretation of change and social relationships. In this chapter I sketch the development of the traditional understanding of religious movements, the reasons for change, and some directions in which this field has moved since the sixties.

In the colonial period, religious movements were seen as attempts to adjust to the problems of "culture contact" in a situation where the replacement of indigenous cultures by the Western ones of the conquerors seemed inevitable, if painful. Scholars wanted to know how, if at all, the movements helped people to cope with the shock and confusion of exposure to modernity. (Linton, for example, assumed that colonised people wanted to assimilate European culture, and developed "nativism" [rejection of new ways and insistence on traditional forms and customs] if the colonisers did not accept them).[5] Anthropologists studied movements throughout the colonised world, and among American Indians. In Africa, Audrey Richards described an anti-witchcraft movement, *mchape*, which she witnessed in 1935. She regarded it as a sort of travelling medicine show, welcomed by the Bemba because they were worried about increasing witchcraft. In her view, *mchape* was a product of the colonial situation, in two ways. First, the strains and insecurities caused by labour migration, the intrusion of missions and administrators, etc., increased witchcraft fears, and this situation was aggravated by the fact that the government had outlawed the usual methods of identifying and punishing witches, and had undermined the power of chiefs on which the Bembas' sense of security depended. Secondly, the new brand of witch finders gained prestige from their connections with the white world: their Western dress and props, and borrowings from Christian ideas. Europeanism, Richards tells us, is something of a cult with the Bemba, and they are always "unusually credulous and unstable in temperament, the first to adopt and discard anything new".[6] But though *mchape* was a result of the colonial regime, Richards did not see it as a protest; in fact, she said the villagers were grateful to the local authorities for allowing the witch finders to operate. In her view, then, witchcraft eradication was a new technique responding to a new situation of strain, but was not a protest against that situation.

In 1950 Marwick observed the Bwanali-Mpulumtsi movement, which was similar to *mchape* except that the leaders did not accuse anyone of witchcraft, thus staying within the law. Instead, they showed that there were a lot of charms about, and offered whole communities a chance to purge themselves by confession and then to receive magic which would kill them if they returned to witchcraft in the future. Marwick felt that the emphasis on "confession and . . . moral rearmament" gave this movement the character of "the religious revival rather than the patent medicine trade".[7]

The transition from these early views of religious movements to their incorporation into the history of nationalism is found in an article by Coleman in 1954, before independence came to dominate the African scene, although it was, of course, in the air. In "Nationalism in Tropical Africa" Coleman placed religious movements in a scheme of political development—a scheme which the writers of the sixties were largely to adopt—but in this scheme such movements were *distinguished* from nationalist politics rather than identified with them, Coleman declining "to place under the cover of 'nationalism' all forms of past and present discontent and organisational development in Africa". He distinguished "traditionalist", "syncretistic", and "modernist" movements, nationalism belonging exclusively to the last category, while "primary resistance" belonged to the first.

Coleman saw some overlap among his categories, either where they contributed (independently or in combination) to the same agitation against the colonial ruler, or where "nationalists have claimed such uncoordinated uprisings, as well as purely economic protest movements, to be manifestations of 'nationalism', when in reality the participants were unaware of such implications".[8] But, he insisted:

These differences are important to the student of African nationalism. Primary resistance and nativism tend to be negative and spontaneous revolts, or assertions of the unacculturated masses against the disruptive and disorganising stranger-invader. . . . Syncretism is different in that it contains an element of rationality—an urge to recapture those aspects of the old which are compatible with the new, which it recognises as inevitable and in some respects desirable. Whereas all forms of protest are politically consequential—at least to colonial administrators—only nationalism is primarily political in that it is irrevocably committed to a positive and radical alteration of the power structure.[9]

This distinction was to infuriate some writers, who felt that it was patronising; in the sixties and seventies the term "nationalism" took on a kind of life of its own, and pride could not exist apart from it. For this reason it became important to call all movements, from the first appearance of the white man, nationalist. This emotional investment in the term had evidently been made by nationalists when Coleman was writing, and soon after by scholars as well. This is interestingly reflected in the language used to describe the movements: while Coleman wrote about the nationalist leaders of Mau Mau manipulating the nativism of the masses,[10] Rosberg and Nottingham were to call "nativism" the "myth of Mau Mau". In their version, the leaders did not "manipulate" "nativism"; instead they used tradition creatively to involve deeply people to whom tradition was important in a modern—and definitely nationalist—movement.[11]

As independence became the topic which in the first place over-whelmingly interested historians, and in the second place identified them as friends of the new regimes, the overlap among the categories which Coleman distinguished became the focus of research in this area, while the categories, which Coleman had placed in an ideal progression, set-tled into a chronological scheme in which traditionalism gave way to nationalism. In this respect, Crawford Young's *Politics in the Congo* (1965) represents a further step in the incorporation of religious move-ments into nationalist history.

Young's book was mainly concerned with the nature of nationalist parties and their interactions, but religious movements were mentioned briefly, by way of background, in a chapter entitled, "The Rise of Na-tionalism: From Primary Resistance to Political Parties". Under the heading "Stages in Development of Nationalist Movements", he in-cluded:

1. Primary resistance movements
2. Messianic and syncretic sects
3. Urban riot and violence
4. Pre-political modern associations
5. Political parties[12]

Note the words "pre-political", i.e., not expressing opposition to the colonial government, and "political" used of nationalist parties. Young went on to elaborate:

Primary resistance . . . was soon succeeded by a second stage, where a syn-thesis of ideas and symbols assimilated from the coloniser and traditional ritual elements was found in messianic and syncretic movements. This represents a period when no secular remedy to the frustrations engendered by the colonial situation seemed available . . . [so they] found temporary remedy through the millen[n]ial dream.

Fortunately, however, "By the 1950s, the religious channel for the venting of frustration tended to be supplanted by the modern, secular nationalism of the Abako". The reason Young gave for the messianic interlude—at least 260 years—was simply that "long contact with Christian doctrine and symbols predisposed the Bakongo to expressing frustrations through the channel of messianism". There is no discus-

sion of what these Christian ideas might have appealed to in indigenous traditions, nor of what the actual content of these movements might
be.

As all this sort of thing was an "apocalyptic dream", there was no
particular reason to present this kind of information. For Young, religious movements were a thing people did because they were prevented
from participating in politics. There was no suggestion that these activities might have been, for Congolese, the *appropriate* response to
the particular kinds of troubles they were having. Thus, while he considered them a "stage in the evolution of the nationalist movement",
Young did not think they were effective in any way. They were political because of their "radical rejection of European domination", but
were not otherwise interesting to a political historian. Nor did he question the idea that they belonged intrinsically to the colonial situation.

At this stage we should make the general point that while many writers
(as well as many participants) considered separatist churches similar to
witchcraft eradication movements, others took churches more seriously as a political force, feeling that they addressed themselves to a
situation of discrimination in a more realistic way. Oddly enough, they
seem to be more associated with "secular" adjustment to the colonial
situation than witch-finding movements were, perhaps because, although their raison d'être was spiritual, Western observers were more
familiar with their institutional forms; they looked more organised. It
is, of course, true that independent church members could also be
"modern" politicians and often were. Moreover, the independent
churches often set up schools, which in Kenya particularly featured in
the development of natior alist politics. Robinson and Gallagher, for
example, while dismissing what we have come to think of as primary
resistance as unrealistic, considered separatist churches a "defter nationalism":

When the time of troubles came to the peoples of China or Tongking or Fiji,
their first response was to rally around the dynasty, just as in Africa the Mo-
roccans and Ethiopians were to group under the *charisma* of the ruler. Movements of this sort were proto-nationalist in their results, but they were romantic, reactionary struggles against the facts, the passionate protest of societies
which were shocked by the new age of change and would not be comforted.
But there were more positive responses to the Western question. The defter
nationalisms of Egypt and the Levant, the "Scholars of New Learning" in
Kuang-Hsu, China, the sections which merged into the continental coalition of

the Indian Congress, the separatist churches of Africa—in their different ways, they all planned to re-form their personalities and regain their powers by operating in the idiom of the Westerners.[13]

The churches were more positive, then, because they were more Western. We find the same idea in *Africa since 1800*, where Oliver and Atmore tell us that mission-educated Africans were the first nationalists, either joining European churches "and seeking the best employment they could get" or forming independent churches "to prepare for an ultimate and revolutionary challenge to the colonial authorities".

Either way, these new nationalisms were thinking in modern terms—not in terms of a reversion to tribal beliefs and tribal organisations, but in terms of Christian churches under African leadership, and of African successor states based on the existing colonial territories, and governed along Western rather than traditional African lines.[14]

Modernity is here equated unequivocally with Western models.

The churches, then, were often taken more seriously as a political force than the less institutionalised, or less Western, "millenarian" movements. The latter were supposed to have their basis in psychological troubles, and their usefulness, if any, in psychological solutions. They were pathological, while the churches were rational and effective.

The incorporation of religious movements into nationalism advanced another step therefore when they too came to be regarded as effective. With Iliffe ("The Organisation of the Maji Maji Rebellion", 1967) we move into this new phase of interpretation. For him, the important question was no longer whether religious movements were anticolonial, and therefore political, in *intent*. What was important was that they lent effectiveness to military efforts against the colonial regime. Thus, he stressed the role of prophetic leaders in Maji Maji in enlarging the scale of the rebellion, and "proclaiming a new religious order to supersede the old, a new loyalty to transcend old loyalties of tribe and kinship".[15]

The difficulty was that while religious leadership could have a unifying effect, it could also be divisive. In some places, the bringers of Maji clashed with the chiefs who refused to surrender their authority in the

larger movement. In some places, people took up Maji Maji as a
witchcraft eradication movement but not as a rebellion.

Thus the paradox of later nationalist movements, the need to use old loyalties
in order to popularise an effort to transcend them, also characterised this earlier attempt to enlarge political scale. The Maji Maji rebellion originated in
peasant grievances, expanded in the dynamism of a millen[n]ial belief which
challenged the old order, and finally came to reflect the cultural and political
divisions of the past. Its changing organisation demonstrates the tension within
a mass movement between ideology and reality.[16]

This approach was still on too general a level to explain very much.
How was Maji Maji challenging the old order? Did this merely mean
that prophets and chiefs faced each other as rivals, or was there something very different about prophetic leadership? What were they asking
the people to do? This might have been relevant to the problem of why
Maji Maji was interpreted in some places as being primarily a witchcraft-eradication movement, rather than an anti-colonial war.[17]

We get the same sort of approach, and the same problems of gen-
erality, in Lonsdale's article, "Some Origins of Nationalism in East
Africa", published the following year. Like Iliffe, he pointed out that

religious appeals . . . in themselves implying a reorientation of society, per-
mitted social mobilisation [in post-pacification revolts] on a wider scale than
appeals by leaders of kin groups. [Later,] . . . it was in the religious field that
corporate action on a lowly social plane retained most vitality in the years that
followed the collapse of armed African resistance and rebellion. Independent
churches and indigenous sects were of many kinds, fulfilling as many social
needs. Some sought relief for the oppressed poor in confused millen[n]ial dreams;
some aimed at social sanity and order at a humble level on earth; others saw
salvation in educational schemes as ambitious as any offered by the mission
churches in which, as may tend to be forgotten, many political leaders continued to find "a place to feel at home". However much these churches differed, they were able to enlist the continuing loyalties of many ordinary Africans, at however local a level, and however prone to further schism and
segmentation. This was a quality more often lacking in explicitly political associations until the late 1930's.[18]

There are hints of something more interesting in the phrases "social
sanity" and a "reorientation of society", but these were not explained. Did he mean something more than an enlargement of scale,

and if so, what? And was a "lowly social plane" just a small or local one? With what was it being contrasted?

Lonsdale too was able to speak of "confused millen[n]ial dreams" as if the actual content of them was clearly unimportant, and to see them as providing "relief" without wondering in what sense that might be possible. To be part of a movement that fails is no relief; there is nothing relaxing about trying to change the world. As I shall try to demonstrate, these movements were anything but an escape. Both Iliffe's and Lonsdale's articles, therefore, raised a number of questions about how the participants themselves understood the movements in which they were involved. But the questions were not answered, because it was the effectiveness of the movements in contributing to the development of nationalism which was considered significant, rather than the actual experience and perceptions of those involved.

If a tendency towards generalisation is noticeable in descriptions of the religious contents of movements, it is far less a problem where the anti-colonial elements are discussed. These were illustrated by quotations from the participants, and some of the flavour came through. There is no question that most of the movements *were* hostile to colonial authorities; the objection here is to the imbalance in so many descriptions of them. The features which historians picked out to discuss in detail—the things which alarmed administrators and thereby contributed to the cause of nationalism—were put forward as the common and most interesting features of the movements. Rotberg wrote, in "The Modern Emergence of Malawi and Zambia":

In both protectorates, chiliastic preachers and the leaders of separatist sects early gathered adherents who were presumably attracted by the apocalyptic message of independence . . . [leaders like] Elliot Kenan Kamwana Achirwa, who promised excited fellow Tongans that they would soon see no more of the British government ("we shall build our own ships, make our own powder, and make or import our own guns") the separatist Charles Domingo ("instead of 'give' Europeans say 'Take away from' ") and John Chilembwe, the American-educated leader of the Providence Industrial Mission of Chiradzulu.[19]

Similarly, Balandier noted in his discussion of Kimbanguism:

The notion of salvation was entirely subversive, and the administration did not know how to react in the presence of this new religion which opposed to its orders the necessity first to obey God. An official document gave an account of the significant words of villagers to their administrative superior: "You, you have only to shut up; the Administrator is not the one to dispense grace. One must not obey the administrator; one must obey God".[20]

When other more "religious" features were mentioned, they were not elaborated on. Roberts mentioned that Jehovah's Witnesses were to earn salvation through baptism and keeping special moral codes; what moral codes?[21] Likewise Richards wrote that the efficacy of the *bamucapi* medicine depended on keeping old taboos, but did not tell us what they were. Balandier too was tantalisingly superficial on the subject of Sundkler's "Zionist" churches[22] as well as on the Kimbanguist movement:

Priests [of these churches] . . . have a more prophetic character, model their role more after that of divine healer and witchfinder than after that of chief, and remain in more direct and close touch with their flock. The cult makes a wide allowance for traditional beliefs and practices; baptism is linked with complex purification rituals; revelation through dreams, taboos, dancing, and fits of seizure play an important role. Religious practice in these churches reaffirms the efficacy of the old social therapies.[23]

While Balandier tried to analyse the political effects of messianic movements, he merely listed the ritual aspects: destruction of fetishes, a "remedy . . . to the proliferation of witchcraft and sorcery",[24] baptism, confession.

What went on in these movements was clearly religious activity. But as far as historians were concerned, its significance lay in what Balandier called its "xenophobic character", and the selection of material is heavily weighted in this way. In the effort to bring religious movements into the history of nationalism, and evaluate their "political" aims and results, other questions suffered because the people who wrote about religious movements were content to notice that they expressed dissatisfaction. They did not look deeply enough into exactly what the participants were dissatisfied *with*, nor why it seemed appropriate to them to look for solutions in a religious sphere. Mostly they did not start with the idea that such solutions seemed appropriate, in any case, but assumed that they were undertaken as a second-best to the normal, secular way of proceeding. With Iliffe, and Lonsdale, religion does not become more interesting, but is accorded more respect only because they have a higher opinion of the effectiveness of religious leadership than previous writers had.[25]

The turning point in the approach to religious movements came only when scholars began to realise that the end of colonial rule did not remove the urge towards religious solutions. Already, by the mid-sixties, examples of post-independence religious protest were not far to seek. A rebellion with a strongly religious character had already occurred in the Kwilu province of the Congo. This area had a history of religious movements, begining, as far as historians of the rebellion knew, in the 1930s, with the "Talking Serpent" sect, which promised liberators from white rule and a collective rising of the dead. Next, Kimbanguism flourished in this region, as well as a third fetish-destroying sect in the 1950s. There had also been a revolt in 1931, arising partly from the exploitation of workers in the palm-oil industry, partly from the raising of taxes and regrouping of villages. The belief in invulnerability in battle, which is found in these earlier movements, arose again in the Kwilu rebellion, whose partisans were protected by "sorcerers" while the rules regulating their discipline were sanctioned by magic. The Kwilu rebellion seems to have been firmly rooted in Congolese traditions of religious movements, then; but it was led by a modern politician, Pierre Mulele, who had been a minister in the independent government of the Congo, and was recruited largely from his party, the Parti Solidaire Africain (PSA). This hardly fits the pattern assumed by historians of religious protest being replaced by Western-style parties; here the party was a failure, and was replaced by the movement. The promises made by the PSA in its campaigns were in fact as all-embracing and unlikely of fulfillment as any millenarian expectations, and when a couple of years had gone by and the PSA had failed to deliver the goods—the roads, free schools, free petrol and vehicles, free education, free medical care, pumps and mills, total employment, and salaries for all which it had promised—then disappointment combined with resentment against the conspicuously thriving elite and the hardships of increasing inflation and unemployment to make the area ripe for a new effort, which was spoken of as the "second independence". The feeling expressed by people in the Kwilu was that the first independence had not really changed things—conditions were the same, only worse. The removal of colonial conditions, then, did not necessarily follow on independence. And if reliance on supernatural aid, while crucial to morale, contributed in the end to military defeat, it would be hard to fault Mulele's understanding of the post-independence situation (paraphrased by the movement's historians, Fox, de Craemer, and Ribeaucourt):

All the wealth of the country is in the hands of [either] . . . foreigners or imperialists [or] persons of the bad government who help them steal the wealth of the country. "Thanks to the aid of foreigners, they live without caring that the majority of their brothers are dying of misery". This class has at its disposal and use the violence of policemen and soldiers. The persons of this group include not only government authorities, but certain functionaries, merchants and businessmen, teachers and missionaries who think, live and act, like the politicians "with the heavy purses".

(Mulele was presumed to have spent time in China and to have learned the language of class struggle there. It does not take a Chinese, however, to see a class struggle.)

It is interesting to note, too, that Mulele's vision of the future is more modest than the earlier projections of the PSA. "When the government is overthrown, we will establish a new regime in which all must and will work in order to eat; in which foreigners cannot come to take the wealth of the country; and in which we cannot steal the wealth of other persons either".[26]

The Kwilu rebellion, then, began to cast doubt on the nationalist interpretation, and soon more movements, mostly concerned with eradicating witchcraft, were observed.[27] Anthropologists at first, and then historians, turned back to local studies to try to find clues to a new explanation, one which could account for the persistence of religious movements when "political" forms of expression were apparently available.

In "Medicines and Men of Influence" (1968) David Parkin introduced a new approach with a critical survey of explanations of movements in Africa and elsewhere (e.g., cargo cults) which emphasised their anti-colonial character. Like earlier writers, he was not particularly interested in the "religious" side of witchcraft-eradication movements. But he argued that it was misleading to place them in the history of nationalist politics as they are *primarily* about local politics, about the power structures of small village communities, where they can be traced back to pre-colonial times, and where they go on even after independence.

If these anti-sorcery movements unite people in a new solidarity, then who is the enemy now? Is it the new establishment, a dominant ethnic group, or an alien commercial class? No doubt it can be shown that these movements are still often expressions of internal solidarity against external pressures. . . . Clearly, also, colonialism is a crucial external factor bringing about change in a society. But it may well be that we should look more closely at the local-level authority structure of those movements for which we have data, in order to understand to what extent any particular movement is inspired by immediate internal pressures as well as general external forces.[28]

He goes on to suggest that witchcraft-eradication movements are basically an idiom for generational conflict. Old men control the use of medicines, and young men lead movements which accuse the elders of witchcraft (or of failing to prevent others from multiplying their witching activities, and so failing in their duty to protect the community). As well as discrediting the elders, the younger men also get them to relinquish their medicines—both harmful ones and those which protect them or ensure their success in various things—and thereby diminish their power. Too much emphasis, then, has been placed on the role of religious movements in *unifying* fragmented communities. "Far from integrating the society", Parkin writes, "the movements illuminate its divisions".[29] This emphasis is shared by Willis, studying an anti-witchcraft movement in Ufipa (Tanzania), which he feels was mainly to do with local politics, specifically the conflict between generations, and likely to be repeated because these conflicts are endemic in village life. The colonial regime increased anxieties in many ways and also pushed people towards *mchape* type movements by outlawing the more usual methods of dealing with accusations of sorcery; but the cycle of aggression is probably an independent one, coming round about every ten years, so that the need for a campaign against sorcery surfaced again in 1964 in Ufipa regardless of the change in government.[30]

Ranger incorporated the new questions about religious movements in an article written in the same year. Though mainly an effort to trace "Connexions between 'Primary Resistance' Movements and Modern Mass Nationalism in East and Central Africa", it considers, as well as the connecting threads, the independent existence of religious movements: the contexts of their occurrence both before and after the period of direct white domination, and also some black-against-black movements within the colonial period.

In the turmoil of the nineteenth century, some East and Central African rulers tried to strengthen themselves against attack by other groups by stiffening their power at the centre. Sometimes religious leaders came to prominence in the resistance against these threats. Sometimes they felt their own authority within their society threatened by the growing power of chiefs or kings, and resisted this instead. "The prophetic and witchcraft eradication traditions were as available to movements of this kind as to later movements of protest against the whites".[31]

During the colonial period, moreover, religious movements were not directed against the colonial authorities alone. They rose also in protest against sub-imperialism by other Africans like the Ganda, Toro, or Lozi, who were able, by virtue of their relationship to the colonial authorities, to extend their own domination of their neighbours further than in the pre-colonial period. Ranger then comes to the problem of movements against newly independent African governments: the Lumpa church in Zambia, which had clashed with the colonial authorities, continuing in opposition to the ruling United National Independence Party (UNIP) after independence; the opposition of the Parmehutu association in Rwanda; and the Kwilu rebellion in the Congo. Why the continuity of religious forms of protest? Ranger suggests that African governments get themselves into a fragile position by making the same kind of unfulfillable promises and demanding the same high level of emotional commitment that religious movements do (the claims of the politicians being complemented, even inflated, of course, by the expectations of their followers). Thus "modern" political movements are not so far from the old millenarian idiom, and the inevitable disappointments of independence provoke reaction in a millenarian style which has not been replaced by modern political methods in the way which was usually assumed. Roberts, studying the Lumpa church which clashed with the ruling party in Zambia, comes to a similar conclusion.[32] With Ranger, Roberts, and Fox *et al.*, we are moving from the idea that religious movements had political uses and were thus part of the independence struggle, to the idea that the independence movements had a religious flavour and were thus part of an African political idiom which included nationalism but did not begin and end with it.

From this point, about 1970, we can see a significant change of emphasis in the study of religious movements. They have moved into the province of the history of ideas and are accorded respect on their own terms instead of in proportion to their resemblance to Western ways of operating. Of course, ideas are not a separate realm; they are ideas *about* something, and the last decade of research into African religious history has been devoted to understanding the relationships between the conditions of life, explored in local studies, and the religious interpretation of them. Ranger characterised this new, intellectualist approach in his report on a conference held in Chilema in 1970, one of a number devoted to the historical study of African religion in recent years:[33] what the papers had in common, in his view, was a stress on

the importance of continuing to turn inward, for continued examination of the religious or ideational aspects of Central African history. The M'Bona cult of the Mang'anja, the Nyau societies of the Chewa, the Mwana Lesa movement among the Lala—these things are important to the political history of their societies not only as factions or foci of political power in themselves, but as sources of *ideas* and symbols. . . . Of course, many of these religious changes were precipitated by the outward, external pressures of political, military, and economic development. But, essentially, most of these changes were inward-looking efforts to *understand* what was happening and through understanding to generate clusters of myth and ritual, and prophecy which might *affect* what was happening.[34]

Or, as MacGaffey puts it, "The independent and syncretist movements embody more or less conscious attempts to resolve the contradictions between two religious 'languages', African and European, and simultaneously to reform the conditions of existence of a class of people who were not doing well in either social sector".[35]

In the context of these new questions about the ways in which Africans have made sense of, and moved to control, changing conditions, Western political procedures are no longer the natural end of a one-way development from bewilderment in local communities to coping on a national scale, but are seen as one of the ways of coping which must be grasped in the terms in which participants conceive of them, rather than taken for granted.[36]

On the face of it, this broader context for the study of religious history would seem to have resulted in a fragmentation of the field. Earlier the province of missionaries or Islamicists on the one hand and of functional anthropology on the other, it was integrated for a while by the theme of nationalist politics. Now, much enlarged, it embraces studies of myths, symbols, spirit possession, pre-colonial territorial cults and prophetic movements, cults of healing, and secret societies; reconsiderations of twentieth-century movements; studies of the intellectual and operational interaction of Christian missions with African religions; studies of Church and State in independent nations, of the churches' role in education, of the liturgies of independent churches; studies of Islam; and studies, including Marxist ones, of the relationship between religious ideas and modes of production. Two points can be made about this apparent fragmentation, however: first, that the integration of religious studies in the sixties was more apparent than real, and second, that while the number and variety of projects have increased, their isolation has been overcome by conferences and resulting collections of work which situate them as part of the same inquiry and make them available together.[37]

It is by no means accidental, for example, that Marxist theories explaining the relationships of African religious forms (as an aspect of "superstructure") to the modes of production with which they are found have appeared since the intellectualist approach to religion gained ground. For many Western Christians, science, and even social science, present themselves as the appropriate means of understanding the mysteries of "real" life, religion having to do with questions to which no other answers can be found: "acts of God". African religions, by contrast, are more intimately concerned with understanding social conditions, and as the ways in which they do so have been more thoroughly investigated,

recent observers have remarked that the leaders of a number of movements have reformulated theories and programs of a social scientific character. Recognition of this dynamic and pragmatic element in these movements has opened the way to studying them as historical phenomena—and, later, to including all religions in this historical perspective.[38]

People who had been seen, rather like experimental rats, as suffering "stress" and "confusion" were now perceived as trying to understand, in the appropriate terms and symbols of their cultures, their changing relationships with nature and with one another. In this way, "belief" was transformed in the eye of the beholder into "consciousness", and brought within the purview of Marxist scholarship. Van Binsbergen, for example, looks at the changing modes of production within which Central Africans have had to operate, and shows how their religions have either complemented these, resisted them, or mediated the stressful experience of people changing the nature of their relationships when they become involved in the articulation, of different modes of production.[39] Territorial cults, for example, reinforce the political incorporation of lineage societies with increasing centralisation. Cults of affliction go with proletarianisation, offering therapy to the individual who is breaking ties of residence and obligation as his life is increasingly defined by his circumstances of employment. The Lumpa church expresses resistance to capitalism, turning its back on the demands of the state and forming its own economic as well as moral community. There is a danger here, when moving from local studies back to generalisations of this broad a scope, that one overweening framework of interpretation will be replaced with another. If the interest in religious movements as expressions of nationalism were simply to be replaced by an interest in them as expressions of class struggle, contradictory data would be likely once again to be subordinated to the demands of theory. So far, however, it seems more likely that the analysis of modes of production is being confronted and asked to deal with questions about how people think, which can only do it good. The apparent mindlessness of actors in Marxist analysis, the feeling that people have been replaced by "isms", makes many people unreceptive to its insights.

Limiting ourselves to the area of witchcraft, we shall see how generalisations like Van Binsbergen's can come out of local studies of belief. This is the other side of the demonstration undertaken earlier, of how such generalisations did not come out of the data in the immediate post-independence period, for it is important to remember that most of the material which will be adduced was available at that time. Indications of its importance were also present in the secondary sources, though unacknowledged for the most part by their authors. This lends support, obviously, to those scholars who are currently arguing the primacy of theory in producing data.[40] Paradoxically, it equally supports "empiricists", inasmuch as the data exist to be recognised when a new "problematic" wants to structure them anew.

We can begin with Ranger's article on the Mwana Lesa movement of 1925, mentioned by earlier writers as an anti-white millenarian movement drawing on ideas of the "Watchtower" Jehovah's Witnesses sect. Taking up the theme of intellectual history, Ranger inquires into the "interaction of a particular form of Christianity with the particular beliefs and customs of the Lamba and Lala peoples among whom the movement spread",[41] using much material from the archives in Lusaka which had been ignored as it added nothing to the history of nationalism. He shows that the idea of Christ's Second Coming fitted neatly with a preexisting local myth; then he spells out the historical circumstances which produced a witch-finding movement from these ideas. Further, he tries to see why witches were killed in this movement and not in others; and decides that the curtailment of the powers of chiefs was particularly frustrating to the Lala and Lamba. They had relied on their chiefs of the Nyendwa clan to protect them against witchcraft, to sponsor the administration of the poison ordeal, arrange for the guilty to be punished, and purify people who had committed acts of violence. With the coming of colonial rule, they could no longer do these things, and at the same time there was more reason to fear witchcraft than usual. Young men were getting a smattering of education and Western wants at the mines, not enough to make them "new men", but enough to frustrate them when they came home, where moreover they feared the jealousy of their elders. They might be suspected of using witchcraft to promote their material success, or they might be bewitched by others who envied it.

With so many men away from home as labourers, moreover, those who stayed behind acquired many more dependents than before, and those dependent felt guilty and so feared witchcraft, even while they were feared by relatives who met the new obligations inadequately or unwillingly.[42] The reason for growing fears of witchcraft, then, lay in the local ramifications of the new organisation of labour in the colonial economy—and also in the opportunities for young men which had not existed before. Thus the particular situation was caused by "colonial pressures",[43] and the Mwana Lesa movement did feature some anti-colonial rhetoric. But what was actually done? The attack was on African wickedness in the local setting, hardly an escape, but not a nationalist offensive either; and Ranger situates it in the local theology and methods of dealing with evil which go back to pre-colonial times. Further evidence of the way in which "colonial pressures" were locally experienced as strain among neighbours comes from Richard Stuart's study of *mchape* on Likoma Island; in this case, strain between married women and the increasing number of women who had to remain single because a large proportion of men were working elsewhere. Their jealousy, it was feared, might come out in witchcraft.[44]

The inquiry into local thinking about witchcraft thus leads back to social history. Through people's experience of the problem of evil we begin to understand both the source of the problem and the logic of their response. The rest of this chapter spells out the implications of this kind of study, the reasons why they went unnoticed for so long, and the reasons why they are likely to be noticed now.

When the analysis begins at the level of the village two things happen. In the first place, we are forced to pay attention to the things which were actually said in the movements and to what people thought they were doing. Their statements focus our attention on the problem of witchcraft, where theirs was usually riveted (with nationalism in the forefront of their minds, historians noticed that these movements had anti-colonial protest in common; pushing it a little towards the back, we must notice that an even more consistent feature was the attack on witchcraft). Once we understand that witchcraft is actually practised and what it is for, we shall see that people had very good reasons for fearing it more and more (and indeed for practising it more, if they did so!). We shall realise, then, how witchcraft-eradication movements were appropriate responses to the problems people were having, and not escapes into fantasy. To see this, we have to look at their problems in the context of colonial rule, reversing the usual direction of analysis. When colonial rule was the big problem that contained all the others, national independence ought to have solved them all. But if we start with the particular problems of people's lives and work back through their causes we see that, while they were a feature of life under colonialism they are equally a feature of life after it ends, and in many cases also before it begins. By starting with the movement and working out and up in this way, we are able to deal with the problems introduced with colonial rule; but we are not limited to these, as when we started with nationalism and worked down, so we can deal with pre-colonial, post-colonial, neo-colonial, or non-colonial problems as well. In this way the localised approach yields *more* possibilities of generalisation, comparing movements in different times and places, than did the nationalist one.

Secondly, when we understand that anti-witchcraft movements are appropriate responses, the dichotomy between religion and politics will disappear, and movements which have been compartmentalised as "religious" or "political" will become more comparable than before.

Let's begin by looking at witchcraft, and the question whether *mchape* movements were vague escapist fantasies, or appropriate programmes of action. In an article on the Fipa, Willis writes, "The suggestion here is that Fipa are unable to formulate objectively the many cross-cutting causes of tension and conflict inside their own society; that their vague awareness of social disharmony is occasionally crystallised into a general tendency to blame the social malaise on the presence among them of practicing sorcerers".[45]

Willis is right in thinking it is not clear to the Fipa who is ultimately responsible for their troubles, but it may be that he should give them more credit for noticing who is immediately responsible. For the first thing we must realise is that witchcraft is no hallucination. People do make objects and say spells intended to hurt other people, or they hire specialists to do it for them. Because we think that these methods do not work, we tend to think they are not employed, and that fears of witchcraft are mere paranoid fantasies. A person falls sick, and blames his uncle for it. We believe that a germ has made him sick, and that his uncle must be innocent. But if we dismiss the whole thing there, we miss two important points. Why does the sufferer suspect his uncle? There must be something wrong between them. There is the potential for witchcraft in the relationship, then. And it is perfectly possible that the uncle is *trying* to bewitch his nephew. He may even be succeeding, if the nephew, who is aware of strain between them, suspects it and makes himself sick. Or the quarrel may only begin when the nephew falls sick, and, casting around for an explanation, thinks of his cross uncle. The uncle meanwhile, may be casting spells and smiling smugly, or he may have done nothing, and feel indignant at being accused.[46] But we should realise that people do *sometimes* practice witchcraft, and if they do, they know that other people do, and there is nothing unreasonable in their suspecting it. The local doctor does not, after all, live on air. And when people think about witchcraft they are pointing to strains in their relationship with others.

What kind of strain? People bewitch others to ensure their failure, or out of resentment at their success. Either way, competition is at the root of it; people bewitch those who have more, and fear the jealousy (and witchcraft) of those who have less; or they bewitch those who threaten them from below, to keep them in their place. Inequalities of wealth, of status, or opportunity, all foster witchcraft and witchcraft fears.

These are felt, particularly, where overt competition and expression of hostility are precluded. The point is made very clearly in Marwick's book on the Chewa, *Sorcery in Its Social Setting*.[47] He shows that witchcraft is resorted to or suspected in relationships in which it is not acceptable to express aggression openly; these are presumably defined differently in different communities, but it is noticeable that a lot of the problems which *mchape* helps to solve arise in relationships which *ought* to be friendly. There are the country people mentioned by Ranger, who feel guilty because they are increasingly dependent on others. This is a situation where the obligation to help is difficult to meet, but should be met, and there is strain on both sides. Another example, again from Ranger's paper, is the young migrant worker from Lingamila village, a Fipa telling about this experience of *Kamchape* (i.e., *mchape*): "My uncle had bewitched me because I had not given him a present on my return from the coast. I was half blind and the skin was peeling off my feet in scales. Yet the witch finder was the person who saved my life. He found my uncle out and got rid of his craft by the methods he applied to all others".[48] Again, someone has failed to meet an obligation of which he is conscious, in a relationship which ought to be friendly. Both cases are clearly results of labour migration, in its turn the result of industrialisation imposed by Europeans. But it is not at all unlikely that people would bewitch each other in these circumstances, and their fears do not indicate an irrational or escapist turn of mind. Some people take advantage of urban opportunities to enrich themselves, others are jealous and are therefore suspected of witchcraft, or else suspect the successful ones of having used witchcraft to get where they are. It has been suggested, by Richards and others, that this may explain why the witch finders take all medicines, good or bad; for magic may ensure success for one person at the expense of others. Ranger quotes Liuli Baraza arguing in favour of *mchape* because it brought peace and "you know that Africans have got the desire to kill one another with their medicines".[49]

Thus whether or not we think witchcraft is actually a problem, we should recognise that Africans, in thinking so, are identifying the local repercussions of larger changes, by pointing to the ways in which social relations are breaking down. This may explain why these movements originate and spread in rural areas rather than in cities. To be sure, people are closer to change in the cities, but they are also further from their close and prescriptively friendly relationships. The relationships they have are ones in which aggression could be more openly expressed, and though Richards says that witchcraft fears increased in the city, Hammond-Tooke and Mitchell both found that this was not the case. (Mitchell found that people in cities were more inclined to attribute illness to the anger of neglected ancestors, while Hammond-Tooke found an increasing tendency to explain misfortunes in the terms of Western science.)[50]

Thus, the historian sees that the villager's troubles are caused by industrialisation, while the villager thinks he ought to be making an effort to get on better with his uncle. Both are right, and the villager is no more vague than the historian.

And when we break down the "stresses and strains" of the colonial situation in this way, to work out what kind of conflict is reflected in a particular case of witchcraft accusation, we find that situations of increasing witchcraft fears are more widely comparable across both time and space. For it appears that the colonial situation was a particular case of a more general problem, rather than the other way around. Wherever witchcraft is practiced and new opportunities are putting strain on old understandings of obligation there are grounds for comparing religious movements. Ranger described an anti-witchcraft movement in a situation where labour migration from a village had increased the dependence of those left behind on the few who were able to help them, so that one lot felt guilty about making excessive claims while the others felt guilty about failure to meet their increased obligations; resentment increased, and therefore the fear of resentment, which amounts to the fear of witchcraft. The fact that this movement happened under a colonial government is by no means irrelevant, for the organisation of labour to meet the requirements of the colonial economy is ultimately responsible for the situation in the village. But if we break down the "colonial situation" to focus on the organisation of labour rather than the presence of foreigners, we can see why independence has not removed the need for action against witchcraft. People are still leaving their villages to look for work in the cities, either pushed by the poverty of village life, or pulled by the promise of greater opportunities in the city, or both. The role of the white industrialist and policeman in this push and pull used to be obvious. If black industrialists and policemen have joined them, that complicates but does not essentially alter the situation.

But if the villager's problems are to be blamed on the organisation of the economy from above, how could an anti-witchcraft movement be anything but a pathetic waste of time?—for it attacks the situation at its lowest level. Ranger said in analysing the Mwana Lesa movement, "The Lala, aware of strain and of evil, internalised it; the cause lay at the heart of Lala society" (rather than in the pressures from outside).[51]

There are two things to be said about this. One is that the Lala recognised both causes, their own failures as well as the "pressures from outside". There *was* an anti-colonial theme in the Mwana Lesa movement, there *was* an intention to attack the highest level as well as the lowest, just as there was in the Maji-Maji rebellion, and as there was in the Kwilu rebellion in the Congo, which took up arms against the new black government shortly after independence, and in a number of others.

The second is that revolutionary movements which demand nothing from their members in the way of personal change have less than brilliant records. Changes in institutions and the distribution of power are necessary, but they are not enough. If the new order is not simply to become a cloak for the old, it must be stabilised by a change in peoples' expectations of themselves and others, based on self-examination.[52] If we call this consciousness-raising, it is respectable enough. To suggest that it is going on in anti-witchcraft movements sounds silly and also contradictory, for witchcraft eradication seems to be based on the finding of scapegoats, the very thing which makes consciousness-raising impossible.

But is it? "The cause (of evil) was at the heart of society". Not in the heart of the ugly old lady in the broken-down hut at the end of the village where the bush begins; to be sure, she has a lot to be angry about, but then she always had. The community-wide movements against witchcraft seem to be a recognition that the problem, felt to be present on an ever-increasing scale, is community-wide. This must be the reason for the technique of the mass ordeal, in which people were purged of witchcraft without being singled out and punished. We do not know to what extent this technique was experimental, because the whole question of the antiquity of witchcraft-eradication movements is not yet clear. For a long time it was taken for granted that these were an innovation of the colonial period, replacing the more piecemeal accusations and trials by poison ordeal of the past, which ended with the accused, if he was found guilty, being executed or expelled. It now appears that witchcraft-eradication movements have been an alternative to the ordeal for at least a hundred years[53] and probably longer. What we need to know now, is under what sort of circumstances the wholesale treatment was undertaken, in preference to the individual trial. There is no reason to suppose that the changes brought by colonial regimes caused large-scale disruption in African communities for the *first time*; we know that many were much more affected by the migrations and conquests of the pre-colonial era. The difference between the two modes of combating evil seems to be that if a person is exposed by the poison ordeal, he is killed, whereas in the mass movement he is received back into the community after he has confessed and has been publicly humiliated. This has been seen (e.g., by Marwick) as representing a growing sophistication in accommodating to the white man's law, which forbade both accusation and punishment of witches. But it may be (and more especially if it should prove to go back before white rule) a recognition that the problems of the community are in the first place general, calling for a solution which takes in everybody, and in the second place not wholly their fault. That is, people are bewitching one another because they are caught in a situation in which anybody might turn nasty, rather than because they are monsters by nature. In many African societies it is believed that everybody has the potential to be a witch, and sometimes that people can *unconsciously* bewitch others, and often there are two kinds of witches, the person who does it for an understandable reason and the one who does it out of sheer gratuitous wickedness. The eradication movements seem to be trying to purge the sin rather than the sinner.[54]

The search for scapegoats for the troubles of everyday life, which certainly goes on and on and on, has turned into a search for the inadequacy within each person which might drive him to witchcraft, the recognition of pressures which bring out these inadequacies, and the attempt to make institutional changes to bolster each person's reform.

All this talk of inadequacy may seem counterproductive. What were the migrant's failures to meet his personal obligations, when compared with the cold-blooded force which yanked him from his village in the first place? In the history of nationalism, it is not the individual's soul-searching in this situation which gives him dignity, but his anger against that force, however dissipated in soul-searching and rendered ineffective by reliance on the supernatural. We know that many of the problems Africans faced were not their own fault; thus, all this wallowing in self-accusation seems wasteful. A victim has much to reproach his exploiter with; why should he reproach himself? But it is this attitude which rolls right over the dignity that *was* there in the movements, not a present from the historian with the benefit of hindsight, but the dignity of a person regarding himself as a whole person. It is true that the organisation of labour is responsible for the draining of a village, but so is the choice that each worker makes. We tend to see the migrants as victims, and they are; but each is still a responsible person, and he or she knows it, and we should know it too. The migrant's success, of which others are so jealous, may seem paltry and pathetic to us; but that does not mean that it seems so to him. Win or lose, he is living a real life; and if he has not got it in his power to affect the lives of executives at UNILEVER, still his decisions are a force in his own family and his own village. It is only right for him, and for them, to question what each of them is doing.

But do the *mchape* movements really involve questioning? Is there an examination of the problem, and an attempt at institutional change? Or do the movements provide a simple blind catharsis, after which everything is just the same as before?

One writer who has thought about these questions is Willis, who asks whether *mchape*-type movements are revolutionary, and whether they *could* be revolutionary. At the end of his article on *Kamcape* in Ufipa, he looks at the means of social control which were suppressed in colonial times, the poison ordeal and public confession, by which people got their feelings of guilt out into the open in order to forestall retaliation. Without these, he says, increasing tensions are likely to

threaten the complete disruption of village society. To this problem there are two possible solutions: revolution, a radical change in the system of social relations; or millenarianism, a general attempt, in the form of a ''revivalist'' movement, to reassert and reestablish the traditional ethos of communal solidarity.

The overt purpose of the *Kamcape* movement, its manifest function, is to eradicate sorcery. Its latent function is to affect a resolution at the psychic level of a generalised sense of internal conflict and to recreate the moral climate of village communities in accordance with the traditional ethos of unity and harmony. But . . . internal conflicts . . . are endemic in village communities. Therefore *Kamcape* can provide only a temporary, and not a permanent, solution of the problem. Eventually the social situation will be ripe for yet another ''millenarian'' movement, perhaps employing new and more elaborate techniques, to appear on the scene.[55]

If this is the case, *mchape* is a substitute for change; it draws off the pressure which years of frustrated resentment have built up. We cannot argue that this was not really the outcome of the movement Willis saw; but we can follow up contradictory threads in a number of movements on which similar judgements have been passed. This evidence is scanty, but that is because it comes from an area which could only embarrass nationalist historians; for while I have argued that self-examination is essential to real change, it is true that it was of no immediate help to the nationalist cause. Historians were more interested in those pushes, both organisational and ideological, which were crowned with success. The belief that if people treated one another better, the enemies' bullets would turn to water, or that black American liberators would come, was notoriously not one of these, and is generally covered with tactful brevity. But this area contains answers to the question, "What was required of people in these movements?" And the answer to this is important because it shows that the analytical distinction between religion and politics is misleading in these contexts and tends to obscure a lot of features which should really be compared from one movement to another.[56]

We have seen the distinction made again and again, with the implication that political solutions would, in the end, succeed, while religious solutions were doomed; they could exist only in the realm of psychology and not for long even there. The historical assumption has been that religious ideas about politics are refined, by repeated confrontations with reality, until people realise that their reliance on supernatural aid is making them ineffective, and cast it off or else reduce it to a lip-service affair. The immediate reasons for supposing this are, first, the examples of failure, the bullets-to-water fiascos, the cattle-killing; and second, the fact that most African nations adopted the separation of church and state, a comfortable concept where religious pluralism exists. But if we think about it, there are outstanding examples of successful religious wars, the Muslim *jihads* (and perhaps the process of colonisation, in which the association of church and state could only lend itself to the idea that the Christian God was active and very effective in war). We can also think of nations in which God plays the same inextricable role in government as was the norm in traditional societies: imperial Ethiopia for one, and of course, the Muslim nations.

Even so, it is likely to be felt by Western observers that religion is simply inappropriate in politics. There is the idea that politics are amoral; the profession of some religion is considered becoming to a politician, like a clean shirt, but if he is influenced by it he cannot be trusted to act out of the same considerations as everyone else. There is the idea that politics is concerned with this world while religion is concerned with the next. And there is the view that religion is by nature a conservative force, and for this reason, too, can only hinder real impulses for change.

It is true, of course, that Christianity (to name but one) has often been used to deflect dissatisfaction, not only by employing the concept of divine rule in this world but by holding out another world, so much more important in the long run, as the real reference for people's lives. The idea that self-reliance depends upon freedom from religion is understandable, then, but it is also ethnocentric. It depends upon the idea that people have a choice whether or not to believe in a god, and this is an idea which many people do not have.[57] To get a perspective on the question of religion and politics, it is as well to remember that most people in the world are religious, and also that political action by religious people is very often successful. If we do not believe in God we think that reliance on religion is irrelevant to success, but very relevant to failure. There is no reason to suppose that people who do believe in God must eventually come round to this point of view.

The idea that religion is an alternative to politics, then, is purely ethnocentric; so is the idea which follows from it, that it is a form of escapism. This depends upon our Christian idea of two worlds. We tend to think that religion has to do with another world, whereas in most African religions the living, the dead, and the spirits inhabit the same world; and for the most part religious movements, whether "syncretic" or not, aim at changing this world, not exchanging it for heaven. The only exception I have come across is the Lumpa church, inasmuch as Roberts tells us that the Lenshina's hymns and sermons urge repeatedly, "Do not look for the things of this world".[58] On the other hand, the main bone of contention between the Lumpa church and the authorities was the question of its survival *as a community*, which is a very this-worldly kind of concern.

The Lumpa church is in fact a good starting point for a discussion of politics in religious movements. Led by Alice Lenshina, a mission Christian whose mission regretfully gave her up when she had visions of Christ, it rejected both the mission and the colonial government, and Lenshina ended in jail; thus it became part of the history of nationalism. Indeed, the connection was more than ideological, for some nationalist politicians belonged to the Lumpa church. But, like the recurrence of *mchape* movements after independence, its ongoing opposition to government was one of the things which forced a rethinking of the place of religious movements in nationalist history. Andrew Roberts, who has studied the Lumpa church, points out its significance for historians "in that its growth coincided with the development of a successful national movement for political independence".[59] It could not, therefore, be regarded as a less satisfying alternative to nationalist politics. As Hooker said of the Jehovah's Witnesses, the Lumpaites's stance was a protest against domination by any non-church authority whatsoever, whether white or black, and their struggle with UNIP and Kaunda's government has been even more bitter than their brushes with the colonial authorities.[60]

What was the imperative that kept the Lumpa community together in the face of persecution? It seems to have been a conviction that it was impossible to live morally outside. Andrew Roberts writes:

The Lumpa church had its own means to personal salvation and communal harmony. Implicitly at least, these rendered superfluous all other techniques of social control. Insofar as it was millenarian, the gospel of the Lumpa church was inherently anarchic—like that of the Anabaptists, or like Marxist prophecy. No other authority, whether derived from ancestral spirits, or Acts of Parliament, was truly valid, but instead it was positively dangerous, inasmuch as it represented a refusal to join with the Lumpa church in being absolved of sorcery.[61]

In independent as in colonial conditions, the need to eliminate the causes of witchcraft continued to be felt. The Lumpa church is only one of the groups which attempted to form a closed community. It confronted Kaunda, as it had the colonial government, on matters concerning its survival as a self-governing community. We have to look at what kind of community it tried to be; and with the more loosely organised movements, which hoped, more ambitiously, to change their larger environment in the end, we must ask what their vision was and what they expected to have to do in order to bring it about.

If witchcraft is caused by jealousy, it is not surprising that the solutions to witchcraft involve visions of a community in which jealousy need not arise, a situation of levelling. This is the word used to translate the Mwana Lesa myth current in the Lala and Lamba country before Nyirenda came on the scene:

So it was believed in the early 1920's that Lesa in his personification as Luchyele would return at dawn and that with him would *return all the dead*. The essential "persons" of the dead, meanwhile, freed from both the body and spirit, rested in the realm of *ichiyawafu*, the "*great place of levelling*". "The dead of all tribes and nations go there, and live in perfect harmony. There is but one tongue, which each person acquires immediately he is greeted by the king [of *ichiyawafu*], there is no distinction of social status; no distinction is made between the persons of chiefs, commoners, and slaves. Even the persons of witches or wizards go to *ichiyawafu*, for their witcheries have been left behind them". All these dead, it was believed, would return with Lesa Luchyele as young males in full health.[62]

Another millennial vision, although its emphasis is on individual self-sufficiency rather than sharing, is one in which jealousy and resentment would not be necessary, because each person would have enough and not have to bind himself in labour or in obligation to any other person. Levelling is implied, certainly, in this Watchtower Tract of 1958:

Everyone who lives through Armageddon . . . will be making something good and useful. No-one will be working for another man . . . [As in Isaiah 65:21–22] "they shall build houses and inhabit them; and they shall plant vineyards, and eat the fruit of them. They shall not build and another inhabit; they shall not plant and another eat; . . . my chosen ones shall enjoy the work of their hands".[63]

Here was a vision of the future, one of many. What would people have to do to bring about the condition of equality, of political autonomy, of economic sufficiency? One reason for thinking that religious movements are politically insignificant was that the participants seem to rely on medicine to solve their problem for them, rather than trying to change anything themselves. Sholto Cross writes,

The preaching of *bamcapi* vendors [i.e., witch finders] . . . tended towards the total conversion of the group, but from the point of view that those who did not buy the medicine or submit to the test were automatically suspected of witchcraft. The supernatural sanctions and myths of origin of the medicine which the *bamcapi* invoked in hawking their wares did not amount to a millen[n]ial claim, however, any more than did the vision of a society cleansed of witchcraft fears amount to a vision of the golden age. The *bamcapi* did not require change, mobilisation or a new form of consciousness for the success of their cult—they operated through persuasion rather than commitment.[64]

The only way to challenge this idea is to look at the statements made in these movements. What in fact did the witch finders require? In every case the people treated had to confess all their witchcraft, as is also the case with the Apostolic churches described by Daneel and Sr. Mary Aquina, in which the ritual does not include medicine but has a similar effect.[65] But this is not all it takes to make the magic work. People think their troubles are their own fault, as a community, and decide that they need supernatural help, but they must first try to deserve it. They must try to be better.

Whether or not this was a *condition* of success (as it is in Melanesian cargo cults, for example)[66] is unclear. Certainly we find frequent exhortations to reform in the literature of witch-finding movements. Ranger quotes Wilson Ngwata on *mchape* in Lundazi in 1933; Ngwata gave evidence that the witch-finders told people not to steal, to share themselves with their wives equally, to live in peace, and not to kill one another.[67] Kunda's evidence on Mwana Lesa[68] was similar: "I used to hear Tomo preaching and teaching the people. He told them to change their hearts, to be hospitable to strangers and treat them well, not to abuse other people, to stop fighting".[69] We have seen that the first Mwana Lesa was remembered as a gentle martyr, who told the people to stop fighting. The evidence on Nyirenda is difficult to evaluate, as at times he talked of taking over the wealth of the whites as they rolled up their railway and departed, at other times blacks and whites were to live together in peace, sharing the wealth as they did in America, where [black] Americans and whites were "sons of sisters". Possibly a more thorough investigation will show where the emphasis lay. Ranger himself stresses the peaceful side of Nyirenda's teaching and the Lala's confrontation with the evil lurking in themselves, rather than the anti-white aspects.

Hooker's evidence confirms Ranger's. Nyirenda told the people to give up adultery, stealing, and fighting in preparation for Christ's return.[70] For other movements there are frustratingly vague hints of something similar. Writing about Anok Simpungwe's Watchtower-inspired church (1919), Roberts mentions that members were noted for their "highly abstemious conduct",[71] but what they were abstaining from he doesn't say. Again, the independent *bamalonda* Watchtower movement which flourished in the Luapula Valley in 1947 followed a "strict moral code". The description of Lenshina's movement is of course more detailed. She attacked magic, beer, and polygamy because they gave rise to quarrelling and ill-feeling (a phrase in one of her hymns goes, "Shout to the desert, shout / leave beer and witchcraft"). Richard Stuart is getting at this idea when he treats *mchape* and the missions as rivals. He ascribes the missions' initial success to their claim that Christianity meant no more hatred and jealousy among the Christian community at least; the old remedies would no longer be needed.[72] He quotes an interview with an African priest in 1972, "We preach to the people to stop *ufiti*, such as jealousy, hatred, things like that, and those who believe, who want to become Christians, they will give up witchcraft."[73]

There is some question, then, whether such movements relied on the mechanics of magic alone. Vansina puts this very well, referring to his material from Zaire: "The term anti-witchcraft cults is too clumsy to convey [the] reality, just as anti-sin cult would not be very satisfactory for some Christian rituals".[74]

A valid objection to all this is that it is no good trying to change one's feelings about other people, unless one also tries to change the nature of one's relationships with them, to remove the causes of bad feeling. The solution to the problem of the labour migrant and his uncle was very incomplete. The young man had been punished by witchcraft for his failure, but it was his uncle who was exposed in the end. The movement seemed to favour the person who was succeeding in the white world and trying to ignore his obligations to those at home. The uncle was "cured" as well as the nephew, but the problem was not solved, for the motive for witchcraft remained untouched.

What evidence is there of reorganisation of social and economic relationships to get rid of the causes of witchcraft?

To begin with, there is the creation of separate communities, the villages of the Jehovah's Witnesses and the Lumpa church among others. In these the community certainly takes control over ideology; in some cases it also forms an economic community aiming at cooperative self-sufficiency. The tendency of the larger economy to accentuate and increase economic inequalities is countered in this way. We should inquire, therefore, into the organisation of these separate villages for production and distribution.[75] (This may not be easy; Andrew Roberts, for example, had to do his very full study of the Lumpa church from documentary sources because the church was undergoing persecution at the time.)

What about social relationships? There are various strands of evidence to be followed up, beginning with changes in the family. Roberts mentions one experiment by the Bamahamutima sect, a Bemba group which broke away from the Roman Catholic Church in 1951:

This movement, led by Emilio Mwalani, sought to create a fellowship akin to that of the early church. It was much occupied with giving to the poor, and it endeavoured at a time of uncertainty and strain in family life, to strengthen the nuclear family by encouraging closer association between husbands and wives. This was an attempt, also made by the Jehovah's Witnesses, to achieve a new and essentially modern equality between men and women. Such a trend was obviously liable to misinterpretation and misrepresentation: rumours of outrageous promiscuity led the government in 1961 to cancel the registration of bamutima branches in Kasama and Mporokoso districts.[76]

It is easy to see how the establishment of greater equality between men and women could strike at the roots of jealousy. It is less easy to see how closer association between husbands and wives could be interpreted as promiscuity. Perhaps two different experiments are at work here. This brings us to the question of experiments with the rules of sexual access. Here we are on very shaky ground, for rumours about this kind of thing are often smears by outsiders, and on the whole have been discounted by historians, perhaps quite rightly.

But there are a few more scraps of evidence in Hooker's article on Jehovah's Witnesses in Northern Rhodesia. He speaks of a "wife-changing heresy" in the 1930s, when sex taboos were lifted, whatever that means, and of cases where incest taboos were deliberately broken. In Central Province, Chief Shiwichinga, the Native Authority, had Watchtower sectarians beaten for sex relations "within the prohibited degree". And after the Second World War the Governor was complaining about free love, "which seems to have been regarded as demonstrating the supreme expression of unselfishness".[77]

We should pay attention to these rumours because sexual experiments have so often been a part of efforts at levelling by utopian communities and even in cargo cults.[78] One of the inequalities which cause jealousies within a community is inequality of access to the opposite sex, and utopians have recognised this and tried to deal with it, often by imposing celibacy, less often by trying promiscuity. In a celibate community, the problem is avoided, because nobody is getting any. In a promiscuous community, the problem is confronted: everyone is getting as much as he or she can attract and handle. These forms appear to be opposites, but they can be seen as efforts to remove something from the field of competition, fitting into a whole pattern of levelling or communalising "resources". In any case, this is one of the things that new studies, or restudies, could look into, for it may be here that we find part of the answer to the question whether people actually tried to restructure their relationships in order to treat each other better, and so deserve the magical aid on which their movement relied.

One problem which all these movements confronted, then, was jealousy. The cause was inequality—between black and white, certainly, but also between black and black in each small community—and the solution was levelling. Whites were to be sent home, and prosperous blacks were to be induced to give up the magic that pushed them ahead of others, or that kept others down, while poorer ones would give up their magic of resentment, and all would be protected from retaliation by the magical disarmament of the whole community. The fresh start would involve moral reform, and in some cases economic and political reforms as well. What could be more political than the effort to raise women to the status of men, or to operate as a separate community in the face of brutal repression, as the Lumpa church people did? What could be less escapist than to withhold taxes or to present oneself for a witchcraft ordeal? (If there was an element of escapism, it was in the hope that getting rid of the Europeans would achieve the levelling which was desired!)

It would be simplistic to suggest that all these movements were about levelling. Sometimes, indeed, people joined Christian churches in order to belong to a new community composed of a new class, while they cut themselves loose from traditional obligations they did not wish to meet (or did not feel they should have to meet).[79] But where the central problem seems to be the eradication of witchcraft, it is reasonable to look for ways in which the movement tries to level inequalities as well as to wipe out magic.

This is one direction in which the study of religious movements could have gone had it not been for the identification of political action with anti-colonial protest. What understandings, then, did the nationalist approach tend to obscure? Because it saw the various kinds of religious movements as stages in an evolution towards Western-style political parties, it was interested primarily in their strengths and weaknesses as forerunners of these.[80] From this point of view, the obsession with witchcraft was a mistake, a distraction; the expectation of "supernatural" participation, an escapist fantasy. Nationalist historians did not consider that witchcraft-eradication movements might be the appropriate response to the profound shifts in status and opportunities brought by colonial rule and the incorporation of Africa into the international economy; that they might reflect a quite reasonable understanding, on the local level, of what these changes meant to relations between people. If they are seen as stages of development which become outmoded and are shuffled off with increasing political experience, it is difficult to see why they should persist through independence and afterwards. If they are seen as appropriate, it is quite understandable. Conditions have not yet been created to dispel the feelings of jealousy and resentment, and probably never will be, so we can expect the need for local-level, communal reform to continue to be felt and expressed in ways which may or may not ever articulate with the political forms at the centre. It must be emphasised that this is only one thread (which I think is an important one) in any of the movements, and that in each of them a great many others will be found. The focus on witchcraft, stemming from jealousy, stemming from increased or unaccustomed patterns of inequality, is not put forward as an automatic or all-embracing approach. It is one approach with which, moving backward, some causes may be better understood, and, moving forward, some experiments with rules or institutions may be compared with others found in seemingly very different circumstances; and I have tried to show that it is an approach which was precluded by the nationalist bias because it seemed tactless, or simply irrelevant, to stray too far down rather sad dead ends.

## NOTES

1. H. Butterfield, *The Whig Interpretation of History* (Harmondsworth, Penguin Books, 1931), pp. 74–75.

2. For a survey of the sort of thing referred to as "religious movements", see V. Lanternari, *The Religions of the Oppressed: A Study of Modern Messianic Cults* (New York, Alfred A. Knopf, 1963).

3. See, e.g., G.C.K. Gwassa, "Kinjeketile and the Ideology of Maji Maji" in eds. T.O. Ranger and I. Kimambo, *The Historical Study of African Religion* (London, Heinemann, 1972), p. 215.

4. R. Linton, "Nativistic Movements", *American Anthropologist*, vol. 14 (1943), pp. 238–39.

5. Ibid., p. 233.

6. A. Richards, "A Modern Movement of Witchfinders", *Africa*, vol. 8, no. 4 (1935).

7. M. Marwick, "Another Modern Anti-Witchcraft Movement in East-Central Africa", *Africa*, vol. 20 (1950), p. 112.

8. J.S. Coleman, "Nationalism in Tropical Africa" in ed. W. Hanna, *Independent Black Africa: The Politics of Freedom* (Chicago, Rand McNally and Co., 1964; reprinted from the *American Political Science Review*, vol. 48 [1954]), p. 212.

9. Ibid, pp. 213–14.

10. Ibid.

11. See C. Rosberg and J. Nottingham, *The Myth of Mau Mau: Nationalism in Kenya* (Nairobi, East African Publishing House, 1966).

12. C. Young, *Politics in the Congo* (Princeton, Princeton University Press, 1965), p. 281. The quotations which follow are all taken from pp. 281–88 of Young's book.

13. R. Robinson and J. Gallagher, "The Partition of Africa" in ed. F.H. Hinsley, *The New Cambridge Modern History* (Cambridge, Cambridge University Press, 1962), vol. 77, pp. 639–40.

14. R. Oliver and A. Atmore, *Africa Since 1800* (Cambridge, Cambridge University Press, 1967), p. 158.

15. J. Iliffe, "The Organisation of the Maji Maji Rebellion" in eds. M. Klein and G.W. Johnson, *Perspectives on the African Past* (Boston, Little, Brown and Co., 1972), pp. 535–36.

16. Ibid., p. 546.

17. Ibid., also T.O. Ranger, "Witchcraft Eradication Movements in Central and Southern Tanzania and their Connection with the Maji Maji Rising" (Research Seminar Paper, Dar es Salaam, November, 1966).

18. J. Lonsdale, "Some Origins of Nationalism in East Africa", *Journal of African History*, vol. 9 (1968). The quotations here come from a version of this article reprinted in ed. R. Collins, *Problems in the History of Colonial Africa 1860–1960* (Englewood Cliffs, N.J., Prentice-Hall, Inc., 1970), p. 384.

19. R. Rotberg, "The Modern Emergence of Malawi and Zambia" in eds. S. Diamond and F. Burke, *The Transformation of East Africa* (London, Basic Books Inc., 1966), p. 347.

20. G. Balandier, "Messianism and Nationalism in Black Africa" in Klein and Johnson, *Perspectives*, p. 468. This was originally published in *Cahiers Internationaux de Sociologie*, vol. 14 (1953).

21. A. Roberts, "The Political History of Twentieth-Century Zambia" in ed. T.O. Ranger, *Aspects of Central African History* (London, Heinemann, 1968), p. 168.

22. Described in B. Sundkler, *Bantu Prophets in South Africa* (London, Oxford University Press, 2nd edition, 1961; first published 1948).

23. Balandier, "Messianism", p. 469.

24. Ibid., p. 472.

25. Michael Banton did in fact criticise this imbalance at the time. In 1963 he wrote: "There has been a tendency to stress the extent to which such movements may serve as vehicles for the expression of political protest and to neglect the question of religious appeal"; and he went on to consider the religious appeal of Kimbangu. This article does not seem to have made much impression on other writers, however; perhaps Banton, as an anthropologist, was less readily absorbed into the nationalist preoccupation than historians were.

26. See R.C. Fox, W. de Craemer, and J.M. Ribeaucourt, "The Second Independence: A Case Study of the Kwilu Rebellion in the Congo", *Comparative Studies in Society and History*, vol. 7 (1965).

27. See H. Turner, *Religious Innovation in Africa* (Boston, G.K. Hall & Co., 1979), p. 302; D. Parkin, "Medicines and Men of Influence", *Man* N.S., vol. 3 (1968); R.G. Willis, "Kamcape: An Anti-Sorcery Movement in South-West Tanzania", *Africa*, vol. 38 (Jan. 1968). More recently in "The Churches, the Nationalist State and African Religion" in eds. E.W. Fasholé-Luke *et al.*, *Christianity in Independent Africa* (London, Rex Collings, 1978), Ranger refers to witchcraft eradication movements in Ujamaa villages in the 1970s (p. 502).

28. Parkin, "Medicines", pp. 424–25.

29. Ibid., p. 428.

30. Willis, "Kamcape".

31. T.O. Ranger, "Connections between 'Primary Resistance' Movements and Modern Mass Nationalism in East and Central Africa", in Klein and Johnson, *Perspectives*, first published in the *Journal of African History*, vol. 9, nos. 3/4 (1968).

32. A. Roberts, "The Lumpa Church of Alice Lenshina and its Antecedents", *Mimeo* (Dar es Salaam, 1967). Shepperson, too, has remarked on the millenarian flavour of a nationalist movement, in the case of Dr. Banda's leadership of his party from the time he returned to Nyasaland. G. Shepperson, "Nyasaland and the Millennium", in ed. S. Thrupp, *Millennial Dreams of Action: Studies in Revolutionary Religious Movements* (New York, Schocken Books, 1970).

33. For example, at Chilema; another on "The History of Central African Religious Systems" at Lusaka in 1972; the "Conference on the Historical Study of East African Religions, Limuru" in 1974; and a series of seminars on "Christianity in Independent Africa" held in London, Los Angeles, and eight African venues between 1973 and 1975.

34. Eds. T.O. Ranger and J. Weller, *Themes in the Christian History of Central Africa* (London, Heinemann, 1975), pp. 37–38.

35. W. McGaffey, "African Ideology and Belief: A Survey", *African Studies Review*, vol. 24, nos. 2/3 (June/Sept. 1981), p. 244.

36. Ranger, "Churches, State, and Religion".

37. The Chilema Conference papers have been published with the title *Themes in the Christian History of Central Africa* (London, Heinemann, 1975), edited by T.O. Ranger and J. Weller. Ranger and S. Cross are editing *The Problem of Evil in Eastern Africa 1870–1970*, incorporating several of the Lusaka papers. Other collections include eds. Ranger and Kimambo, *Historical Study*; eds. Fasholé-Luke *et al., Christianity*; N.D. Booth, *African Religions: A Symposium* (New York, NOK Publishers, 1977); and *African Perspectives* 1976/77, issue titled *Religious Innovations in Modern African Society*. See also the journal, *African Religions Research*, published in the 1970s.

38. MacGaffey, "Ideology", p. 233.

39. W. van Binsbergen, *Religious Change in Zambia* (London and Boston, Kegan Paul, 1981).

40. See the discussion of Marxist scholarship in Chapter 6.

41. See T.O. Ranger, "The Mwana Lesa Movement of 1925" in Ranger and Weller, *Christian History*.

42. Ranger is drawing here on ideas from A.D.J. Macfarlane, *Witchcraft in Tudor and Stuart England: A Regional and Comparative Study* (London, Routledge and Kegan Paul, 1970). Macfarlane looks at the situation in England, when the provision for paupers was undergoing change and people were uncertain what their obligations to the poor should be, and afraid of retaliation when they turned from the door beggars whom they previously had fed. For a brief presentation of these ideas see Macfarlane's article in ed. M. Douglas, *Witchcraft Confessions and Accusations* (London, Tavistock, 1970).

43. Regarding "colonial pressures": we have seen that labour migration is a fruitful area to look into, but it is only one. Land reform might be another; or reformulation of laws to do with marriage or ownership of property. The conversion or partial conversion to cash-cropping is also likely to be accompanied by a changing distribution of wealth, leading to increased witchcraft fears and accusations. This occurred in Giriama (see Parkin, "Medicines").

44. R. Stuart, "Anglican Missionaries and the Problem of Evil: Mchape and the U.M.C.A. 1933", unpublished paper given to the Lusaka Conference on the History of Central African Religious Systems (Aug./Sept. 1972).

45. Willis, "Kamcape", footnote on p. 12.

46. Or, if he is a Zande, he may admit that he *was* cross so he might have caused the other's misfortune by *unconsciously* directing a barrage of effective malice against him, and agree to stop it now that it has been drawn to his attention. (See Evans-Pritchard, *Witchcraft, Oracles and Magic among the Azande* [Oxford, Clarendon Press, 1937]).

47. M. Marwick, *Sorcery in Its Social Setting* (Manchester, Manchester University Press, 1965).

48. T.O. Ranger, "Mchape and the Study of Witchcraft Eradication", unpublished paper presented to the Lusaka Conference on the History of Central African Religious Systems (Aug./Sept. 1972), p. 18.

49. Ibid., p. 8. The identification of witchcraft with jealousy was expressed by one of Nyirenda's victims, one of many who submitted to testing and execution out of belief in their own guilt. Lipereto had come to Nyirenda hoping to become a Watchtower preacher. "Tomo said to him, 'You have come, Lipereto? Today you are going to die.' Lipereto said, 'All right, if I am a wizard, I must die'. . . . Lipereto submitted without struggling or resisting—He said, 'I must die: I have a little horn of jealousy.' " Ranger, "Mwana Lesa", p. 59, quoting the Evidence of Chisenga, 8 Oct. 1925, KSM 3/1/1. National Archives, Lusaka.

50. C. Mitchell, "The Meaning of Misfortune for Urban Africans" in eds. M. Fortes and G. Dieterlen, *African Systems of Thought* (London, Oxford University Press, 1965); and W.D. Hammond-Tooke, "Urbanisation and the Interpretation of Misfortune: A Quantitative Analysis", *Africa*, vol. 40 (1970).

51. Ranger, "Mwana Lesa", p. 67.

52. Hodgkin recognises this in his essay on "Mahdism, Messianism and Marxism in the African Setting" in eds. P. Gutkind and P. Waterman, *African Social Studies: A Radical Reader* (London, Heinemann, 1977):

The revolution, as [Messianic-Mahdist movements] conceived it, must involve the total transformation of society, and of man as a social being; the assertion of a new ethic and a new basis of human relationships; the ending of all forms of oppression, not merely those specific forms of oppression associated with external domination or the colonial state. (p. 318).

53. T.O. Ranger, "Mchape", p. 30.

54. Stuart thinks this idea is new with the missions, but in view of long traditions of spirit possession, if not witchcraft eradications, this view is probably mistaken. Often, if a person is behaving badly, expressing greedy desires or discontent or a longing to break rules, he is treated sympathetically; it is assumed that a spirit possesses him, and is asking for these things, so they are granted to the spirit and the possessed person is then expected to calm down and buck up, as if he had been ill. He has got what he wanted, just this once, and the ideal of good behaviour has been preserved. Communal witchcraft-eradication movements are comparable, in that people are bad, are purged and forgiven, but are given no encouragement to go off and be bad again. See I.M. Lewis, *Ecstatic Religion: An Anthropological Study of Spirit Possession and Shamanism* (Harmondsworth, Penguin Books, 1971), Ch. 3.

55. Willis, "Kamcape", pp. 11–12.

56. Again, Hodgkin is unusual in recognising that a reliance on supernat-

ural aid did not necessarily imply an attitude of passivity. He makes an interesting analogy with the Marxist reliance on "History":

"Millenarian movements", Hobsbawm argues, "share a fundamental vagueness about the actual way in which the new society will be brought about". (Hobsbawm, *Primitive Rebels* [Manchester, 1959], p. 58.)

But while this contention is no doubt in general correct, I think he exaggerates the extent to which "pure" millenarian movements have tended to adopt a passive, or "waiting" attitude to revolutionary change": their "followers are not makers of revolution. They expect it to make itself". This is certainly not true of Mahdist movements, nor, I think, of most of the non-Muslim movements referred to here. They are closer to the classic Marxist position that revolution is at the same time historically necessary and dependent upon the beliefs and actions of revolutionaries. Their difficulty was rather that of all Utopian movements: the lack of a clearly defined strategy of revolution, reliance upon a variety of methods—*jihad* or armed rebellion, magical-religious techniques (such as the *maji* water-medicine), *hijra* or withdrawal from the European-dominated political order, expectation of external support (e.g. from American Negroes)—inadequate to achieve their revolutionary objectives. ("Mahdism", pp. 319–20.)

57. "The believer does not believe himself to be such; it is the unbeliever who believes that the believer believes in the existence of God".—J. Pouillon, "Remarques sur le verbe 'croire' " in eds. M. Izard and P. Smith, *La Fonction Symbolique* (Paris, 1979); quoted in MacGaffey, "Ideology", p. 230.

58. A. Roberts, "The Lumpa Church of Alice Lenshina" in eds. R. Rotberg and Mazrui, *Protest and Power in Black Africa* (London, Oxford University Press, 1970), p. 540.

59. Ibid., p. 563.

60. J. Hooker, "Witnesses and Watchtower in the Rhodesias and Nyasaland", *Journal of African History*, vol. 6 (1965).

61. Roberts, "Lumpa Church", p. 543.

62. Ranger, "Mwana Lesa", p. 55. Ranger's source is C.M. Doke, *The Lambas of Northern Rhodesia: A Study of their Customs and Beliefs* (London, G.G. Harrap and Co., 1931), pp. 226, 231–32.

63. N. Long, *Social Change and the Individual* (Manchester, Manchester University Press, 1972; first published 1968), p. 221.

64. S. Cross, "The Watch-Tower, Witch-Cleansing, and Secret Societies in Central Africa", unpublished paper for the Lusaka Conference on the History of Central African Religious Systems (Aug./Sept. 1972), p. 11.

65. M.L. Daneel, "Shona Independent Churches and the Eradication of Wizardry", unpublished paper presented to the Lusaka Conference on the History of Central African Religious Systems (Aug./Sept. 1972) and Sr. Mary Aquina, "The People of the Spirit: An Independent Church in Rhodesia", *Africa*, vol. 37 (1967).

66. See K. Burridge, *Mambu* (London, Methuen, 1960), passim.

67. Ranger, "Mwana Lesa", p. 5.

68. At his own trial for assisting Nyirenda in the execution of witches.
69. Ranger, "Mwana Lesa", p. 57.
70. Hooker, "Witnesses".
71. Roberts, "Lumpa Church", p. 520.
72. Stuart, "Anglican Missionaries", p. 19.
73. Ibid., p. 23.
74. Vansina, quoted by Ranger in "Mchape", p. 29.
75. Van Binsbergen thinks that a split began to develop in the Lumpa communities between a religious elite and the common members; if this is so, it would contradict my suggestion, so it will be interesting if more can be discovered on this point. W. van Binsbergen, "Religious Innovation and Political Conflict in Zambia: The Lumpa Rising" in van Binsbergen, *Religious Change*.
76. Roberts, "Lumpa Church", p. 522.
77. Hooker, "Witnesses", p. 104.
78. For material on cargo cults, see note 54. Relevant material on American Utopian communities, both celibate and promiscuous, can be found in M. Holloway, *Heavens on Earth: Utopian Communities in America, 1680–1880* (London, Turnstile Press, 1951).
79. Indeed, people may convert to Islam apparently for the same reason. Giriama studied by Parkin are a case in point. When some became wealthy through the adoption of cash crops, they began to be afflicted by Muslim spirits, possessing them, making them ill, and demanding that they convert to Islam as the only cure. Lewis explains:

Conversion . . . obliges the new Muslim adherent to observe the Islamic requirements in diet and to abstain from traditional intoxicants, thus isolating him from his neighbours and enabling him to escape from customary commensual obligations, at the same time, the risk of being offered ensorcelled food at parties by jealous neighbours or kin is also reduced. . . . The ambitious progressive Giriama . . . at one blow . . . legitimises his anti-social ambitions of personal aggrandisement and protects himself from the malicious envy of the less successful. And all this is done in the form of a cure for a possession illness for which he cannot be held accountable. (Lewis, *Ecstatic Religion*, p. 130.)

80. In a recent article, Wyatt MacGaffey demonstrates that magic and "modern" politics are coexisting idioms for dealing with the same problems. The Zairians he refers to do not outgrow magical interpretations and methods and take up party organisation instead; rather, they bring one or other technique to bear, depending upon the context in which they are operating in their "plural society", like a bilingual person switching from English to French and back. MacGaffey's discussion of "pluralism"—he uses the word to describe Africans living in a variety of situations simultaneously, some of which are defined and controlled by Europeans, others by Africans—directly challenges

ideas about the transition from "traditional" to "modern" ways of life found in most African histories. See W. MacGaffey, "African History, Anthropology, and the Rationality of Natives", *History in Africa*, vol. 5 (1978), especially pp. 112–16.

# 4

# HISTORY BY AFRICAN
# ACADEMICS

So far no distinction has been made between black and white historians in this discussion. Indeed, for the purpose of illustrating most of the points made here, no distinction is necessary, for most of the values we are examining seem to be held in common. This is something which needs to be discussed in itself, however, for it runs counter to a widely held assumption of the sixties, made by black and white students alike: that the replacement of white historians of Africa by black ones would automatically mean the replacement of colonial and neocolonial ideology by an authentically *African* historiography. Blacks would bring a point of view which even sympathetic and well-intentioned whites could not contribute, because the experience of being African was felt to be an essential ingredient of this point of view. It would be one, moreover, which would effect a restoration of pride in the past, both the need and the means of which could only fully be understood by blacks themselves. This is still articulated and gains support from the character of Black Studies in the United States. This is not considered just another branch of history, but a means by which blacks may discover and share bases for pride in their race and for confidence in its future.[1]

If we look at history written by Africans, however, this assumption is not really borne out. In the first place, there is no dramatic cleavage between black and white historians' points of view. Old glories, ancient dignity, and the continuing courage and vigour of Africans throughout the colonial encounter are as much a part of white as of black writing, as we have seen; nor can it be said that Africans have brought any unique slant to these topics.

Secondly, differences among African writers must be distinguished. The significant difference in approach which emerges from a study of history written by Africans in the sixties is not one between whites and blacks but a difference between (English-speaking) East and West Africans. The writers who appear to have been most free of the desire to use history as a means of restoring pride, even when it meant distorting the past, were West Africans, particularly Nigerians. Their work lends very little support to the idea that Africans needed the new history to give them confidence in themselves; no such need is reflected in the cold light the Ibadan historians throw on many aspects of the African past.[2]

After a decade of writing in the spirit of nation-building, however, East Africans became far more critical in their approach. Like some East African poets and novelists,[3] East African historians were to react more sharply, on the whole, than their West African colleagues to the disappointments of independence. By the late seventies, a number of them were taking up a Marxist approach and stressing the necessity for studies of class, peasants, and the workings of neo-colonialism. Others, while not committing themselves to Marxist analysis, write with bitterness of the betrayal of the nationalist struggle, particularly in Kenya, and see a need to go back to its history, which had been seen in the light of a people's victory, with new questions.[4] Here, if anywhere, a difference can be felt between African and European writing, a personal need to understand rather than an ideological requirement to convince.

While the main focus is on writing in the post-independence decade, some explanation will be sought of the contrast between these orientations of East African writing, as well as between East and West African viewpoints. I say "orientation" because, while a broad change over time is discernible, no firm periodisation is possible, just as it is impossible neatly to divide East from West African writers (and so one should hope). There is a variety of views on either side of the continent, and of course scholars from either side have frequently been working and writing away from their place of origin. The observations put forward here, therefore, are of a general nature, and are intended to stimulate, not to enrage.

To begin with the contrast between East and West African writing in the sixties:

Both overtly, and often in their structure as well, East African writings at this time were largely defensive. Historians took up one or another accusation made against Africans by colonial writers, and wrote an article or book refuting it. Ogot, for instance, devoted two articles, one in *Emerging Themes of African History*, the other in *The Historian in Tropical Africa*, to refuting the Hamitic hypothesis.[5] Kimambo, too, was at pains, when writing about the centralisation of power in Ugweno and Usambara, to show that diffusion of ideas was no more significant than evolution in either case.

There is a need to recognise the efforts, initiative and even success achieved by the people of Tanzania even in that distant past. The time for tracing influences from outside for everything achieved in Tanzania has passed. Certainly it is becoming clear that the Tanzanians of that period were much more in control of their own affairs than has hitherto been allowed. They were able to create political ideologies which suited their own environments and needs. It is from the realisation of such achievements that the Tanzanians of today must draw inspiration and courage as they strive in developing a modern nation founded on their own culture.[6]

In another piece, this time a pamphlet in the Historical Association of Tanzania's series, Kimambo wrote,

It has been assumed that the pre-mass party "tribal" revolts against colonial policies were spontaneous and unorganised. The main aim of this study is to illustrate how the *mbiru* protest reveals a clear combination of traditional methods of resistance against oppressive rulers with modern techniques learned from the colonial period to achieve specific ends.[7]

One is reminded of East African literature, which took longer than that of West Africa to relax from its defensive posture and take up themes other than the one of colonial injustice and the fight for freedom. East African historians seemed still to be demonstrating the independence of their countries, and confirming its reality, by injecting it into their history. We shall see that West Africans were less given to this, which seems rather odd, as West African thinkers must have been more intellectually colonised, and come from a longer background of intellectual domination by the West, than East Africans had. The difference is probably explicable, however, in terms of their relationships to European culture. West Africans had more of the things Europeans admired at the time of their early interaction, than East Africans had; thus, although they suffered very heavily in other ways, perhaps they suffered less from cultural comparisons. Their longer exposure to European dominance also meant that they had a longer time in which to succeed within that system. West African intellectuals had the confidence of belonging to a class, with more than a generation of Western-style professionals behind it. In terms of Western models, therefore, they had less to be defensive about, in either their pre-colonial past or their adjustment to colonial rule, than East Africans had. (The case of French-speaking West Africans is altogether different, for the cultural offensive of the French in their colonies was far more drastic, hence the reaction of Negritude.)[8] It seems, therefore, that the people who had the least glorious past, in Western terms, needed it the most; they also had the most difficulty in knocking one into shape. Thus it was the East African historians who insisted on seeing the success of African peoples, in the past as in the present, in European terms. If nationalism was the approved technique of liberation, then Africans must be shown to have been nationalist from the earliest moment possible; if resistance was part of this, then everyone must have resisted. If the facts did not seem to bear any such interpretation, the labels of nationalism and resistance were not discarded; they were redefined until they could be used to describe the facts, whatever they were.

This is what we find, for instance, in some of the contributions to *A History of Tanzania*, which, we should remember, was not an official publication but an academic work, and was aimed at teachers as well as students.

In his contribution, Temu objected to the idea that nationalism was a relatively recent development in Tanzania. He criticised Lonsdale, among other Europeans, for taking the view (in his article "The Emergence of African Nations")[9] that nationalism was the effort to take over power at the centre, in this case the colonial legislature.

In their haste to dismiss the early phase of our nationalism lightly (and it is understandable that they should do so), they have picked on this central characteristic in order to assert that African nationalism is a post-world war phenomenon.[10]

Nationalism in Tanzania began long before the end of World War II, the period often mistakenly cited. Indeed our nationalism began with the onset of colonialism for it was then that, threatened with German invasion, the people of mainland Tanzania rose to defend their country against colonial invasion.[11]

He redefined nationalism, in fact, so that its "content", not its "focus", was what was important; the thing which early and later resisters had in common, "their desire and attempt to remove European rule and so to govern themselves, is certainly the central feature of our nationalism".[12]

Why "of our nationalism"? Why not "of our reaction" or "of our politics"? "Nationalism" already meant something, and Temu could hardly object to Europeans using the word as it is defined by them. It *is* defined by them; it is an English word. What was odd was that he seemed to think Tanzanians' efforts were not interesting in themselves unless they were nationalist, even at a time when the idea of a nation was unknown in Tanzania.

Even more extraordinary was Gwassa's attempt to redefine the concepts of "resistance" and "collaboration".[13] Like Temu, he stressed the continuity of Tanzanian nationalism from early beginnings, again starting from a defensive position: "African resistance was dismissed as merely foolish, fanatical and retrograde or simply as the work of the uncivilised. . . . In this chapter an attempt is made to establish that the African resistance was reasonable and secondly that European colonisation was not always as easy as has often been believed."[14] He divided resistance into active and passive resistance, "African adaptation", which was what we usually call "collaboration", and "the mercenary technique" employed by people like the *ruga-ruga* thugs.

Passive resistance is a familiar enough concept. We use it to mean non-violent noncooperation: withdrawing labour, refusing orders, and so forth. Gwassa redefined it to embrace the attitude of anybody who did not like the Germans, whether they gave any indication of it or not. Was it really so surprising that so little attention had been paid to this area, as Gwassa complained? Not that there was not passive resistance in the usual sense; Kimambo's book about Mbiru, when the Pare assembled, sat down for two months, and refused to pay a tax, is a case in point.[15] But then why should Gwassa have to argue from the psychology of the individual? Nobody, he reasoned, likes to be ruled by foreigners, so Tanzanians could not have liked German rule, and if they did not, they were passive resisters.

He moved on to consider how inadequate is the word "collaboration" to describe the alliances that Africans entered into with Germans against other Africans. Collaboration implied, to Gwassa, that the Africans concerned wanted colonial rule, whereas in reality they wanted freedom. Collaborators were simply twice as freedom-loving as active resisters, for they wanted freedom from neighbouring Africans as well as from foreigners, and saw their chance to use the Germans in pursuit of the first of these goals. This he called "African adaptation". The naive Germans did not understand local African politics, and so they allowed themselves to be used time and again. They were used by each Chagga chief in turn to defeat his rival, mere pawns in a game in which they found themselves eventually in control of the players, a fact which Gwassa did nothing to explain. One of the chiefs, Marealle, "continued to make use of the Germans. By 1900 he had convinced the Germans that chiefs of Kibosho, Moshi, and his other rivals were plotting against the new authority. Such tactics precipitated the execution of 19 chiefs".[16] Well done, Chagga resistance. Then there were the real collaborators, those who fought as mercenaries for the Germans. They, however, were not "lovers of African independence".[17] But if collaboration means positively welcoming colonial rule, knowing what it meant, it seems strange that Gwassa should credit *ruga-ruga* with this any more than anybody else.

I take no pleasure in pointing out that Tanzanian history was among the worst products of the new history. It is extraordinary how often intellectual leaders who say that power should belong to the people simultaneously decide that the people are willing, good-hearted, but too simple-minded to cope with being properly informed.

Thus we find in Tanzanian, and some other East African writings, many of the characteristics familiar to us from European histories of Africa. There was the same defensive stance. There was the feeling that Africans, like children, should not be told harsh truths lest it shatter their self-esteem. There was the preoccupation with how the colonial encounter reflected on Africans, whether it spoke well or badly of them. There was the approval of Africans who were important, for whatever reason. There was the reverence for tradition, coupled with a reverence for nationalism. Interestingly enough, the Africans did not all share the European enthusiasm for centralised authority. Although

Kimambo was happy to see it where it did exist—he wrote of the "revolutions" which brought about centralised authority in Ugweno and Usambara that "they introduced reforms which improved the political system which already existed"[18]—Gwassa pointed out that Tanzania, while she had no large kingdoms like Buganda and Bunyoro, "alone provided, in the Maji Maji rising, the most widespread and fierce single resistance to colonial domination and this fact suggests that state systems were not always necessarily more dangerous or stronger than stateless ones".[19] Dike likewise defended stateless systems, in his book on the Niger Delta. He objected to the idea that the Niger Delta peoples were "low in the scale of political organisation", and quoted Piddington, who wrote that "no human community is any lower, earlier or more ancient than any other. All represent highly specialised human adaptations, the product of millen[n]ia of traditionalised cultural life".[20] Viewed in this light, said Dike, "the Delta and the eastern Nigerian political organisations served well the needs of their day".[21] This was all to the good; but it seems to be a difference of views between people from centralised and from stateless societies, rather than between Africans and Europeans.

Let us turn our attention now to the West Africans. They had their defensive moments, certainly—we have just seen one of Dike's. But these seem often to be formal pieces included out of a sense of obligation, and their interest in various subjects did not appear to be determined, or even given shape, by their defensive urges. East African articles were often *structured* as refutations, West African ones seldom were. This seems to be largely because they had a different perspective on their past, in which the colonial experience was important, but not overwhelming; action-packed, certainly, but not very long in duration. The claim that West Africans seemed concerned to refute, in the main, was the claim that the African past was static.[22] There was a lot going on, Ajayi reminded us, before the Europeans took over:

large scale migration . . . with attendant conflicts, absorption of some ethnic groups by others, the creation of new polities . . . internal wars, domestic slavery and centuries of external slave trade. . . . In relation to linguistic, cultural and religious change and the cultivation of new ideas and new ways of life, new economic orientations and so on, colonialism must be seen not as a complete departure from the African past, but as one episode in the continuous flow of African history.[23]

Thus Ajayi reasoned that the people who argued endlessly about whether African institutions continued or were disrupted through the colonial period were wasting their time—both those who welcomed the disruption because they thought pre-colonial Africa was uncreative and static, and those who subscribed to the

myth which assumes that Africa had a glorious past, but that nevertheless so strong was the European impact and so effective was their malice that in the brief duration of the colonial period, the whole glorious past of Africa was disrupted, leaving the poor African paralysed and helpless, a lonely man lost between two worlds.[24]

Both views, he said, made Africans less than human.

Once we have broken the myth about the colonial period and we establish that Africans, even under colonialism, were human beings, people, and not just Natives, it seems hardly very profound or significant to go on arguing about whether or not their institutions had any continuity in the 70 or 80 years— often much less—of colonial rule.[25]

History is change, said Ajayi, and of course there was change, and of course there was continuity in the colonial period as in all the time before it. What should interest the historian is *how* people adapted to change.

So Africans were people like any others, and their historical experience was comparable with others. As Tamuno pointed out, Nigeria was ruled by Britain for a shorter time than the United States, India and Ireland.[26] Seen in this perspective, the Good African and the Bad European disappear, just as the Bad African and the Good European once had to do. In Nigerian writings on pre-colonial times, Europeans were just another lot of people who were present at the coast. They spoke favourably of missionaries (as does Katoke in his history of the Karagwe kingdom).[27] For the rest, the white man was just another entrepreneur or chief. Several writers stressed that Africans felt the presence of European traders to be beneficial as long as they were easily manageable, which they were for varying lengths of time.[28] And, like other chiefs, they might be called upon to mediate in African disputes, or invited into alliances against neighbours.[29] In these ways, Europeans became influential in African affairs before they turned their energies to conquest. But it was never suggested that there was anything special about Europeans that enabled them to take over power—they were not more cunning, more malicious, or less scrupulous than blacks in comparable positions. Thus, although Adeleye, for one, organised his book around the question, How did it come about that the Caliphate was conquered? he saw the conquest, not as a sudden crushing blow to a Caliphate that was getting on all right otherwise, but as a normal event, explicable in terms of the problems of defence that the Caliphate had experienced throughout its rule. There was no question of whites being superior in themselves, only in their weaponry,[30] and their knowledge of what was happening over a much larger field than the Caliph could have been expected to know about.[31] Perhaps this is why Adeleye could refer to the conquest as "the whole stirring episode".[32]

Adeleye, in fact, made it clear in his preface that he had chosen to narrow his scope to events within the Caliphate. Thus the activities of Europeans in the Caliphate were relevant to his concerns, but not the policies of their home countries or the diplomatic exchanges between European rivals "except where the picture would be blurred without a mention of them". This policy on the treatment of Europeans in African history seems to have been followed by most of the writers of the Ibadan series of books. There is a legitimate objection to this way of handling the European presence, which would probably be raised by Marxist writers. It cannot give a realistic picture of what was happening in the world, that is, of the place of events in Africa in the whole global scene. Ayi Kwei Armah, for example, sees many of the same events the Ibadan writers treat of, in a radically different perspective:

Most of the actual work needed to decimate the continent's human resources was done *in place* by Africans—leaders and chiefs being in the vanguard. So that an assessment that does not focus on the exocenter, the metropole also but concentrates on Africa would be misleading, presenting as it would the semblance of a series of independent self-acting societies, when in fact the reality was that a subordinate sub-system was being torn apart in Africa to nourish and entertain a dominant metropole.[33]

The Ibadan writers did not seem to see it this way. Akinjogbin, for example, wrote, "The European directors were not left out of [Dahomey's] administrative organisation. Tegbesu recognised that they were

very important to the national economy".[34] Armah would probably say
that Tegbesu's was not a national economy, but an appendage to an
international one, and that the essential thing to note about the relationship was that Tegbesu was important to the Europeans, not the other
way round. But Tegbesu was not to know that. All of these are local
studies, and they have the particular virtue that they give us a picture
of what the situation may have looked like to the people who were in
it, without which we cannot understand what they did. We can then
combine this with what we know of the international situation; but it
is the first kind of picture, which has real people in it, that makes interesting history. There are times, however, when the African side makes
no sense by itself. This is particularly noticeable in some articles about
the granting of independence to African countries, when the only evidence produced is statements by politicians about what they want and
what they consider right and just, and the next thing you know, the
metropolitan power is acceding to their demands with no reason given
in the article why it should want to, or feel that it had no choice. Two
of the articles in the issue of *Tarikh* devoted to "Independence Movements in Africa" were like this, Tamuno's on "The Independence
Movement in Nigeria" and Ukpabi's on "The Independence Movement in the Sudan". In the latter, a point is reached when Egypt agrees
with the rival factions in the Sudan to leave the choice between complete independence, or association with Egypt, to the Sudanese. "Since
the British Government had always professed the right of the Sudanese
to self-government", Ukpabi wrote, "it had no alternative but to accept the agreement already reached by Egypt and the Sudanese political parties".[35] This is too formal, too mechanical, as it is bound to be
when questions of power and necessity in the largest relevant context
are left out. There are limitations, then, on what can be done with an
African-sided (rather than African-centred) approach.

In addition to adopting a less defensive approach to their past, the
Nigerians took a far less reverent attitude towards the trends on which
European and East African historians placed such value. After making
the literary tour of the admirable African kingdoms on so many occa-
sions, it is refreshing to come across Akinjogbin's throw-away remark
that "Dahomey was more than yet another African kingdom".[36] Lack
of reverence, indeed, is the hallmark of Tamuno's inaugural lecture as
Professor of History at the University of Ibadan in 1973, an occasion
on which he might have been expected to be more gracious than to

take the recent civil war as the proof of the Nigerian pudding. But that is what he did. "No matter how courageous we are as individuals and historians", he said—an interesting use of "courageous"—"we cannot ignore the continued existence of the national emergency in Nigeria". Had Nigeria's past really been so edifying, he argues, the present situation could harldy have come about. And, indeed, a survey of topical events in the last hundred years would show that, while not all "the history-makers could be called villains, heroes were few and far between".[37] He takes us through the resistance to colonialism, in the midst of which he does not scruple to identify collaborators. Although his claim that "even those who cooperated with the new British rulers did not abandon their natural wish to be free" sounds like Gwassa, it is not the same, for he does not consider those people to be resisters. He moves on through the amalgamation of Nigeria in 1914; the problems arising from the combination of different peoples under one government for the brief period of British rule, problems not solved then or since; the failure of representation due to electoral violence and corruption; and the hypocrisy of the nationalist leaders. Elsewhere he notes that many of the chiefs joined the nationalist cause purely to protect themselves.[38] While Nigerian responsibility in the government was increased in the fifties, there was "accelerated economic and social development [because] . . . the leading politicians found it necessary to satisfy the needs of the masses—the workers, farmers, fishermen and others—who had supported the agitation for independence. Hence began the practice in Nigeria of using politics as a game of rewards and penalties".[39] In this lecture, again, he writes:

Nigeria's political leaders . . . were so eager to control and monopolise the machinery of government that they encouraged rivalries which resulted in playing off one ethnic group against another. Moreover, in their bid to assume or retain power, these same leaders winked at corruption, recklessness, victimisation, and other mal-practices which embittered their opponents to the extent of threatening revenge or secession. In post-independence Nigeria, as elsewhere in Africa, the charismatic leadership of the advocates of decolonisation failed to ensure the stability of the newly emergent state.[40]

Interestingly enough, Tamuno does not consider participation the most important ingredient of the legitimacy of a government; but on the other counts of security, stability, and welfare, he finds nothing to redeem

Nigeria's management before the coup. There is no attempt here to confer legitimacy on the nation, nor on the struggle for independence, although there is much in the latter that Tamuno admires, and when he does, he says so.

It seems to be because they were in no doubt that there were moments of strength in African history that the West African historians could accept that there were also moments of weakness. Akintoye wrote about the missionary arbitration of the Ibadan-Ekitiparapo War, for example, as something the combatants badly needed, not as an instance of interference by Europeans. The Yoruba could not put their house in order, he said[41]; fair enough. They chose the most mutually acceptable mediators they could get hold of. Choice is of course the crucial thing here. West Africans had a very long time to interact with Europeans, and experiment with their ways and their things, before African sovereignty was threatened. Ajayi emphasised that the things of Europeans were not felt to be bad in themselves; some people wanted Christianity and Western education, for a variety of reasons; some tried and then rejected them. "The normal intercourse between nations leads to such spread of religion and new social and political ideas. Because of the loss of sovereignty, however, the changes of the colonial period were not normal".[42] Loss of sovereignty, he said, undermines peoples' self-respect and their confidence in their own choices, to the extent that they are allowed to choose.[43] But many West Africans were at least in a position to know that the power of white men depended on political circumstances, and not on any special attribute of their race. For many East Africans, the moment of meeting was also the moment of conquest, and the conquerors and their things and habits were then all one phenomenon. Perhaps this accounts for the relative lack of self-confidence in the East Africans' historical writing.

Another aspect of this greater self-confidence is that when West African writers described the societies of earlier times they did not feel called upon to show that whatever arrangements existed were beneficial to everybody. It was enough to show that, for various reasons, some edifying, others not, they were acceptable to enough people to keep them going; or that they were not, in moments of upheaval.

Thus Dike outlined the distribution of power in Delta societies, which depended on slavery and on wealth got by trading. He explained the role of Calabar's Egba society, which acted instead of police, and added that "similar organisations existed in communities of divided authority, such as the Cameroons, primarily to protect the privileges of the nobility against the insurrection of the lower orders".[44] He concluded, later, that "Delta society in the nineteenth century rested on a foundation of slavery; terror and despotism were normal features of a system that had to keep the masses in subjection. Yet if house rule may be judged from its practical results, on the whole it met the needs of the day".[45] This was because slaves could get rich as well as free men, so for the most part they caused little trouble. And in fact when slave rebellions did come (partly because of the influence of missionaries in Calabar),

these rebellions lingered on from 1848 to the late seventies because after more than three centuries of despotic rule, the political ideas and religious sanctions which sustained that despotism were difficult to eradicate; they had become part and parcel of Delta life and thought. Another impression derived from detailed investigation is that what some of the rebels attacked was not the political system as such; they strove to win a place in that system and to secure full life within it for themselves. . . . No sooner were the ex-slaves emancipated politically than they might become despots in their turn.[46]

Similarly, the Yoruba wars were presented more as empire-building efforts, as we understand the term, than as attempts at any sort of centralisation for the common good. Ajayi wrote of the Ijaye war:

Economic considerations featured prominently in this struggle. The basic ingredients of power were land and taxable peasants. Each state sought to win control over as many towns and villages as possible, and to tax them. It also tried to capture slaves in war, who were valuable both for work on the farms and service in the ranks of the armies.[47]

Akintoye likewise describes the effects of Ibadan's expansion and centralisation in rather the same way that historians write about the effects of Portuguese hegemony on the East coast of Africa. The provincial administration of Ibadan's empire was more extortionate even than was good for it.[48] Ibadan could not enlist the loyalty of subject towns which it was "endlessly raiding, sacking and despoiling", nor could it come to any cooperative arrangement with its neighbours who controlled the trade routes going to the coast. Akintoye puts Ibadan's ultimate failure down to its inability to control this "constant aggression".[49]

There is a lot of nastiness described in these and other passages, but they are not particularly critical in tone. Just as these writers were not concerned with justifying their past, they were not concerned with attacking it either. I do not think this is due to a lack of any bias so much as to a bias which most of them appear to share—one in favour of the individual. Developments which gave more scope to individual enterprise, and which made merit of more importance than kinship or inherited position, were noted with approval. Alagoa and Dike both stressed this aspect of the "house" system in the Niger Delta, where lineages turned into "houses" which comprised numbers of followers and slaves as well as kin, within which advancement was by merit, not by age or position in the lineage. Akinjogbin suggested that a similar trend was responsible for Dahomey's initial success, although in this case individualism was encouraged for the purpose of strengthening the monarchy. Loyalty was supposed to be felt to the king directly, not to and through the lineage, in hopes that a sense of citizenship might emerge. Promotion in the king's service was by merit, not through lineage connections.[50] Akintoye attributed the rise of Ibadan in the nineteenth century to the same kind of thing:

[From 1863 on] there became apparent in the actions of the Ibadan leaders the dream of a vast empire comprising all the Yoruba and having Ibadan as its centre. The very nature of the town—composed as it was from the 1850's of elements from practically all sections of the Yoruba, considerably free from inhibitions imposed by traditions and highly geared towards achievement—seemed to set for it just such a destiny.[51]

The opposition to Ibadan, however, was at no disadvantage, for they too cast off the fetters of tradition to form a confederacy led by a new type of military man, willing "to forget traditional sub-group differences and place emphasis on sheer experience and ability" and to act on their "own initiative".[52] A word like "merit" in these contexts has no moral load; it is measured more by success than goodness. For the characters in West African history are, by and large, people who made waves, and their "greatness" is judged pragmatically. Occasionally a false note is struck, as when Ikime (in *Tarikh*, significantly enough)[53] finishes his biographical sketch of Nana, the keynote of whose career was sheer self-interest, by calling him a "patriot" because he fought the British—since they, among others (indeed, egged on by Nana's African competitors) happened to get in his way.[54] But at least it *is* a false note, and not the organising theme. The main point here is that if you think individual achievement is the important thing in history, you do not have to cover up for systems in which the general good was at something of a discount. Consequently, we can learn more about such systems from the Ibadan school than from the Western champions of centralisation.

The same pragmatism is evident in these authors' writings on slavery and the slave trade, which, like human sacrifice, harsh punishments, and summary executions, were not played down in the Ibadan books. Far from trying to prove that slavery was mainly the result of contact with Europeans, Daaku, for example, wrote that it would be "difficult to argue that sub-Saharan Africa was unique in not developing this common human institution of slavery".[55] Dike documented the opposition to Britain's efforts to abolish the slave trade, which led to riots in the Gold Coast. "The king of Bonny, Africa's greatest slave market, spoke for the rest when he declared to Captain Crow in 1807: 'We (i.e., the king and Council) think that this trade must go on. That also is the verdict of our Oracle and the priests. They say that your country, however great, can never stop a trade ordained by God himself' ".[56]

Nana, too, ignored attempts to get him to stop—quite naturally, in Ikime's view.[57] Ajayi and Akintoye, writing about the Yoruba wars, both argued against the usual view that the wars were caused by entanglement in the slave trade—on the contrary, they said, the wars were about power and wealth, and the antagonists captured slaves to finance their wars rather than having the wars to capture slaves.

Akinjogbin's treatment of the slave trade was entirely practical. He considered its role in Dahomey's political reorganisation. Tegbesu loaned money to the European trading houses, and increased the comforts of their personnel, which,

together with the administrative and constitutional steps being concurrently taken, increased the export of slaves through Whydah port and enriched the king. By about 1750 there was an air of prosperity in Dahomey. The slave trade was efficiently organised and it looked as if it was the answer to all the economic ills of Dahomey.

What was wrong with it—all that Akinjogbin showed was wrong with it—was that it did not work. "What the Dahomean authorities failed to realise (and even today scholars are still arguing about it) was that the slave trade was destructive of itself and of every other economic activity. Human beings were not bred as cattle for sale".[58] Thus, if they were sold, they could not farm. Daaku raised the same objection, saying that slave-trading "sapped the energies" of states in the long run.[59]

Again, we are being told about how things were at the time—not, that is, about how we ought to interpret them from the point of view of our present historiographical concerns, dictated by current politics—independence and the colonial encounter. Well, almost. I did come across one passage which sounded like Fage on the slave trade or Marks on the *Mfecane*. Akintoye wrote of the sixteen years of fighting between Ibadan and the Ekitiparapo:

In terms of human suffering, the effects of all this were grave. The wars and the raids resulted in widespread insecurity, while the migrations, the flights and the forcible seizures of people led to the desertion of homes and means of livelihood, the breaking up of families and the scattering of their members in different directions. Whole towns and villages became deserted and large areas of farmland were reclaimed by jungles.

This, however, is only the negative side of a movement which deserves to be regarded as a revolution. Some of the communities (like Abeokuta, Ibadan, Oyo, Ilorin, Madakeke near Ile-Ife and Aiyede in Ekiti) created by this revolution have survived to our day as important socio-political local entities in the wider unity of one Nigeria.[60]

Doubtless they have. But that is no reason to use the word "only" in the second paragraph. There was little of this, however, in West African history, and it did not dominate Akintoye's, or others', presentations. To it we could oppose Tamuno's thoughts on the Biafran struggle:

Experience during and after the Nigerian Civil War reminds one of the relevance of an East African saying, "when elephants fight it is the country that suffers". Again, experience after the same war suggests the applicability to Nigeria of a German proverb: "A great war leaves a country with three armies—an army of cripples, an army of mourners, and an army of thieves".

This quotation, he says, "easily lends itself to flexible interpretations".[61]

Which brings us to my last point: that these writers did not go out of their way to lend support to present regimes. We have seen that they did not fish much for legitimacy in the past; and there is certainly a kind of statement about present legitimacy in Tamuno's last sentence. He could, of course, have ended his lecture with the thought that the evils of the first independent regime would now be put right by the present one, and if he had, his criticisms which have been quoted already would not be so significant. In fact, he *asked* for enlightened leadership, but at the same time warned:

Yet, in contemporary Nigeria, where the new laws of the new lords are followed by new tricks, the careful observer is bound to ascertain how far the leaders are trying to prevent a repetition of the loss of public confidence which touched off the momentous events that resulted in the civil war. . . . If the past in Nigeria has any abiding lesson, it is that leaders come and go, their ideas and achievements last as long as they enjoy general acceptability, but the people remain.[62]

It is pretty obvious from all of this that West African historians did not need the new history to give them self-respect. But when it comes to writing books for schools, they often take it up as a style and as an organising theme. If they, who grew up without sovereignty, do not need it, today's children, supposedly growing up sovereign, could hardly need it more than they. When West Africans write school books with an underlying message about legitimacy therefore, they can only be doing it for political and not educational reasons, and we need not tell ourselves that this is what the children need. It is what the nation needs. It is in the school histories, not surprisingly, that the tone of post-independence West African writing most closely resembles that of academic East African writing at the same time.

If we look at more recent writing by East African historians, however, we find that the nation-building fervour has frequently been replaced, not by the more distanced posture of West African writing (which has continued with a proliferation of close studies of West African localities), but by a reexamination of nation-building designed to uncover dishonesty and mystification.[63] (It is not without mystification of its own, in that neo-Marxist language can often, in itself, place "new insights" beyond the realm of understanding; but it is the line of attack which we are concerned with here.) The general thrust of Marxist Af-

rican history is considered in another chapter. What is of most interest
here is why East Africa should be the setting for the feeling which lies
behind both Marxist and non-Marxist reassessments of the contradictions between formal independence and continuing informal structures
of dependence on Western capitalism. The development of Marxist
orientations in East Africa probably owes a great deal to the role of
Tanzania, first in attracting the presence and commitment of scholars
with high hopes of African socialism, second in providing a venue for
the expression of Marxist scholarship, and third in disappointing such
scholars over a number of years, in which they turned from supporters
to critics.[64] More generally, an explanation may be sought in the same
terms in which the earlier contrast between East and West African writing
was drawn. East African writing has been more strongly ideological,
in whatever direction, because much more was expected of independence, of leadership, of ideology itself. Tamuno was critical of Nigerian national politics, but not surprised. A longer tradition of experience with urban living; centralised politics; interaction with Western
capitalism, culture, and political forms; playing for higher stakes—
perhaps this accounts for the greater cynicism of West African writing,
and the lesser degree of either commitment or disillusionment.

## NOTES

1. Orlando Patterson, "Rethinking Black History", *Harvard Educational
Review*, vol. 41, no. 3 (1971), p. 298.

2. By the "Ibadan historians" I do not mean only historians at Ibadan. A
number of Nigerians and Europeans, some of whom teach at the University of
Ibadan, have published books in the Ibadan series, which are published by
Longmans.

3. African literature is discussed in the next chapter.

4. See the *Kenya Historical Review*, vol. 5, no. 2 (1977), a special issue
on *Some Perspectives in the Mau Mau Movement*, with an introduction by B.
Ogot.

5. B. Ogot, "Kingship and Statelessness among the Nilotes" in eds. J.
Vansina, R. Mauny, and L.V. Thomas, *The Historian in Tropical Africa*
(London, Oxford University Press, 1964); and "The Role of the Pastoralist
and the Agriculturalist in African History" in ed. T.O. Ranger, *Emerging
Themes in African History* (Nairobi, East African Publishing House, 1968), p.
130.

6. I. Kimambo, "The Interior Before 1800" in eds. I. Kimambo and A.

Temu, *A History of Tanzania* (Nairobi, East African Publishing House, 1969), p. 33.

7. I. Kimambo, *Mbiru: Popular Protest in Colonial Tanzania* (Nairobi, East African Publishing House, Historical Association of Tanzania Paper no. 9, 1971), p. 8. See also pp. 26–27.

8. This, too, is discussed in the next chapter.

9. J. Lonsdale, "The Emergence of African Nations, A Historiographical Analysis", *African Affairs*, vol. 67 (Jan. 1968).

10. A.J. Temu, "The Rise and Triumph of Nationalism" in Kimambo and Temu, *Tanzania*, p. 208.

11. Ibid., pp. 189–90.

12. Ibid., p. 209.

13. It is unfortunate that the word "collaboration" carries the connotation of its use in the Second World War, for people who cooperated with the Nazis. Another word would be preferable, certainly, but the criticism of Gwassa's argument must stand.

14. G.C.K. Gwassa, "The German Intervention and African Resistance in Tanzania", in Kimambo and Temu, *Tanzania*, p. 85. For a good illustration of the difference suggested here between the East and West African approaches to history, compare Gwassa's with the much less defensive account of the same events by A.C. Unomah of the University of Ibadan, "The Maji Maji in Tanzania (1905–07): African Reaction to German Conquest", *Tarikh*, vol. 4, no. 3 (1973), *European Conquest and African Resistance* I.

15. Kimambo, *Mbiru*.

16. Gwassa, "Resistance", p. 110.

17. Ibid., p. 97.

18. Kimambo, "Interior", p. 28.

19. Gwassa, "Resistance", p. 86. Similar sentiments are expressed, with a flavour of acephalic patriotism, by A.E. Afigbo of the University of Nigeria at Nsukka, in "Patterns of Igbo Resistance to British Conquest", *Tarikh*, vol. 4, no. 3 (1973), *European Conquest and African Resistance* I. Since Igboland was not organised under one authority, he argues, it had to be conquered piecemeal and at tedious length, which "was very irritating to the British. Long after the much fancied Fulani, Kanuri and Yoruba empires had been forced to accept British rule, the British were still sending military forces round and about Igboland in pursuit of 'naked savages' " (p. 23).

20. Quoted in K.O. Dike, *Trade and Politics in the Niger Delta* (London, Oxford University Press, 1956), p. 43 of the 2nd edition (1966).

21. Ibid., p. 43.

22. J.F.A. Ajayi, "The Continuity of African Institutions under Colonialism", in Ranger, *Emerging Themes*, p. 193; I.A. Akinjogbin, "The Expansion of Oyo and the Rise of Dahomey 1600–1800" in eds. J.F.A. Ajayi and

M. Crowder, *History of West Africa* (London, Longman, 1971), vol. 1, p. 343; J.F.A. Ajayi and R. Smith, *Yoruba Warfare in the Nineteenth Century* (Cambridge, Cambridge University Press, 1964), p. 128. This comes out in *Tarikh*, as well; see J.A. Atanda, "Government of Yorubaland in the Pre-Colonial Period", *Tarikh*, vol. 4, no. 2 (1973), *Government in Pre-Colonial Africa*, and, in the same volume, E.A. Ijagbemi, "A Note on Temne Kingship in the Early Nineteenth Century".

23. Ajayi, "Continuity", pp. 193–94.

24. Ibid., p. 191. It is interesting to read Orlando Patterson's parallel observations on black American history, which he says is seen in terms of either "catastrophe" or "survival"; some historians think the Negroes' African past was completely wiped out by slavery, others that it survived and continues to be relevant in blacks' lives. (Patterson, "Rethinking".)

25. Ajayi, "Continuity", p. 192.

26. T.N. Tamuno, *History and History-Makers in Modern Nigeria* (an inaugural lecture delivered at the University of Ibadan, 25 Oct. 1973, Ibadan University Press, 1973), p. 7.

27. S.A. Akintoye, *Revolution and Power Politics in Yorubaland 1840–1893* (London, Longman, 1971), p. 173; I.K. Katoke, *The Making of the Karagwe Kingdom* (Nairobi, East African Publishing House, Historical Association of Tanzania Paper no. 8, 1970), p. 29; E.A. Ayandele, "Traditional Rulers and Missionaries in Pre-Colonial West Africa", *Tarikh*, vol. 3, no. 1 (1969), *Christianity in Modern Africa*, pp. 31–32; Dike, *Trade and Politics*, pp. 154–55.

28. R.A. Adeleye, *Power and Diplomacy in Northern Nigeria 1804–1906* (London, Longman, 1971), pp. 163–64; E.J. Alagoa, "The Niger Delta States and their Neighbours 1600–1800" in eds. J.F.A. Ajayi and M. Crowder, *West Africa*, p. 305.

29. See Akintoye, *Power Politics*, p. 173; Akinjogbin, "Expansion of Oyo", p. 320; and O. Ikime, "Nana Olomu: Governor of the Benin River", in *Tarikh*, vol. 1, no. 2 (1965), *African Leadership and European Domination*, p. 42.

30. Adeleye, *Power and Diplomacy*, pp. 286–87.

31. Ibid., pp. 168–69 and 112–13.

32. Ibid., p. 213.

33. A.K. Armah, "A Mystification: African Independence Revalued", *Pan-African Journal*, vol. 2, no. 2 (Spring 1969), p. 149. A note on terminology: Marxist writers often refer to a colonising country as "the metropole" and to its colonies as "the periphery", in order to compare the way in which the former is supported by its colonies with the way in which a city is supported by the countryside around it. This is explained more fully in Chapter 6.

34. Akinjogbin, "Expansion of Oyo", p. 336.
35. S.C. Ukpabi, "The Independence Movement in the Sudan", *Tarikh*, vol. 4, no. 1 (1971), *Independence Movements in Africa* II.
36. Akinjogbin, "Expansion of Oyo", p. 315.
37. Tamuno, *History*, p. 5.
38. T.N. Tamuno, "The Independence Movement in Nigeria", *Tarikh*, vol. 4, no. 1 (1971), *Independence Movements in Africa* II, p. 5.
39. Ibid., p. 13.
40. Tamuno, *History*, pp. 9–10.
41. Akintoye, *Power Politics*, p. 171.
42. Ajayi, "Continuity", p. 197.
43. Ibid., p. 196.
44. Dike, *Trade and Politics*, p. 34.
45. Ibid., p. 36.
46. Ibid.
47. Ajayi and Smith, *Yoruba Warfare*, p. 125.
48. Akintoye, *Power Politics*, pp. 70–75.
49. Ibid., p. 20.
50. Akinjogbin, "Expansion of Oyo", p. 315.
51. Akintoye, *Power Politics*, pp. 41–42.
52. Ibid., pp. 76–77, 139.
53. The objectivity which characterises West Africans' writing at a higher level is often not in evidence in their writing for schools, and *Tarikh*, although a valuable source, runs to rather fulsome biographies.
54. Ikime, "Nana Olomu", p. 48.
55. K.Y. Daaku, "The Slave Trade and African Society" in Ranger, *Emerging Themes*, pp. 139–40. My point here is not that slavery *is* a universal institution, but that Daaku does not feel any need to play down its existence as an *indigenous* institution in West Africa.
56. Dike, *Trade and Politics*, p. 13, quoting H. Crow, *Memoirs* (London, 1830), p. 137. Dike paraphrases the original pidgin.
57. Ikime, "Nana Olomu", pp. 43–44.
58. Akinjogbin, "Expansion of Oyo", p. 337.
59. Daaku, "Slave Trade", p. 137.
60. Akintoye, *Power Politics*, p. xviii.
61. Tamuno, *History*, p. 12.
62. Ibid., pp. 12, 17.
63. E.g., B. Ogot, "Towards a History of Kenya", *Kenya Historical Review*, vol. 4, no. 1 (1976); Ogot cautions that a search for unity and success in Kenya's past should no longer be allowed to obscure the dissidents, losers, and "little people" whose experiences were an important part of the nation's

experience. See also E.S. Atieno-Odhiambo, "Synthesising Kenya's History" in his *The Paradox of Collaboration and Other Essays* (Nairobi, East African Literature Bureau, 1974).

64. See C. Ake, "The Congruence of Political Economies and Ideologies in Africa" in eds. P. Gutkind and I. Wallerstein, *The Political Economy of Contemporary Africa* (Beverly Hills and London, Sage, 1976).

# 5

# THE WIDER CONTEXT

If we now put the nationalist phase of African history in a wider context, we can see how it fits into a pattern of responses to intellectual domination. Many other peoples have gone through a similar struggle to establish self-esteem, as they think about why they have been ruled by someone else and how they have, to a greater or lesser degree, forced their rulers to make room for them. African history is only one of a number of new histories produced by peoples who are trying to wrest power from rulers who are physically different from themselves. As well as people whose oppression, like that of Africans, has been justified by racial arguments (one thinks of Indians, West Indians, American blacks, American Indians, Australian aborigines, New Guineans), there are women, oppressed on the basis of their sex; all are writing about their pasts, and about their liberation. What do they consider important? Are there similarities with African history? It is suggested that a very rough pattern is discernible in new histories, involving a development of explanations in terms of the innate qualities, or identities, of the two sides concerned, a growing doubt about the truth of this kind of explanation, and a subsequent search for some other kind. If we look at movements which have gone along a similar path to that discerned in African history, we can get enough perspective to see that it *is* a path, and will also be able to suggest why nationalist history seems often to give way to Marxist history in the post-independence period. Any gains in perspective, moreover, may be suggestive for younger liberation movements, for whom identity still appears to be a fact of nature.

If we look at the recent historiography of India, whose cultures are very different from any in Africa, but whose experience of imperialism has been in many ways similar, we are immediately struck by the familiar pattern of representations of the past. Here is the concern to find a racial identity with which to confront Britain's sense of manifest destiny (Indians opposed a supposedly "spiritual", mystical personality to the force of British arms), coupled with the attempt to re-create a past of urban empires to compete with those of European history.

Narayanan tells us that during and, increasingly, after, India's independence, scholars rejected the colonial picture of her past and concentrated on reconstructing ancient glories, heroes, kingdoms, and empires.[1] Like the intensified research into African kingdoms, this produced more detailed knowledge, and corrected errors which had had their origin in white racism. But the narrowness of focus, together with the tendency to idealise, could only give a false impression of the past. Nationalists affirmed the kind of past which imperialists had denied; as Narayanan says, there was no significant shift of perspective.

A shift occurred, however, as it became impossible to sustain the idea of a national past in the face of continuing conflict among India's many sectional traditions, and above all in the face of the shock of Partition. Historians were forced to re-examine the clichés of heroism, of dark ages and golden ages, of the uniquely spiritual quality of India. Attention turned to the lower orders of society, and to Marxism for the tools of conceptualisation.

Mysticism, nationalism, and Marxism in India; Negritude, nationalism, and Marxism in Africa; is this just a succession of fads, or does it involve a change from one way of thinking about history to another? On the face of it, any shift from the first to the second position would seem to be an important one: from the emphasis on cultural difference to the organisation of political action in the international arena. Nationalism and Marxism seem more alike, and they are, of course, often found together. I suggest, however, that a shift from a nationalist to a Marxist approach to explaining the relations between ruling and emerging groups may, particularly in the colonial situation, be more significant. Often, in this kind of situation, both cultural separatists and nationalists seem to think that the most important factor influencing their fate is what kind of people they are—their identity—while Marxists see this not as given, but as a thing created by material circumstances. This is a fundamental difference between ideas of causation in history.

What is the role of identity, then, in the struggle against rulers who are ethnically different? It can be the answer to the question, "How did we get into this situation?" We might imagine a greatly simplified dialogue, in which the ruling group answers: "Your societies are technologically backward, insufficiently militarised, and insufficiently commercialised, all due to a weakness in your racial character; you are passive". One response is: "It is true that we could not fight you with your own weapons, but what you see as a weakness is a strength in the moral sphere, something to take pride in. We have a racial virtue you have not got". Indians, for example, lay claim to a spiritual approach to life, Africans have Negritude, blacks in exile have Soul, American Indians and Australian aborigines have a harmonious relationship with nature. The creation of this kind of self-image is appealing because it attacks the ruler's grounds for self-confidence, provides a positive racial basis for unity, and does not toady to the ruler's values. It does, however, accept the notion that his success in worldly terms is related to his values, and also that his values, and his qualities, are what he says they are.

The next question, however, is, "How are we going to get out of this situation"? To this, too, the ruler has an answer: "You cannot get out from under, because you have not got the necessary qualities. You are not fierce enough to fight, nor rational enough to rule yourselves". The opposition to this, too, therefore comes in terms of identity: "We, too, have had strong, rational, far-ranging systems of authority, institutions of government like yours, and we are a fierce people, we resisted you from the beginning". This is where nationalist history, of the kind we have seen in Africa, comes in, and it seems to play a similar role in India. "We will defeat the ruler with his own weapons, and take over and manage his institutions, because we are also that kind of people, and our history proves it". Once again, a certain version of the imperial personality is accepted, only this time, the underdogs are claiming to share it too.

The dialectic between these ideas of identity is not a simple one. They often seem to coexist, unresolved; in the long term, perhaps, there is a shift towards the nationalist position because it is more easily translatable into action of the kind with which rulers are prepared to negotiate. This seems to be the one with which the leadership embarks upon independence, in any case, and the first few years of power are spent in consolidating it. The roots of the present situation, in which the heroes of the people are managing institutions created by someone else, are sought in the distant past. Nobody is suggesting now that gerontocracy, hunting and gathering, communion with the dead, contempt for the material world, or whatever, is more appropriate to the new rulers' racial identity than representative institutions and development. A return to the rhetoric of racial identity may come later, sometimes in a move towards less representative government. Alternatively, or sometimes by way of opposition, there may be a rejection of the idea of identity as a prime mover in history, and this is the trend I want to consider here.

In the broadest terms, it is suggested that some participants and sympathisers of the movement become disillusioned with both uses of identity once the movement has begun to succeed. On the one hand, there is disappointment in the failure of those in power to exhibit the special virtues claimed for their race. On the other hand, the myth of the ruler's qualities cannot be sustained when one gets to know him and to share his position. The imperial personality proves to be merely the facade of a people with the same tendencies towards social and personal contradictions as any other. Neither side can field an identity consistent enough to be regarded as the mainspring of history, and the realisation that this is so leaves an explanatory gap which, it is suggested, Marxist explanations, among others, may fill.

To illustrate this process, let us look at the intellectual liberation of two categories of people who used to be regarded as quite different from their masters. One of these is women, the other African writers. Women are not, of course, an ethnic group, but, like non-whites, they have had to struggle with the idea that their obvious physical differences from their masters imply a different and inferior personality, moral, emotional, and intellectual.[2] Like African writers, they have identified this personality, embraced it, rejected it, and finally come to regard it and its opposite both as irrelevant, ideological creations, which appeal and repel, but do nothing to interpret the realities of human experience.

The ideology of women's liberation has been rather like that of African liberation. The position which women rebelled against was that in which they were regarded as inadequate to perform the roles considered by society to be the most important, involving work outside the home and public decision making and executive functions, while they were supposed to be uniquely suited to the work of servicing the sex which took those roles. These different abilities were supposed to be sex-linked, just as the relegation of Africans to the service role—serving the European personally or serving his economy—was justified on the grounds of race. Interestingly enough, the booby prize for women was a compensating ideology—since labelled the "feminine mystique"[3]—which closely resembled the ideology of Negritude. To be sure, Negritude was intended as a rebellion, while the feminine mystique helped to keep women in their place; but it has since been said that Negritude unwittingly did that to blacks. Like the spokesmen of Negritude,[4] many women agreed that they were different, and glorified in their differences. Their supposed inability to think as rationally or intelligently as men was compensated for by a greater emotional sensitivity and depth of feeling. The compassion which made them incapable of decision-making in a tough world suited them admirably to caring for husbands and children. The physical weakness which kept them out of the work force made them rewarding partners in bed. Through the tantalisingly mysterious quality of their natures, and their greater beauty, they could manipulate men to gain their limited ends, which gave them a small but, they thought, sufficient sense of power.

A greater sense of power came when the Second World War sucked many more women into the work force, and the subsequent boom enabled many to stay there. With changed economic circumstances came a change in consciousness, the germ of which had of course been there for some time. Women felt the challenge to prove to men, as well as themselves, that they were men's equals. In the present this meant aspiring to traditionally masculine jobs and despising feminine ones even if the latter were sometimes more pleasant and more satisfying. Women did not question the prevailing notions of what qualities were involved in "men's work", nor did they question the idea that men possessed these qualities. They accepted the industrial context and asserted that they could succeed within it, because they were really more like men than anyone had supposed. They would compete by the rules, not dividing their time between work and family, nor changing the conditions of work, but adding work to family or else denying family. Personal ruthlessness and material ambition were among the new virtues, as these were what made that pinnacle of masculine achievement, the business executive.

In this effort, history provided some inspiration, but it was not history which looked at what the mass of women's lives had been like. Women on the rise thought instead of individuals who had succeeded at things which were normally thought of as masculine achievements. Unlike the majority of women, who (like the Nuer or the Dinka) had not *done* anything, these great women of the past were writers, painters, soldiers, scientists, political figures, and their lives were proof that women could succeed in men's terms.

Forging ahead with this new identity, however, some women began to feel that it had little to do with the realities of power and wealth. They could prove that women were strong, tough, brave, rational, ambitious, and competitive, but economic equality did not necessarily follow, not because their role performance was in any way deficient, but because men have an economic as well as an ideological interest in maintaining their control of work. Second, they found, as their familiarity with the world of work increased, that manly qualities were very unevenly distributed in men, and were not in any case correlated with success, even for men in a man's world.

After some years of experience as liberated women, then, a new theme began to appear, with many socialist adherents and stronger in Britain than in America. The truth, which many encountered, particularly as boom turned into slump, was that a man's world was not the promised land. This did not mean that the traditional woman's world was any better, of course; but it meant that the old values which went with male dominance, accepted by women who wished to join them at the top, had to be reconsidered. Men were expected to bring strength and endurance to their work regardless of whether it gave them anything more than their living, and they were largely unable to challenge their situation because they were responsible for their families' survival as well as their own. And not only survival was involved; the value system required a man to sacrifice his leisure, his interests, his peace of mind to provide an ever-increasing standard of material comfort and ostentation. For those brought up in these values, there was no opting out—most people were not prepared to be hippies—and there was no approved way to live on the earnings of another person, as there was for a woman. Moreover, any failure in this system was a deeply personal one, a crisis of identity, because it was a failure as a man. What kind of life was this, then? If the values which had justified the domination of women by men in reality oppressed men as well as women, then whom did they serve?

They were seen to serve the few at the top of the economic pyramid. Men's strength was strength to work for another's profit; their endurance kept them at it. The lack of emotionalism contributed to a stoical acceptance of the conditions of work. The material ambition provided the incentive to stay in the system, while the pressure on men from their women to sustain their masculine role made the prospect of refusal really appalling.

Looked at in this way, of course, the values cease to be absolutes. Correspondingly, the "feminine" virtues become available again for freely choosing, and a liberated woman does not have to despise them. At the same time as women began to realise that men and women both were oppressed by the ideology of male superiority, they dropped some of their expectations of men and invited men to join them in struggling to find some ultimately easier way. Women's history developed a socialist strain to go with this; it was not men's low opinion of women that was of primary interest, nor was it necessary to dredge up exceptional women to prove that the mass did not deserve this treatment; of more interest was the fate, and the alternatives, of women and men in the larger system and its changes over time.[5] This is not by any means the dominant strain in the literature of women's liberation and in fact is regarded by some as an evasion of the real issues.[6] It is, however, a strong development, and one that offers women the possibility of exploring their pasts with questions other than the ones about what they lack, or what they have, as human beings.

A certain similarity between the "feminine mystique" and the ideology of Negritude has been suggested, and we pass now to a consideration of the experience of African writers as they went through a phase of creating various versions of African identity in response to the coloniser's picture of them, and later rejected this effort as a proper raison d'être for literature.

It is particularly interesting to study the changes in African literature because African writers themselves have thought and written so much about it. African authors stand out from their people in a special way because the degree of literacy they have attained is comparatively rare, and also because they tend to write in the colonial languages rather than in the vernacular (this makes sense both in terms of their education and of the languages of literacy of their readers, both foreigners and fellow-countrymen, but it makes for an ethnographic slant in their writing). The role of the writer as spokesman of his people has re-

ceived a lot of attention, therefore; and part of this role, for a long
time the most compelling part, was to mediate between native and foreigner, and between past and present. Identity was all-important, and
the past was felt/to hold the key to it. This feeling, which was noted
earlier in this chapter as one which historians share, is stated by Ngugi
wa Thiong'o in an essay on "The Writer and His Past":

Here I want to argue that what has been—the evolution of human culture through
the ages, society in motion through time and space—is of grave import to the
poet and the novelist. For what has been, especially for the vast majority of
submerged, exploited masses in Africa, Asia and Black America, is intimately
bound up with what might be: our vision of the future, of diverse possibilities
of life and human potential, has roots in our experience of the past.[7]

The problem of identity, vis-à-vis the white man and defined by the
past, produced roughly two kinds of literary responses. The differences
between these—the French-speaking school of Negritude and the English-speaking literature of a broadly nationalist character—are related
to the different assimilation policies of France and Britain. French colonial education was more French than British education was British.
The aim of higher education was to produce black Frenchmen, whereas
the British were not so enthusiastic about black Britons. The flavour,
as well as the degree, of assimilation was different. The French believed their civilisation superior to any, white or black, and offered it
to a select few of their subjects who could, on demonstrating a high
degree of assimilation, become French citizens, with the legal and vot-
ing rights of whites in France. British-educated Africans were less isolated, in terms of special status, of the content of their lessons, or of
numbers. A higher proportion of them went through secondary and
tertiary education, so their experience was shared and understood by
many around them.

All this meant that, in various ways, the few Africans (and West
Indians) who gained sufficient education in French to embark upon literary careers were more closely identified with the culture of their rulers than were their counterparts in British colonies. They had been
separated from their backgrounds in the process of assimilation, and
their educators had strongly emphasised the gulf between what they
had been (what the mass of their people remained) and what they had
become. But when they tried to be black Frenchmen, they felt rejected

by white Frenchmen, and they realised that, while they had lost one identity, they had not actually gained another. Thus their reaction against the rulers' culture, when it came, was more extreme than that of Anglophone intellectuals, while the identity to which they claimed to be "returning" was really one which they were compelled largely to create. Anglophone writers, however strongly they were aware of being placed "between two worlds" by their education, were more firmly rooted; they might feel they had left the world of their childhood, in some respects, but they did not romanticise it to the same extent. Both kinds of writers addressed themselves to Europeans, writing in European languages and using the images and allusions of those cultures as well as of their own, and they wrote about what Europeans had done to them; but, while Francophone writers were more concerned with the shock of the journey away from their cultural home, British Africans were more interested in its stages. Thus, in writing about the meeting between black and white, Anglophone writers focussed on issues and incidents, producing the historical or sociological novel, which can be contrasted with the rather mystical exploration of supposed polarities contained, more often in poetry, in Francophone writing. Chinua Achebe wrote about the clash between traditional authority in Iboland and that claimed by the missions.[8] Ngugi wrote about the same thing in Kikuyuland, where the missions lost many adherents through trying to combat female circumcision, and about the Mau Mau struggle.[9] Senghor, meanwhile, wrote about the beauty and vitality of blackness.[10]

Both kinds of writing could be very good. The contrasts invented by the poets of Negritude might be false as descriptions of black and white, but as expressions of the way some blacks *feel* about black and white, they can certainly involve and convince the reader. Exaggeration is not out of place in poetry, which communicates, often, by developing one facet of reality, or fantasy, and excluding all others. What was wrong with Negritude, therefore, was not the quality of the writing, but the fact that it could not produce more than one kind of literature. There is no prosaic license; a novelist's creations may be people of limited or mistaken vision, but the novelist is supposed to have a firmer grip on reality, to see things that his characters do not see. Exaggeration in poetry may be understood to be deliberate, whereas in prose it seems merely ignorant. And when the style of polemic is brought to bear on historical events, the result can only be bad literature, as in Senghor's play, *Chaka*, which takes Chaka as the embodiment of the heroism of blackness against the white menace. Here, he is supposed to have directed all his efforts towards building up a military machine, imbued with mystical power, for the sole purpose of defeating the white man! Even his murder of the woman he loved is presented as a sacrifice to give him strength towards this end. Thus a piece of history which in reality can have had little to do with the confrontation between races, is nevertheless seen entirely in terms of such a confrontation.[11] The conflicts of Negritude are external ones, so that those involved in being one human being, of whatever race, need not be explored. It is this limitation for which Negritude has been criticised by Anglophone writers. It would be a mistake, however, to suppose that African literature in English has been free of the same limitations.

Some of it has, certainly; there are books about the meeting of black and white in which both sides are fully human. In Achebe's *Things Fall Apart*, for example, the primary focus is on the contradictions of Okonkwo's life, presented in the context of the advent of white missions and government, but not represented as arising solely from this change in circumstances. Okonkwo wishes desperately to succeed as an elder in the traditional mould, but this is not because of the perfection of tradition, but because he is afraid of being like his father, who failed in just that role. Achebe does not seem to identify himself with Okonkwo: Okonkwo does not speak for him.

Not all novelists in English have approached Achebe's realism, however. Often we find a nostalgia for a simpler, more virtuous, more dignified existence, before the white man came to divide and corrupt. This is characteristic of Ngugi's *The River Between*,[12] in which all the action, characterisation, and philosophy have to do with the problem of what to accept from the white world and what to reject, and how to maintain the purity of the tribe. Ngugi's hero is larger than life, with glittering eyes, imbued with an exceptional authority, confused and wavering, but only between one virtuous course and another. His characters, like his landscape and society, are more essence than reality. One represents tradition, one modernity, one ambition, one service to the tribe. This oversimplification is even more marked in a play written later in his career, which is one of the more simplistic products of Anglophone nationalistic literature. *The Trial of Dedan Kimathi* is coauthored by Micere Githae Mugo, and possibly the fact of joint authorship accounts for the shallowness of the play. Coming between two extremely insightful novels of Ngugi's, *A Grain of Wheat* and *Petals of Blood*, in which the characters are fully human and the effects of Mau Mau on its participants analysed, rather than simply celebrated, this is a play in which the forest fighters are godlike figures, the nationalist woman is all that is womanly, the collaborators cringe and fawn, and the whites are big beefy boors. Here is a refusal to treat either side as human beings, in case such subtlety confuses the audience and makes them think that the issues are less clear-cut than they are represented, as if oppression would be justified if those on top were not all bad and those beneath were not all good.

Most of the writing in English in the fifties and sixties avoided this degree of artistic barrenness, but a lesser limitation must be mentioned. Nearly all the fiction written at this time was about the clash of African and European cultures, so that the exploration of African characters was largely in terms of what that clash brought out. There were few attempts to write about indigenous ideas and events, which is reasonable as the authors' own experiences were necessarily, and to a much greater extent than many others', those of individuals being educated into a culture which despised their own. That was what they knew best, and was very relevant both to them and their contemporaries, and to the families which made the decision to educate them. The pictures of indigenous culture which we get at this time, therefore, are largely the work of Europeans who are interested in Africa.[13] People like Ulli Beier and Jan Knappert collected folk tales, poetry, and proverbs, with a quite different flavour from the self-conscious soul-searching of contemporary fiction.[14] It is only later, when the definition of African identity loses its urgency, that we get the pre-colonial historical novel, or novels set in early colonial times which concentrate on everyday African affairs in the larger proportion in which the characters are likely to have been concerned with them.[15]

Some of the criticisms in the discussion of Negritude which follows, therefore, are relevant to aspects of Anglophone literature as well. But against these must be set the greater realism of much of the writing in English, the sense that the observer in the author is always in dialogue with the committed interpreter of historical experience. Thus it is that the criticism of French-speaking writers comes chiefly from writers in English. They condemn romanticism, because it leads nowhere, neither outwards against real enemies, nor inwards towards the real self.

The founders of Negritude, however, intended their movement to have just this double thrust, to be both political and artistic. On the one hand, the revelation of the value of black personality and its artistic expression would so impress Europeans that they would henceforth treat with Africans on equal terms. "If Europe has now begun to reckon with Africa," Senghor wrote, "it is because African traditional sculpture, music, dancing, literature and philosophy have compelled recognition from an astonished world".[16] On the other hand, the rejection of European values would free black intellectuals to discover the full truth about their racial personality and give this truth a literary form.

Senghor, writing about the beginning of the Negritude movement in Paris in the 1930s, stresses that it was the only beginning possible for French-educated black intellectuals.

We were . . . plunged with some other Negro students in a sort of panic desperation. The horizon was plugged up, no reform in prospect and colonisers legitimated our political and economic dependence by the theory of clean sweep. They esteemed that we had neither invented, nor created, nor written, nor sculptured, nor painted nor sung anything. To set our own and effective revolution, we had first to put off our borrowed dresses, those of assimilation, and affirm our being, that is, our negritude.[17]

So what was Negritude? It was, says Joseph Okpaku, "the re-affirmation of precisely those aspects of African culture that the Western world held in disdain".[18] Its spokesmen (inventors) were Leon Damas of Haiti, Leopold Senghor of Senegal, and Aimé Cèsaire of Martinique. It is Cèsaire who states the case most baldly in his long poem *Return to My Native Land*:

those who invented neither gunpowder nor compass,
those who tamed neither steam nor electricity
those who explored neither sea nor sky
but without them the earth would not be the earth. . . .
those who give themselves up to the essence of all things
ignorant of surfaces but struck by the movement of all things
free of the desire to tame but familiar with the play of the world . . . [19]

The white world knew, the black world felt; the white world was "weary with effort", resounding with "grandiose alibis"; the black world innocent, as it were without memory. For what was there to remember? Sheikh Hamidou Kane, in *Ambiguous Adventure*:

Strange dawn! The morning of the Occident in black Africa was spangled over with smiles, with cannon shots, with shining glass beads. Those who had no history were encountering those who carried the world on their shoulders. . . .

From shock, the one side made no resistance. They were a people without a past, therefore without memory. The men who were landing on their shores were white, and mad. Nothing like them had ever been known. The deed was accomplished before the people were even conscious of what had happened.

Some among the Africans . . . brandished their shields, pointed their lances. . . . Then the cannons were fired. The vanquished did not understand. [20]

The things that chiefly seemed worth saying, for several years, were about the meeting of black and white and what it meant. [21] Gerald Moore writes:

Up to about the late 1940s or early 1950s, the literature of Negritude is in a posture of facing towards the white world. The expression it wears on its face may vary; it may be one of reconciliation; it may be one of bringing gifts to enrich the common store; it may be an expression of hatred; it may be an expression of hope; it may be one of disappointment; it may be one of grief; but the face is towards the white world, towards Europe. [22]

It would have to be, indeed, for the only people who could be in need of a definition of black personality were either Europeans or blacks living in European situations which exiled them to some extent from their origins. What happened, then, to make African writers lose interest in defining the difference between black and white identity? The rejection of Negritude was on both political and artistic grounds, both arising, it seems, from the course of events following independence. The success of neo-colonialism in Africa was the measure of the failure of Negritude: while Europe had justified her colonial exploitation with arguments of racial superiority, she subsequently proved willing to accept claims of racial equality, and carry on domination by economic means. Racist ideology had been a useful, but not essential, tool of domination; racial pride might therefore be a useful, but by no means sufficient, tool of liberation. Meanwhile, the nature of society in the independent nations did not bear out the poets' version of the black personality. Pride, dignity, mutual support, and personal security were not restored by independence. Relations of exploitation, political impotence, impersonal violence, were all still there, and the black personality must be accorded another dimension to explain these evils. As Mbella Sonne Dipoko writes:

From the beginning, politics was central in the works of French-speaking African writers. If they talked so much of love and dignity and the past it was because they were dissatisfied with the present as administered by the colonial administration. And injustice and oppression came to be identified with the white man. But as if history decided to expose these writers before their people, the anti-imperialist struggle made headway and Africans, including some writers, found themselves in positions of power. At last they could concretise the dream of the ideal city. . . . But that city was not founded. And more and more it is becoming futile to blame everything on the white man, futile even to continue to sing the past. Thus the exercise of power brought with it the occasion for a new realism in African literature.[23]

One strand of the argument against Negritude, then, was that it took the ideology of domination too seriously, distracting attention from the more lasting reality behind it. As Dipoko puts it, "Poets tended to see colonialism solely in terms of racial oppression, forgetting that it was merely a mechanism of a certain kind of force, the logic of minority power; and that white people had done the same to each other through the centuries, were still doing it even today".[24]

Similarly, Ezekiel Mphahlele points out that though colonialists hit at African culture, colonialism was not about culture, it was about power, and Negritude—"the delegation of the negro to the slow rhythm of the fields, at the treacherous hour of neo-colonisation"[25]—is no weapon against power. "You will never make colonialism blush for shame by spreading out little-known cultural treasures under its eyes".[26]

Europe's oppression of Africa, then, had not begun with racial contempt and would not end if and when Europe conceded cultural equality. Thus cultural offensives were limited, at best; and some writers feared that to concentrate on this aspect of liberation would be to invite humiliation of a new kind. Whites had not taken them seriously when they denied their equality, and now they did not take them seriously when they accepted it, because it was not *political* equality that was being contested. Mphahlele wrote,

Neither Senghor nor his African peers nor his imitators really understood the essence and workings of white power—political and economic. They thought that as long as they could reconstruct in their minds an Africa that was beautiful, innocent, non-violent, bountiful, vibrant, and announce it to the white man they could diminish his power. They did not . . . realise that the white man can easily concede your black pride, give you the freedom to do your song and dance while he manipulates you from a position of political and economic strength. For we have passed the stage when, as Fanon said, colonialism . . . distorted and tried to destroy the past of the oppressed people. Today . . . the white world promotes the rediscovery of the past, encourages you to tell it frankly what it did to you, asks to be invited to your mammoth ''negro arts festivals''. . . . You glory in your corporate blackness, you keep telling the white world about yourself, your inscrutable ''being'', you do nothing to decolonise the minds of your elite, to put more effort into the social and economic welfare of the masses. And you still do your song and dance for the amusement of the white world.[27]

The search for pride in this direction, then, is merely a mystification. Achebe warns against the possible consequences of this in his poem, ''Beware, Soul Brother'':

We are the men of soul
men of song we measure out
our joys and agonies
too, our long, long passion week
in paces of the dance. . . .
But beware soul brother
of the lures of ascension day
the day of soporific levitation
on high winds of skysong; beware
for others there will be that day
lying in wait leaden-footed, tone-deaf
passionate only for the deep entrails
of our soil; beware of the day
we head truly skyward leave
that spoil to the long ravenous tooth
and talon of their hunger. . . .
Take care
then, mother's son, lest you become
a dancer disinherited in mid-dance
hanging a lame foot in air like the hen
in a strange unfamiliar compound. Pray
protect this patrimony to which
you must return when the song
is finished and the dancers disperse;

remember also your children
for they in their time will want
a place for their feet when
they come of age and the dance
of the future is born
for them.[28]


So much for Negritude as a tool of liberation, then. Neocolonialism
has made African writers skeptical of its power. It brings an emotional
satisfaction which is by no means worthless, but the situation calls for
an ideology linked to action. A further problem is that action is now
seen to be needed against those in power in independent Africa, as
well as against the whites with investments there, and Negritude actually blocks the development of any consciousness of what is wrong
with black governments. This is Dipoko's real reason for objecting to
what he calls "cultural diplomacy", the

tendency of trying to prove something to Europe, of parading the charm and
specific qualities of the homeland. . . . [One] result of this ambassadorial pose
is the refusal to criticise custom and tradition in public. . . . Hence most of
the writers of French-speaking Africa are the uncritical servants of old Africa
which they glorify, beautify, and often romanticise—not a bad thing in itself
given the nature of colonialism, the hurt it inflicted on African self-pride. It is
when this attachment to the past and its emotional reconstitution becomes in-
discriminate that the whole thing could become reactionary.[29]

There is nothing radical about blackness itself, but people are easily
persuaded that there is, and will accept reactionary ideologies and
repression put forward in its name. Acts which would be recognised
as oppressive elsewhere are regarded as among the "growing pains"
of nations being built with a speed, energy, and singleness of purpose
made necessary by their late, and disadvantaged, arrival on the international scene. Wole Soyinka urges African writers not to join in the
self-deception. The point could hardly be put more powerfully than in
his article in *Transition*, written following the massacre of 30,000 Ibos
in Northern Nigeria in September, 1966:

The consideration that brings me, personally, hard to earth is the thought of
the Angolan or South African writer either in exile or stretching out his last
feeble twitches before the inexorable maul of a desperate regime ends him. . . .

And he sees, and he understands for the first time that, given equal opportunity, the black tin-god a few thousand miles north of him would degrade and dehumanise his victim as capably as Vorster or Governor Wallace. This fact has been ever present, this knowledge is not new and the only wonder is that the romancer and the intellectual myth-maker have successfully deleted this black portion of the human equation. . . . We whose humanity the poets celebrated before the proof . . . are now forced by disaster, not foresight, to a reconsideration . . . and . . . the . . . African writer must have the courage to determine what alone can be salvaged from the recurrent cycle of human stupidity.[30]

This brings us to the question of the repercussions of all this debate upon African literature. Would there be an exaggerated reaction to Negritude, a literature of self-blame in which the more sinister side of the African character is brought to the fore instead of being denied? Both Achebe and Soyinka see this as a danger. They note the enthusiasm with which white critics welcome books in which Africans play a destructive role; such works, they say, enable Europeans to shift the responsibility for Africa's ills onto black shoulders, congratulating the authors on their "mature, responsible" attitude as they do so.[31] Does this mean that the developing strength with which African writers face and depict African realities is really a weakness? I do not think so, and Soyinka's work is itself proof to the contrary. He writes in an African as well as an English idiom, he incorporates traditional art forms into his drama, he is concerned to bring out the uniqueness of his culture, and considers this a duty. But he does not equate uniqueness with virtue, and he stands without mystical or pseudo-historical crutches. Indeed, when Nigeria was celebrating its independence, Soyinka's literary offering was wholly out of step with the mood of self-congratulation. In his play *A Dance of the Forests*,[32] he brought the past to bear on the present, not as an inspiration but with a view to dispelling political mystification in both directions.

In this play, ancestors are called up to lend glory to the Gathering of the Tribes, called to celebrate "The accumulated heritage. . . . Mali. Chaka. Songhai. Glory. Empires. . . . " But their visit backfires, for they are mainly concerned to recreate the circumstances of their deaths, "inflicted upon them at the ancient court of Mata Kharibu by the forbears and historical prototypes of those who have now sent for them".[33] Robert McDowell comments:

Most interesting here is Soyinka's reaching back to the dead court of Mata
Kharibu and the satire on the impulse men have toward stuffing their ancestors. . . . *A Dance of the Forests* attacks a blind reverence for things past. . . .
Instead of a grandeur called to mind by the name Chaka, or greatness suggested by the old nations of Songhai and Mali, the play exposes the same hid-
eous sins demonstrated by the historical counterparts of [its modern charac-
ters]. . . . The "dead" characters, along with the living, display propensities
toward violence, insensitivity, insincerity, cruelty, lust for power, hypocrisy,
superstition.[34]

Soyinka is unstintingly critical here, but he is not making whites look
better by making blacks look worse. There is not a limited stock of
vice and virtue in history, and the vices which "responsible" writers
depict in their characters are not borrowed from the whites' account.
What they are doing is simply to accord full humanity to their characters, which makes them more, not less, important. This has been a
conscious development, with various writers advancing reasons for it.

From a purely artistic point of view, there is the problem that writers who wished to portray their black characters in the most admirable
light possible were not left with very much to say about them. Where
were the interesting conflicts, the tragic flaws? Mphahlele pointed out
that for some years the best of the non-white figures created by white
authors—Aziz, Joe Christmas, Nina, and Aissa—had far more reality,
greater "freedom of movement" than most of the characters of black
African literature, because "they are not there to justify themselves,
to vindicate themselves and their race. As a result they can be carried
through several emotional states and react to different situations in various ways that indicate a development".[35]

The flatter, more symbolic figures of Negritude were not as satisfying. The poets insisted that the world accept black people as they
were, with all their difference, but they were not being honest about
what they were. It may be that any formulation of identity would have
to be limited and thus partially false; in any case, Soyinka offers a
simple solution: any formulation is quite unnecessary. "A tiger does
not proclaim his tigritude", says Soyinka, "he pounces. . . . When
. . . you see the skeleton of the duiker, you know that some tigritude
has been emanated there".[36] This has been taken to mean that Soyinka
considers African identity unimportant, but he does not; he is saying,
rather, that whatever special qualities a writer has, racial, cultural, or
personal, would automatically be reflected in his work, and need not

be selectively worked into an ideology. Thus, maintaining that Africa did not have to respond to European prejudice, Tigritude asserted that Negritude was motivated and limited by precisely the Whititude it sought to overcome.[37]

Then, about 1965 came the New Generation, ironically, thanks to the groundwork of its predecessors. These young men refused any patronage, denounced the Negritude-Tigritude debate as irrelevant. . . . Africa could avow Negritude, Tigritude, Mother Earth, or even Virgin Mary, if she so desired. In short, Africa was going to be Africa in her own style, and the Western world, racist or "liberal", could accept it or forget it.[38]

These writers do not say identity is unimportant; they say, rather, that it is not to be dictated by ideologies of race, which dig for evidence in the pasts of white and black continents.

This does not mean, of course, that henceforth African writing will deal only with the present. The past continues to be a subject for examination, but less and less for rehabilitation. There are now a large number of novels set in the past whose characters are presented not as representatives of Africans but as human beings first and foremost. The European presence comes into some of these but never dominates them or distorts the characterisation or the action. One thinks of Elechi Amadi's novels, *The Concubine* and *The Great Ponds*, or Buchi Emecheta's *The Slave Girl*.[39] Writers like these have risen to the challenge Gerald Moore talks about in *The Chosen Tongue*:

Faced with the proposition that one's great grandfather was a benighted savage in desperate need of salvation, the temptation is either to agree or to seize the open end of the dialectic and maintain that he was a paragon of all the virtues. Insofar as this argument was a political and cultural one conducted by publicists, it would have seemed intolerably flat to show only that one's great grandfather was a man like other men; it is the artists who will appreciate that this demonstration is the most relevant and difficult of all.[40]

This is not the end of the political novel. The literary depiction of reality is a truly political activity. It is simply that insight into life's conflicts is the more convincing, the more realistic—and therefore complex—is the treatment of them.

An excellent example of this is Ngugi's novel, *Petals of Blood*, published in 1977.[41] His themes are intensely political; he brings out the betrayal felt by Kenya's freedom fighters when the rewards of independence went not to them nor to the common people for whom they had fought, but to the men who had remained loyal or aloof in the Emergency and acceded to wealth and position in the new nation. How, Ngugi asks, does such an outcome fit with ideas of past and future glory, or of the simple conflict between white oppressors and black liberators? Questions about the relevance of history recur insistently throughout the book (which should be compulsory reading for African historians); but they are dealt with through the confused and shifting efforts of the characters to understand their personal histories, in which the conflicts, while occurring in the context of the Emergency, are felt as personal ones. In this way, Ngugi makes the connection, so often elusive, between political situation and human action, creating at the same time a moving story, a masterful whodunit, and a treatise on the possibilities and limitations of political action, all conveyed not by simplifying but by exploring the complexities of his characters and their situation.

Both the increasing complexity of Ngugi's work, and the time span involved, call attention to an interesting difference between East and West African writing. How is it that Soyinka could greet Nigeria's independence with the cynicism of *A Dance of the Forests*, while Ngugi's *Petals of Blood* appeared only in 1977? Part of the answer may be that the experience of competition for power in Nigeria, even before an African government took office, was as disillusioning as the exercise of power in the post-independence period in Kenya. In neither country did Britian hand over power to a properly representative government, but a Kikuyu radical in Kenya had more reason to be optimistic than a Yoruba radical in Nigeria. The Kikuyu had fought for independence and won, and in taking office their leaders claimed to be holding power in trust for the whole nation. The overriding concern for sectional interests was more obvious in Nigeria. The regions (the East, the West, and the North) were the foci of political organisations, rather than the country as a whole, and the political problem for each area was how to protect itself against domination by the others when power was handed over. This could not be concealed by the rhetoric of unity; there were ethnic riots, and there was political dealing. In the end, the most conservative (the Northern) forces took office, while in Kenya the first head of state was the hero of the revolution. It is not surprising, therefore, that disillusionment had to wait a few years in Kenya. When it comes it has the feel, not of a worldly skepticism reconfirmed, but of the genuine questioning of hope disappointed. (In the previous chapter it was suggested that Nigerian historians for a long time approached their past with fewer illusions than East African historians, and this too might be traced, in part, to the same experience.)

How relevant, finally, is this examination of African literature to the representation of the past by historians? To be fair, it is not possible for historians to reconstruct the characters of African history with anything like the complexity which fiction allows a novelist. With a few exceptions, the sources do not exist for such a degree of understanding of anybody before the twentieth century, nor of most people then. What I have criticised is not the failure to discover the contradictions within Africans of the past, but the tendency to write them up larger, simpler, and stronger than life. Finding the same tendency in other kinds of defensive literature, we can see that it is not just a problem in historical writing, but has more to do with the ways that whites in this century have thought about themselves. The questions are something like: "Since we are different physically, does it mean that we have different levels of ability, different mentalities, or different characters? If so, what are the differences? If not, how can we prove it"? And African history, like feminism, like African literature, went through a phase of involvement with these questions to the detriment of others.

In all these cases, the exploration of the relationships between past and present which are truly relevant to the domination of one group by another, has been limited by the mystification of associating identity with physical type. Once an understanding has been established, however, that, whatever their physical differences, people in similar situations behave similarly, the way is open for other explanations. Marxism is one to which people turn. Instead of postulating that people occupy the positions they do because of the way they behave, Marxist theory explains that they behave the way they do because of the positions they occupy, and offers an historical explanation of these positions. Ngugi is inclining towards Marxism; and, as we saw, Indian and feminist historians are too. In the next chapter, therefore, let us look at the socialist strain, mainly Marxist, which is developing in our field of African history.

## NOTES

1. M.G.S. Narayanan, "Modern Indian Historical Writing on Ancient India: Some Problems of Conceptualisation", paper presented to the Institute of

Commonwealth Studies, University of London, Postgraduate Seminar in ''The Writing of History in New Nations'', 17 Feb. 1975.

2. It is *not* suggested, of course, that differences of colour are comparable to the physical differences between men and women. The analogy is based, rather, on the idea that in neither case is the person's physical nature correlated with the particular abilities and inabilities imputed by the dominant sex or race.

3. B. Friedan, *The Feminine Mystique* (Harmondsworth, Penguin Books, 1965; first published by W.W. Norton in 1963).

4. Excerpts from Senghor's writings on several aspects of Negritude: see the ''prose'' section of eds. J. Reed and C. Wake, *Senghor: Prose and Poetry* (London, Oxford University Press, 1965).

5. See, for example, S. Rowbotham, *Hidden from History* (London, Pluto Press, 1974). An interesting discussion of various lines of thought within the movement, including the socialist strain, can be found in J. Mitchell, *Women's Estate* (Harmondsworth, Penguin Books, 1971), Ch. 3, 4.

6. On pages 94–95 of *Women's Estate* Mitchell contrasts the position of the ''Abstract Socialists'', as she calls them, with that of the ''Radical Feminists'', who feel that psychological oppression in every system is the fundamental problem, rather than economic oppression.

7. Ngugi wa Thiong'o, *Homecoming* (London, Heinemann, 1972), p. 39.

8. C. Achebe, *Things Fall Apart* (New York, Obolensky, 1959); *No Longer at East* (New York, Obolensky, 1961); *Arrow of God* (London, Heinemann, 1964). The first two are also available in Heinemann's ''African Writers Series''.

9. J. Ngugi (now Ngugi wa Thiong'o), *Weep Not Child* (London, Heinemann, 1964); *A Grain of Wheat* (London, Heinemann, 1967); Ngugi and M.G. Mugo, *The Trial of Dedan Kimathi* (London, Heinemann, 1976).

10. See Reed and Wake, *Senghor*.

11. L.S. Senghor, ''Chaka'' in Reed and Wake, *Senghor* (from L.S. Senghor, *Ethiopiques* [Paris, Seuil, 1956]).

12. J. Ngugi, *The River Between* (London, Heinemann, 1965).

13. Some exceptions must be mentioned, e.g., C. Ekwensi, *Burning Grass* (London, Heinemann, 1962); F. Nwapa, *Efuru* (London, Heinemann, 1966); B. Diop, *Tales of Amadou Koumba*, trans. D.S. Blair (London, Oxford University Press, 1966).

14. E.g., ed. U. Beier, *The Origin of Life and Death* (London, Heinemann, 1966); ed. U. Beier, *African Poetry: An Anthology of Traditional African Poems* (Cambridge, Cambridge University Press, 1966); B. Gbadamosi and U. Beier, *Not Even God Is Ripe Enough* (London, Heinemann, 1968); J. Knappert, *Traditional Swahili Poetry* (Leiden, E.J. Brill, 1967).

15. E.g., the novels of Amadi and Emecheta listed in note 44.

16. L.S. Senghor, *L'Esprit de la Civilisation ou les Lois de la Culture Né-gro-Africaine (Présence Africaine*, June/Nov. 1956; excerpted in Reed and Wake, *Senghor*, p. 71).

17. L.S. Senghor, quoted in O. Taiwo, *An Introduction to West African Literature* (London, Nelson, 1967), p. 15.

18. Ed. J. Okpaku, *New African Literature and the Arts* (New York, Thomas Y. Crowell Co., in association with the Third Press, 1970), I, editor's preface, p. xi.

19. A. Cesaire, *Return to My Native Land*, trans. J. Berger and A. Bostock (Harmondsworth, Penguin Books, 1969; first published with the title *Cahier d'un Retour au Pays Natal* by Présence Africaine, 1956).

20. C.H. Kane, *Ambiguous Adventure*, trans. K. Woods (London, Heinemann, 1972; first published with the title *L'Aventure Ambigue* by René Julliard in 1962), p. 48.

21. Various aspects of this kind of writing are discussed and illustrated with quotations by G.C.M. Mutiso in his book, *Socio-Political Thought in African Literature* (London, Macmillan, 1974); see Chapter 9, "Interpretations of the Past, the Present and the Future". This book contains a particularly full bibliography of African literature, listing both primary and secondary sources (i.e., criticism, statements by African writers, etc.). Jon Povey, too, discusses the preoccupation with "culture conflict" to the exclusion of other themes, with reference to West African literature in English as well as French, in his article "Changing Themes in the Nigerian Novel" in ed. J. Okpaku, *New African Literature and the Arts* (New York, The Third Press, Joseph Okpaku Publishing Co., 1973), vol. 1.

22. G. Moore, "The Politics of Negritude", in eds. C. Pieterse and D. Munro, *Protest and Conflict in African Literature* (London, Heinemann, 1974; first published 1964), p. 38.

23. M.S. Dipoko, "Cultural Diplomacy in African Writing", *Africa Today*, vol. 15 (Aug./Sept. 1968), p. 11.

24. Ibid., p. 8.

25. S. Adotevi, "Negritude Is Dead: The Burial", in Okpaku, *New African Literature*, vol. 3, p. 90.

26. E. Mphahlele, *The African Image* (London, Faber and Faber, revised edition 1974; first published 1962), p. 93.

27. Ibid.

28. C. Achebe, "Beware, Soul Brother", in his book *Beware Soul Brother; Poems* (London, Heinemann, 1971), pp. 29–30.

29. Dipoko, "Cultural Diplomacy", pp. 9–10.

30. W. Soyinka, "The Writer and the Modern African State", *Transition*, vol. 31 (1967), p. 13.

31. Though Soyinka has criticised aspects of the African past repeatedly

and courageously, he does not wish to be identified with a movement towards a universalism he sees as false. He and Achebe both have expressed suspicion of the new writers who reject the idea that they ought to represent the unique character of the African communities about which they write, asserting instead that Africans are just like everybody else; and suspicion, too, of the white literary critics who welcome this movement. The way these writers are offering, and being urged, to represent their characters and their backgrounds is, say Soyinka and Achebe, not universal but merely Western, and writers who aspire to universalism of this kind are betraying their people in the desire for Western approval. Wishing to be considered mature and responsible by a Western audience, moreover, they choose to write about the worst aspects of Africa and her past. Soyinka writes:

> The . . . route of negation is, for whatever motives, an attempt to perpetuate the external subjugation of the black continent. There is nothing to choose ultimately between the colonial mentality of an Ajayi Crowther, West Africa's first black bishop, who grovelled before his white missionary superiors in a plea for patience and understanding of his "backward, heathen, brutish" brothers, and the new black ideologues who were embarrassed by statements of self-apprehension by the new "ideologically backward" African. Both suffer from externally induced fantasies of redemptive transformation in the image of alien masters.

("Preface" in his *Myth, Literature and the African World* [Cambridge, Cambridge University Press, 1976], p. xiii.) The solution, he feels, must be "a reinstatement of the values authentic to [African] society" (p. x) and the "continuing objective re-statement of . . . [the] self-apprehension [of African writers] . . . to call attention to it in living works of the imagination, placing them in the context of primal systems of apprehension of the race" (pp. xi–xii). The point Achebe and Soyinka make about the false identification of universal with European values is well taken. They are also quite right to insist on cultural difference; as Soyinka puts it, "Man exists . . . in a comprehensive world of myth, history and mores; in such a total context, the African world, like any other 'world' is unique" (Ibid., p. xii). But if this is coupled with an insistence on racial difference, I am sure it is a mistake. However, if the non-racial movement in African literature turns out to be an ephemeral phase like Negritude, this would affect the argument of this chapter, so the reaction against it must be noted here. A pointed and witty discussion of these points can be found in Achebe's article, "Colonialist Criticism", the first essay in his collection *Morning Yet on Creation Day* (London, Heinemann, 1975).

Another article in the same book, "Africa and Her Writers", also deals with these themes. The preface to Soyinka's *Myth, Literature and the African World* states his thoughts on the error of universalism, and the rest of the book tries to explain various aspects of the "African World".

32. W. Soyinka, *A Dance of the Forests*, in his *Five Plays* (London, Oxford University Press, 1963).

33. G. Moore, *The Chosen Tongue: English Writing in the Tropical World* (London, Longmans, 1969), p. 134.

34. R.E. McDowell, "African Drama, West and South", *Africa Today*, vol. 15 (Aug./Sept. 1968), p. 26.

35. Mphahlele, *African Image*, p. 131; the reference is to Aziz in E.M. Forster's *A Passage to India*; Joe Christmas in William Faulkner's *Light in August*; Nina in Conrad's *Almayer's Folly*; Aissa in Conrad's *An Outcast of the Islands*.

36. From a tape of Soyinka's speech at the Berlin Conference in 1964, quoted in J. Jahn, *A History of Neo-African Literature* (London, Faber and Faber Ltd., 1966), pp. 265–66.

37. Okpaku, *New African Literature*, vol. 1, editor's preface, pp. xii–xiii.

38. Ibid.

39. E. Amadi, *The Concubine* (London, Heinemann, 1966) and *The Great Ponds* (London, Heinemann, 1969); B. Emecheta, *The Slave Girl* (London, Allison and Busby, 1977). Jon Povey, in "Changing Themes", mentioned four works in particular whose appearance in the mid-sixties he regarded as a sign that West African writers were shaking off their preoccupation with "culture conflict". These were: N. Nwankwo, *Danda* (London, Deutsch, 1964); C. Ekwensi, *Beautiful Feathers* (London, Hutchinson, 1963); G. Okara, *The Voice* (London, Deutsch, 1964); and W. Soyinka, *The Interpreters* (London, Deutsch, 1965).

40. Moore, *Chosen Tongue*, p. 134.

41. Ngugi wa Thiong'o, *Petals of Blood* (London, Heinemann, 1977).

# 6

# MARXIST AFRICAN HISTORY IN THE PERIOD OF NATIONALISM: TWO STEPS FORWARD, ONE STEP BACK

In recent years, Marxist African history has undergone a great expansion, both in terms of the volume of writing by Marxists on increasingly diverse topics and periods, and in terms of the influence which the "political economy" approach has had on the thinking of non-Marxist scholars.[1] In the period with which this book is chiefly concerned, however, Marxist scholarship was in an uneasy state of transition. It was given great impetus by the growing recognition of the former colonial powers' success in maintaining, after independence, the economic relationships which had been important to them. In the atmosphere of the sixties, however, Marxist analysis was not easily acceptable (to its proponents or to their audience) unless it could be combined somehow with nationalism, in which a strong emotional investment continued. They were combined, for a time, in various forms: in the ideologies of nationalist movements in the Portuguese colonies; in the superficial socialist rhetoric articulated by some regimes and their supporters, appealing to values such as "traditional socialism" or communalism, while ignoring contemporary economic and political realities; and in the early formulations of dependency theory.[2]

Attempts to combine nationalism with Marxism entailed great contradictions, however, which have been picked up and debated as scholarly disillusionment with the performance of independent regimes has grown, and the futility of socialist ideology without significant structural change has become obvious. Out of this debate have come advances in Marxist theory itself. The gap between rhetoric and reality in "socialist" states has led to questioning of the historical reality of "communalism"[3] and focussed attention on the structure of the post-colonial state.[4] The continuity of African history, from pre-contact times to the present, has been explored, chiefly by way of attempts to elucidate pre-industrial African modes of production[5] and their articulation with the modes introduced by contact and colonial rule.[6] When it became possible to apply Marxism consistently in the study of African history, dependency theory was criticised for its contradictions, both within itself and in relation to more orthodox Marxist theory, which insists on the primacy of relations of production rather than relations of exchange, on which dependency theory was focussed.[7] Some Marxists have rejected dependency theory as non-Marxist, while others have refined and elaborated it.[8] On the other hand, orthodox Marxism has been found inadequate to describe the economic forms which have emerged in Africa. The articulation of different modes of production has not brought about a simple replacement of pre-industrial life by peasantisation or proletarianisation, as some scholars expected. "Traditional" ways have proved tenacious, and all the modes have been reexamined, requiring some conceptual innovation:[9] hence the elucidation of a "colonial capitalist mode of production", for example.[10]

The situation is somewhat complicated by the transposition of a debate from European Marxist scholarship, between Althusserian Marxists and others. The methodological proposals of the Althusserians are characterised by a combination of crossness and vagueness, according to which empirical work cannot proceed, because of the dangers of empiricism, until a firm problematic has been acceded to.[11] It is quite true that facts do not speak for themselves, and that material is selected by historians according to their interests and interpreted according to their convictions,[12] both of which are related to their social position and to the times in which they live. (This understanding is not limited to Marxists; furthermore, it can presumably be applied to Marxist scholars as to others, although it seldom is.) It is also true that Marxism does not simply offer some interesting ideas that historians can use along with any others they may hold.[13] It is a coherent theory, negating, rather than adding to, some others. To call a halt to empirical research and conceptualisation until the confrontation between Marxism and "bourgeois" scholarship has been satisfactorily resolved, however, does no service to Marxist studies, and fortunately many more scholars have seen a need to make the insights attainable through Marxist analysis concrete by a proliferation of local studies within the framework of "political economy", as it has come to be called.[14] This chapter deals chiefly with the contradictions between nationalist and Marxist history which marred Marxist writing in the sixties, but we shall also look at the broad changes in the orientation of African history to which Marxist scholarship has contributed.

In the 1950s and 1960s Marxist writers spoke for the African revolution in the anti-colonial form which it took at that time. In the seventies they spoke for the revolution against Europe, as before, and against the African agents of neo-colonialism on the African continent itself. This periodisation, however, should not be taken too far, for there is a good deal of overlap. Which view a writer takes depends upon whether he sees the nationalist leaders as attacking or abetting imperialism; many, but not all, writers took the former view in the sixties and the latter in the seventies.

Up to a point, the interests of nationalists and Marxists coincided. Nationalists attacked imperialists, while Marxists attacked imperialism. The immediate enemy was the same; furthermore, many African nationalists espoused socialist ideas, and in view of the relatively fluid class situation in many places it seemed possible that they might establish socialist regimes after independence. For a few years after independence, indeed, it seemed possible that they were trying. Nowhere was it easy to get socialist ideas accepted and institutionalised; there was a period, therefore, before the left withdrew its support from the new nations. Thus it is that we get Marxist writing of a nationalist flavour in the 1960s and on into the 1970s, when it is joined by a more critical strain. Now we find Marxism in the role which was discussed in the previous chapter, that of a new explanatory system to which people are turning as they become disillusioned with the outcome of the struggle between races. While European historians generally have been taking a greater interest in Marxist history, the enthusiasm with which historians of Africa have taken it up in recent years must be seen as a product of liberal disillusionment.[15] If the nationalists' picture of ancient Ghana as the land of commercial and intellectual opportunity is being replaced by a Marxist picture of it as a place in which inequalities had a chance to grow, it is because what one thinks went on in ancient Ghana is still determined by what one thinks goes on in mod-

ern Ghana. In historical writing, the difference may be seen in the way
earlier writers stressed the unity, later writers the diversity, of African
interests, both in the present and in the past.

It will be argued that the latter emphasis is the more consistent with
Marxist analysis; and the attempt to combine a loyalty to the nationalist movements with a Marxist orientation toward history both limited
what was written in the sixties and gave rise to some inconsistent
thinking. In this chapter we shall look at what Marxist history has to
offer, as an explanatory system; at the ways in which their identification with nationalism prevented some Marxist historians from understanding and presenting their theoretical position as a genuine alternative; and at how these constraints began to disappear, leaving the way
open for research which would have embarrassed the nationalists.

In trying to establish a picture of the kinds of contributions we might
expect from Marxist historians, there is once again the danger of becoming embroiled in factional disputes. At the general level of this
discussion, however, it is possible to point to assumptions, and elements of an historical approach, which are held in common.

What characteristics of Marxist historical interpretation, then, are
relevant to this overview? It has been argued that African history was
bedevilled, following independence, by the continuing preoccupation
with that struggle and the two sides involved. The world was dominated by white men, who stood at the pinnacle of cultural evolution as
they themselves conceived of it; and the reality of Africa's success
against them seemed to depend upon a reassessment of her role in that
evolution. Thus questions about what particular Africans or groups of
Africans had done, and its significance in their own time and situation,
were subsumed under questions about what "Africans", a more homogeneous party, had done in the evolution of the world.[16]

With Marxism, to be sure, we do not turn our backs on the evolutionary view of history. Marxism is an evolutionary theory, like the
one we have been looking at so far, and it should be noted that, in
this respect, it shares some of the limitations of "Whig" histories. Like
them, Marxism postulates an end which is considered both inevitable
and desirable. This is bound to influence the selection and interpretation of materials from the past.

In the case of Marxism (as with nationalism), moreover, Eurocen-
trism is an obvious hazard. The theory originates in Europe. Furthermore, Marxism is not an eclectic tradition; variations are often re-

garded as deviations, an attitude which may serve to shore up Euro-centric assumptions.

The importance of Marxist history as an alternative, therefore, is not that it is non-evolutionary, but that both the goal in Marxist theory and the process by which it is achieved are quite different from those of nationalist history.

Perhaps the most important difference, from the point of view of this discussion, concerns the role played by the nationalist struggles in the whole perspective of history. For many historians in the sixties, national independence was the event which seemed to dominate the formulation of questions about both past and future: what was the nature of pre-colonial independence, how was it lost, how was it fought for, how was it regained, how was it to be consolidated, how could it be turned into an article of heritage? With these questions in mind, it was natural that Africans should be seen as a side, not only in the nationalist struggles, in which they *were* one side and Europe the other, but throughout their history, as if preparing for this particular conflict. In this view, progress meant a process of increasingly empowering themselves as a side in an internationally competitive struggle. Increased control over both nature and population was the key to success in these terms; hence the stress placed on unification and the central-isation of economic resources and political power.

The perspective of Marxist historians, on the other hand, is dominated by a different goal, the establishment of socialism; and they expect it to be reached not by gradual improvements, building on general efforts and redounding to the general good, but by revolution resulting from an increasing awareness of irreconcilable conflicts of interest. In terms of these expectations, the key to understanding history lies in the disparity of interests discernible at any time. This is quite different from the idea that unity is the basis of progress; and it throws up a different set of questions.

Thus (to take the most recent period), while nationalist historians saw the post-independence period as a time when the unities which were the object of their search would be recognised, strengthened, and institutionalised, for Marxist historians it should be, equally, a time for further division, and that too should be progress. The ultimate conflicts to which this will lead will be, on the most immediate level at least, between black and black; and a history which seeks the roots and the growth of black unity, without at the same time analysing the growth of internal contradictions, will not be able to address itself to these.[17] In Marxist history, therefore, blacks cannot be amalgamated to make up a side, and if they could, it would be a bar, rather than a spur, to progress.

It is essential to understand that when Marxists speak of progress they are not using the word in its usual sense. The most important difference may be that, unlike the nationalists, Marxists are not celebrating the process they seek to explain. They do think in terms of levels of civilisation, and of progress from one to another, but quite without the idea that each step forward is an improvement in the sense of being in the best interests of society as a whole. In Marxist thought, obviously, there can be no best interest of society *as a whole* (unless or until it is classless).

The unusual view of progress involved here is vividly expressed in the following passage from Engels:

> Civilisation achieved things of which gentile society was not even remotely capable. But it achieved them by setting in motion the lowest instincts and passions in man and developing them at the expense of all his other abilities. From its first day to this, sheer greed was the driving spirit of civilisation; wealth and again wealth and once more wealth, wealth, not of society but of the single scurvy individual—here was its one and final aim. If at the same time the progressive development of science and a repeated flowering of supreme art dropped into its lap, it was only because without them modern wealth could not have completely realised its achievements.
>
> Since civilisation is founded on the exploitation of one class by another class, its whole development proceeds in a constant contradiction. . . . Whatever benefits some necessarily injures the others; every fresh emancipation of one class is necessarily a new oppression for another class. . . . And if among the barbarians, as we saw, the distinction between rights and duties could hardly be drawn, civilisation makes the difference and antagonism between them clear even to the dullest intelligence by giving one class practically all the rights and the other class practically all the duties.[18]

This is not, then, the picture of progress with which we are so often presented, in which state systems grow because there is a "need" for greater authority at the centre, exercised for the benefit of all. Such mystifications are explicitly rejected in the paragraphs quoted above, and Marxists cut through them by asking, "What kind of need? What kind of benefit? And for whom"?

The kinds of questions they ask shed light on all levels of society, and on the differences, reconcilable and irreconcilable, among them. They want to know how things were produced, what technology there was, who owned the land, the tools, the capital, who did the work, and if owners and workers were not the same people, what were the relations between them?[19] And to what moral and intellectual patterns did these relations give rise?[20]

Since Marxists and nationalists both see history heading in the same direction, up to a point, they see the same kinds of events as being "historical". But they have different reasons for thinking the same events are important. The development of the medieval states of Africa, for example, was seen by non-Marxists as proof that Africans could govern themselves before Europeans came on the scene. Thus they quoted the accounts of Arab travellers to the courts of kings, describing the things the king had, the honours that were paid him, the extent of his territory, international recognition of his importance, and so on. But for Marxists, these kingdoms show that some Africans were governing others, that whatever the economic basis for this stratification it was no longer a communal one, and the next question is, what was it? Was it slave-based, feudal, transitional between the two, or something else? What was the class structure, who owned the means of production, and in what ways could they be said to "own" them? What were the obligations of people to their government, what were their economic opportunities, how might they perceive their situation? What were people getting out of the system? To what extent could class antagonisms have developed? What were the long-term strengths and weaknesses of a state, judging from the continuing productive potential of its economic base?

This line of questioning differs from the "mainstream" followed by the nationalists in at least two ways. First, it focusses attention on the lower as well as the upper levels of society. The second difference concerns the *kind* of attention each receives. The admiration with which it had become customary to speak of nearly everybody in the African past was sustained partly by omitting, or redefining, things which might embarrass historians and their readers, such as "domestic" slavery, or human sacrifice. In a materialist analysis, these aspects have to re-emerge, both because slavery, for example, had economic, political, and social importance, whatever moral perspective one wishes to adopt, and because oppression should not be a public relations headache for historians whose central interest is in class conflict.[21] Thus, the conditions of life for ordinary people should become more visible as the idealisation of both leaders and followers declines. Apparently this is just the result which Marxist scholarship produced in the field of Indian history, as oppression connected with the rule of kings, slavery, and the caste system became part of the historian's concerns.[22]

Any investigation which can find out more about the commoners (or sub-commoners) of African history helps to fill a gap which has its origins both in the scarcity of information about them, and in a bias in favour of rulers. The latter seems to be twofold: there is a feeling that rulers are more interesting, and also a supposition that the society is in a sense encompassed in, or represented by, its rulers.[23] This is, of course, the surface impression given by those oral histories which are solely or principally royal chronicles, and it has been congenial to scholars who wished to see "traditional" African societies as strong and harmonious systems. Leaders may often have been considered "at one" with their people, therefore, not because the bases of their authority have been thoroughly explored, but because they have been taken for granted.

If a Marxist analysis undermines the picture of African leaders solving the problems of their societies, however, it does not (or should not) replace it with a picture of peasant, slave, or working classes in a continual ferment of progressive political action. It is not logical, but it is probably possible, to make "the underdog" into a side, but it would not further the purposes of Marxist analysis.

For, although Marxists provide a theory for revolutionaries, they are not only interested in historical processes which make for change, but also in those which work against it. As Hobsbawm puts it, Marxism is a structuralist and functionalist explanation of societies with a "dynamising element", reflecting "the simultaneous existence of stabilising and disruptive elements".[24] From an activist as well as from an academic standpoint, this makes sense; in order to attack a situation one must understand what it is, and this means knowing its strengths as well as its weaknesses. The understanding a nationalism requires is not as complex as that which a socialist movement must have. For nationalists, the relevant situation is one of domination by a foreigner, the goal is the transfer of power, and the rewards can be represented as accruing throughout the society. In the struggle towards socialism, however, the enemy is not only the people who must be overthrown, but is contained in a whole system of structural relations between people, usually of very long standing, with ramifications in the realms of social life and of political, moral, religious, and other cultural ideas as well as in the economic activities in which they have their base—some aspects of which must also form the basis for cooperation in struggle. These relations are fundamental, therefore, to people's expectations, and the system rewards most people to some degree as well as exploiting them, while for many any radical change would be a disaster. This explains why a history looking back from the triumph of nationalism is likely to be more limited in its scope than one based on Marxism, which looks forward to a struggle for socialism. That which constrains people from struggle—not only outside force, but the situation in which they are most deeply involved—is as interesting as that which propels them into it, and is something to be understood rather than to be ashamed of.

These aspects of the Marxist approach have been selected to show how Marxist historians could have been expected to improve upon nationalist African history. In part, the suggested benefits can be stated negatively. There should be no distortion of the past through the projection of nationalist preoccupations where these are inappropriate; in particular, history should not be represented as a competition between an African and a European side. The materialist organising principle which would replace this ought to provide a more complex analysis of the societies of the African past, paying greater attention to their lower levels, and attempting to find the bases for both stability and conflict, without emphasising either at the expense of the other.

To what extent, then, has Marxist writing borne out these expectations? First of all, it must be said that it did not, in the decade following independence, supply a real alternative in the sense we are discussing here (with the important exception of some of Rodney's work, which will be discussed below). A number of Marxists, like nationalists, tried to superimpose on history too neat a scheme of development, so that, instead of asking new questions about Africa's past, they simply put their own labels on the configurations which had already been described.

Also, like nationalists, they tended to see Africans as a side in an age-long competition with the West. This is not surprising, for Marxist historians originally were drawn to take an interest in Africa because African countries were in conflict with capitalist Europe. As a short-term political tactic, therefore, the historical vision of black-against-white made sense. Furthermore, as an interpretation of the particular conflicts which were their chief foci of interest, this vision contained a large part of the truth. What it omitted, however, was of crucial importance, and this has become more obvious with the passage of time. The refusal to see Africa as participant, as well as victim, in the transformations brought by imperialism, rendered any interpretation of nationalism too short-sighted to stand the test of time. The rest of this chapter will look at these problems, and at their passing.

First of all, the projection of nationalist ideas into the past was replaced, to some extent, by a projection of Marxist expectations. Marxism provides a method, a programme for investigating the nature of societies in history; and, while little was known of the "primitive" world, it seemed to provide a broad outline of history as well. The succession of stages had been produced as a result of contemplating European (and, to a lesser degree, Asian) history, and Marxist historians in the fifties and sixties were faced with the problem of placing what they knew of African history within it. Africa does seem to offer problems to those who think that all societies must pass through the same stages, and much energy was spent on arguing about whether it was possible (almost, whether it was permissible) for some African countries to "skip" stages. Samir Amin, Idris Cox, and Potekhin all wrote about this, Cox, for example, holding out hope that Africans might be able to dispense with capitalism altogether, because the Soviet Union provided a model of socialism which they could copy, whereas Russians themselves had no such model when they began their revolution.[25] There was also much discussion as to whether African communalism could be turned into African socialism. Could not Africans share prosperity without moving away from the values and traditions with which they used to share poverty?

One way of dealing with the problem, then, was to argue for gaps and bridges in the road to socialism. Another way was to bring together examples of recognisable way stations from the continent as a whole: here there was communalism, elsewhere there was feudalism, and this suggests that "African societies" move from the one to the other, although we were not sure how.[26] It was, of course, the poverty of sources for early African history which made this dominance of assumptions possible. Marx and Engels said little about Africa, recorded history said little about Africa, and for some time contemporary Marxists were not in a position to carry out much original research in Africa. Waterman points out that some of the reasons for the character of Soviet and Soviet-oriented writing, "whose apparent aim is simply to illustrate a pre-existing theoretical or political position",[27] lie in the conditions of scholarship. Apart from South Africans and some French writers, officially Communist Africanists have generally had to work outside of Africa.[28] Their obligations to the system which employs them and its priorities of scholarship must also be borne in mind, especially in the case of Soviet writers.[29] In place of historical analysis, therefore, we got the more superficial procedure of matching authority with example. Waterman cites

the numerous contradictory (and often self-contradictory) Communist analyses of the Nigerian civil war, replete with citations of Stalin on the national problem, Lenin on minorities, and examples taken from Europe in the nineteenth century . . . [as well as] Kubbel (1968) and Malowist (1966) seeking feudalism in the great states of the Sudan, or Olderogge (1959) finding early feudalism in pre-*jihad* Hausaland, or Suret-Canale (1969) discovering Marx's "Asiatic mode of production" in pre-colonial Africa.[30]

Endre Sik, indeed, offers the following justification for taking the time to work on African history at all:

A study of the history of Black Africa is of particular importance in view of the fact that it brilliantly substantiates and most vividly illustrates a whole series of theses maintained by Marx, Lenin, and Stalin in the field of historical science (e.g., the doctrine of Marx on primitive accumulation; the Leninist teaching about the colonial policies of pre-imperalistic and imperialistic capitalism; the teaching of Stalin about the origin of nations and of the national problems, etc.).[31]

What did not fit in with Marxist theory is simply not seen as a problem for historians; it is seen, rather, as irrelevant, or "prehistorical".[32]

Fortunately, this dead end, the result of a reverence for authority, was opened up by a reinterpretation of authority. The *Grundrisse*, a body of Marx's writing which indicated greater flexibility in his thinking about stages of development, became more widely available,[33] and the effort to transpose Marx's history to Africa gave way to efforts to apply Marxist method. Accordingly, there was a shift from trying to make Africa mesh with the European and/or Asian evolution of modes of production, to an effort, by anthropologists as well as historians, to elucidate one or more African modes of production. Indeed, this is an area in which African studies may do more for Marxist thinking than the other way round; Crummey and Stewart suggest that "the terrain of precolonial African history", though "largely ignored" by Marxists, "is the terrain *par excellence* of precapitalist modes of production", and that to study it "would very substantially illuminate major questions of contemporary concern to Marxist theory", too narrowly focussed thus far on capitalism.[34]

A more serious blind spot, perhaps, resulted from the overgeneralised loyalty which made Africans into one homogeneous side. The effect of this was to conceal the very things Marxism offers to explain, i.e., the bases of differentiation and conflict *within Africa* as well as between Africa and Europe. In our period, some Marxists seemed to see Africa as one side in a race for progress, in the same way that nationalist writers did. Rodney wants us to know that there were public baths in the Maghreb at a time when Oxford dons refused to wash.[35] Basil Davidson, as we have seen, emphasises the correspondence between Africa and Europe at various times, and the moments when Africa was "ahead". Similarly, Cox writes that

recent evidence indicates that parts of Africa enjoyed a higher level of civilisation in the early Middle Ages than existed at that time in Europe. Feudal states and kingdoms were in being in Songhai, Mali, Oyo, Benin, Ghana and Zimbabwe. . . . Africans are justified in their pride that their forefathers reached a higher level at a time when parts of Europe were almost in a state of barbarism.[36]

And Suret-Canale confirms, "Until the sixteenth century, black Africa, following its own path of development, had already produced developed civilisations; in the eleventh century, at the time of Ghana, the comparison with contemporary western Europe had been in many spheres to its advantage".[37]

To their credit, these writers were not unaware of a contradiction in their espousal of an African side. Cox follows his apparent endorsement, above, with the qualification: "But these medieval states had little in common with the principles of a communal and egalitarian system". This seems self-evident; who would expect them to? Cox's

singular use of "but" here would be unnecessary, had he not introduced the un-Engelian idea of whole societies "enjoy[ing] a higher level
of civilisation". In fact, the unity of African societies, an idea pro-
pounded by historians with national liberation and subsequent nation-
building in mind, is one which some Marxist historians seem unable
to resist. Rodney, for example, regards Shaka as an example of what
Africans could be when they were not interfered with by Europeans,
and, in recruiting him for the African side, he finds it necessary to toss
out the dialectic and bring back the "society as a whole". "All com-
mentators on Shaka (both African and European)", Rodney writes,
"frequently compare him favourably with the 'Great Men' of European history". In the nineteenth century, apparently, "senior clan heads
began to recognise the need for a political structure to ensure unity,
the maximisation of resources and the minimisation of internecine conflict".[38] And fortunately,

Shaka was able to invest his talents and creative energies in a worthwhile en-
deavour of construction. . . . It was a tribute to the organisational and agri-
cultural capacity of the society as a whole, that it could feed and maintain a
standing army of 30,000 men, re-equip them with iron weapons, and issue
each soldier with the full-length Zulu shield made from cattle hide.[39]

In support of his claims for Shaka's achievement in imposing a "sense
of security"[40] over so large an area, Rodney quotes European travellers, excited by the sight of such "disciplined . . . savages", by the
cleanliness, order, and absence of theft in Shaka's domain.

The explanation of this kind of writing would seem to be that some
Marxists, like nationalists, wished to inspire Africans with confidence.
The struggle for which it was needed was not the same in both cases,
and this ought to have made a difference to the sources of inspiration
they chose. Like the nationalists, however, these Marxist scholars saw
themselves as dealing with a racial inferiority complex, and sought to
combat it in the usual way, by creating a picture of Africans as an
achieving race. Thus, Rodney stressed that the Interlacustrine states were
"*African*"[41] (Rodney's italics), and not just the product of "light-
complexioned" culture carriers from the North,[42] while Potekhin en-
dorsed the approach of

African historians [who] are now concentrating attention on distant times, on
the historical epoch when the African peoples lived a life independent of the

European powers—the epoch of the great empires of Ghana, Mali and others. They rightly see in a description of the great deeds of their forebears a means of restoring the national dignity of their peoples trampled into the dust by the colonialists.[43]

The question was not raised as to what sources of inspiration were relevant to Marxists' interests. The sources were already established, and the historian simply associated himself with them. The emptiness of such an association is shown by Onoge's appropriation of Macemba in an article entitled "Revolutionary Imperatives in African Sociology".

If sociology is to be relevant to the contemporary African situation [it must be an approach] . . . that searches for the strategies for structural disengagement from the capitalist system. . . . Political, intellectual, and financial obstacles will be put in the way . . . [but] if courage is what we need, there are several sources of inspiration in the African past. In 1890 when the Yao people were given the ultimatum of voluntary surrender or invasion by Hermann von Wissman, a German imperialist, their chief, Macemba wrote back in Kiswahili in the following words:
"I have listened to your words but can find no reason why I should obey you—I would rather die first. I have no relations with you and cannot bring it to my mind that you have given me so much as a *pesa* (fraction of a rupee) or the quarter of a *pesa* or a needle or a thread. I look for some reason why I should obey you and find not the smallest. If it should be friendship that you desire, then I am ready for it, today and always; but to be your subject . . . I do not fall at your feet, for you are God's creature just as I am . . . I am sultan here in my land . . . and if you are strong enough, then come and fetch me".[44]

Stirring words, certainly, but what is the logic of quoting a chief of the foremost slave-trading people of the area to inspire people today "towards a revolutionary sociology", as Onoge's title has it?

It was the apparent logic of projection, by which socialism acquired a past in the same way that nationalism has done. The oppositions of the present were projected into the past, so that present resistance to imperialism was represented as having its roots in past resistance to the white man for whatever reason.[45]

Thus Marxists, nationalists, and Macemba could all be on the same side. Could this approach be justified in terms of strategy? It might win some superficial popularity for socialist writers, in the short term;

but, to the extent that the past has been simplified to provide inspiration and increase confidence, it will be a false confidence, easily manipulated and easily disappointed. History which misrepresents the past by glossing over contradictions does not, in fact, serve socialists.[46] It makes their task more difficult by raising people's expectations of easy success and playing down obstacles, with roots in history and continuing into the present day, which they must still overcome. Thus, as Genovese puts it, "the 'role' of the socialist historian is to be a good historian.[47] . . . Only ruling classes . . . have anything to gain from the ideological approach to history".[48] In this connection, Bernstein and Depelchin make the further point that any appeal to the past which represents it as harmonious and classless creates a mystification which

is a component of the very process of class formation and class rule, whereby the unity and harmony of the current social order (under the benign leadership of the State) continues a tradition that is authentically African. The glaring contradictions of the social order are accordingly externalised as the effects of "imperialism" in its contemporary form of "neo-colonialism".[49]

The real incompatibility between "good" Marxist history and what Genovese calls an "ideological approach" can be illustrated, for our period of African history, by a comparison between the bulk of Walter Rodney's writing and his study of dependency, *How Europe Underdeveloped Africa*.[50] Rodney was mentioned above as a writer who does, often, fulfill our expectations of a Marxist historian. Paradoxically, however, when consciously addressing his work to a Third World and partially non-academic audience, he withholds the kinds of questions he asks elsewhere, and tries to popularise a Marxist idea by presenting it in an essentially non-Marxist way. The inadequacy of the result shows both the poverty of such tactics and, more importantly for this study, the contradictions between Marxist and nationalistic history.

In *A History of the Upper Guinea Coast*, published in 1969, Rodney begins with a picture of the economic life, and social and political organisation, of the coastal peoples up to the time of their involvement with Europe, paying particular attention to relationships of inequality, which are to become very important in the situation of expanded opportunity which Atlantic trade brought to African rulers. In his description of that trade, and of the various transformations it brought to different coastal societies, Rodney never loses sight of the complexity of African responses in his insistence that their economic systems were being brought into the orbit of a capitalist system directed from without. Nor, in his picture of this system, does he simplify the turmoil of competition, success and failure, and adjustment within it. European agents are part of a system discernible by the historian, but their own understanding of what they were doing is simultaneously conveyed. Similarly, though the overall effect of the relationship is seen as devastating to African societies, these are not represented as either homogeneous or passive. The changes within each society are documented, and Rodney explores the interaction of internal factors (the history of the society before the advent of European trade, the various kinds of economic resources and organisation for their exploitation, relationships with neighbouring polities, influences from the interior, particularly the spread of Islam) with the demands and opportunities of the external trade. He examines the effects of the trade (and of Islam) on existing patterns of stratification, and the rise of a new class, the mulatto traders. He constructs a picture of coastal society up to 1800 which, without heroes, villains, or victims, provides a basis for understanding both the role which Africa was to take in the world economic system, and the development of commercially oriented social configurations at the coast. The contradiction between cooperation with European commerce and development which could benefit the mass of Africans is clearly represented; but Rodney does not make Africans and Europeans into opposed homogeneous sides in the process of establishing this contradiction.

*A History of the Upper Guinea Coast*, therefore, represents the fulfillment of many of our expectations of Marxist scholarship in the period with which we are concerned (as does an article Rodney published in 1968, *"Jihad* and Social Revolution in Futa Djalon in the Eighteenth Century"*, which shows how the contradiction between increasing economic capacity and continuing political subjection led to a *jihad* aimed at seizing secular power, comparable with those in Northern Nigeria). In a recent chapter in the *Cambridge History of Africa*, likewise, he looks at the internal contradictions in African societies, and especially at the oppositions between royalty and nobility, in a way quite different from the nationalist stress on the growth of unity, central authority, and constitutional balance between king and advisers which make African kingdoms such promising precursors of African nations.

*How Europe Underdeveloped Africa*, by contrast, is the only one of Rodney's historical writings which fails as Marxist history, although it is the only one which represents itself as Marxist analysis. It fails because it tries to persuade an African audience of the relevance of dependency theory by making it mesh with the simplistic version of the past already popularised by nationalist historians. In this attempt to appeal to a recently established national pride we see the surrender of many of those Marxist insights which inform Rodney's other work.

In the sense that Rodney's book did popularise dependency theory, it was of course a tactical success. Inasmuch as it left out so much that is essential to dependency theory, however, it did no real service either to the theory or to its readership, and this is important because it was so influential. Marxist writers were beginning to propound a view of underdevelopment which directly challenged both the method and the conclusions of nationalist history, but in Rodney's best-known version of it, this challenge disappeared. To understand why this is so, it is helpful to look at the debates within African history which formed the context for the emergence of *How Europe Underdeveloped Africa*.

Particularly in the 1960s and early 1970s, Marxist scholars, like others, concentrated on explaining the gap between Africa and Europe. Their explanation, and the remedy they offered, were quite different from those of most non-Marxist economists and historians concerned with the problem of underdevelopment. They wrote about the economic relationships between Africa and Europe created by early trade, slave trade, colonial rule, and neo-colonial association, and their ramifications in African societies, with the object of debunking the consensus of liberal economists that development is something capitalist countries help their backward neighbours to achieve, and showing instead how the wealth of capitalist countries is founded and continues to grow on the active underdevelopment of others.[51] They drew on the dependency theory of André Gunder Frank, a Marxist studying underdevelopment in Latin America, where aid and investment by wealthier countries had not resulted in a commensurate degree of development.[52] According to this theory, the effect of the relationship between developed and underdeveloped countries is actually to widen the gap between them. Whether before, during, after, or (as in the case of the United States) outside of a colonial relationship, the investors generate wealth only, ultimately, to repatriate it, so that the dependent country is never given the means to control its own resources. It provides raw materials, labour, and a market for manufactured goods; in these respects it is comparable to the rural areas of an industrialised economy, and Marxists speak in terms of the metropole (a developed country) and its periphery (the underdeveloped countries dependent upon their economic relationships with the metropole). Any benefits to the periphery are small compared with those which the relationship affords the metropole; thus instead of closing the gap between rich and poor countries, the relationship will necessarily increase it. Thus, Frank argues, the countries usually referred to, with either tact or optimism, as "developing", are *not* developing in fact; they are being actively underdeveloped by their foreign rulers and/or trading partners. Political dependency goes with economic dependency, and only radical political action can be expected to change the relationship. A colonial power may use force to prevent such action, but a neo-colonial power generally does not have to, for its relationship with the periphery creates and sustains a privileged class which derives considerable benefit, by local standards, from its middleman position. This class can only lose by any disruption of the relationship, for the creation of a self-sustaining economy in a former colony cannot be achieved without considerable hardship, if not revenge, on the middleman class.

To understand the difference this theory has made to the conceptualisation of African history, we must contrast it with the prevailing view of non-Marxist scholars in the sixties. Generally speaking, they tended to see the history of economic relations—with their political concomitants—in terms of different periods, each with its own evils and benefits. These are the periods (1) of early trade on equal terms; (2) of the slave trade, which was morally inexcusable and on the whole detrimental to Africa's development (though Fage has tried to show that it had some "positive" effects, in that it enabled strong states to grow stronger at the expense of others)[53] (3) of colonial rule, during which the administrations created in their colonies an economic infrastructure, mines, factories, roads, railways, tools and training, and well-established trading links with markets overseas (the benefit accruing to Africans from this transformation of their economic life being limited by the profits appropriated by the metropolitan countries and their settlers, and mitigated by the social disturbance which goes with industrialisation); and (4) the post-independence period, when Africans are finally able to use this heritage of improved technology and extensive links with the wider world, which continues to furnish aid, to develop their countries along "modern"—that is, Western—lines. The emphasis here is more on the transfer of technology than on the nature of the economic relationships between European and African countries. If international trade is taken to be mutually beneficial, then the strategies for development centre on technological improvement and the obstacles are factors like ignorance, conservative values, or disease in the countryside (one cannot get much more Africa-centred than this!).[54]

For Marxist historians, on the other hand, all the phases of Africa's relations with Europe were parts of a single process which, with or without direct political domination, reduced Africa to a supplier of materials and labour for Europe's industrialisation. This is the framework for understanding the picture as a whole. Without in any way belittling the importance of Africans in the period of involvement with Europe, they must still seek the causes of underdevelopment outside Africa, in European exploitation of Africa's resources. To focus on politics as separate from economics, to get caught up in nationalism and the achievement of independence, is merely to distract attention from the fact that this relationship between Africa and Europe has not changed; it was not overturned by independence.[55]

The truth of this viewpoint, obviously, does not depend upon its appeal, but on the evidence which can be found to support it, and this varies with the area, the period, and the sector of the economy one is looking at. What is important is that it proposed an entirely different approach to the problem of underdevelopment, and raised a different set of questions for historians to work with.

At the same time, however, it raised new problems for sympathetic historians of Africa. Nationalist history had replaced the old picture of stagnation, or unproductive enterprise (of "unrewarding gyrations", in fact), with a reconstruction of bold, creative, profitable pre-colonial trade all over the continent.[56] In the trade with Europe, the rum-loving slaving chiefs of an older stereotype were replaced, more positively, with entrepreneurs. For later periods, the "half-educated" blacks were more properly pictured as burgeoning new elites, struggling to gain what advantages they could from the colonial situation, organising meaningful political movements which wrested genuine independence from reluctant colonial governments, and initiating nation-building programmes.

It has been felt that the "development of underdevelopment" thesis must undermine these positive orientations of nationalist history, by revealing the weakness of pre-colonial economic systems, and by em-

phasising the cooperation of elites with neo-colonialism, rather than
their opposition to it. The international dimension seemed to threaten
the nationalists' emphasis on the recovery of African initiative.[57] Ranger
articulated the problem in 1968 in *Emerging Themes*, in the following
terms:

The historian who persists in treating national movements as something of
genuine importance and formidable energy; who sees the African peoples win-
ning their independence in the face of colonial reluctance and suppression; who
believes that mass participation was at various points crucial; has to argue his
case against a wide belief that national independence was an episode in a com-
edy in which the colonial powers handed over to their selected and groomed
bourgeois successors and in which nothing fundamental was changed.

In this view, the development of new elites, with new ways of life,
appears as the domestication of an exploiting system, the struggle for
independence a bit pathetic, the victory partial at best, and nation-
building a deception.

This would seem to me to have become the fundamental debate both of contemporary African politics and of much of African historiography. Can Africa
help itself or is it powerless until the whole pattern of the world has been changed
by revolution? And looking back into the past this revived pessimism casts
doubt upon the ability of African peoples to shape or affect their fate over
hundreds of years. The Africanist historian . . . who emphasises African activity, African adaptation, African choice, African initiative, will increasingly
find his main adversaries not in the discredited colonial school but in the radical pessimists.[58]

We must not be too quick to agree with these views of the pessimist
problem. Why should Africans be ashamed if their ancestors failed to
initiate effective programmes of development, when development was
not a contemporary idea? It is only nationalist history which has made
harbingers of development out of people who must have had a variety
of ideas about what they were doing. The problem is at least partially
created, then, by projection of the kind Rodney is doing when he writes,
"The ideals of Muhammad Ali could be related in the idiom of modern social science as being the creation of a viable, self-propelling
economy to provide the basis for national independence".[59] Why should
they be? The only reason to describe them in this way could be to en-

hance Muhammad Ali's reputation with twentieth-century readers, and we can only be disillusioned with his performance in these terms, if we have accepted definition of his intentions in these terms. The "harbingers of development" were traders; the nationalist movements comprised a great many different people, with a great variety of intentions, performances, and careers. Marxist historians need not deny the value of African initiative, therefore, but could analyse its nature and variety in its *contemporary* context.[60] Colonialists and nationalists both regarded "initiative" as a good thing, and were concerned, from different points of view, to know how good it was in Africa. It would be more properly historical to ask what it was, and here Marxism has a good deal to offer. In all of this, pride and shame have no logical place.

When we consider long-term results rather than contemporary aims, however, there are grounds for pessimism. As Ranger says, if Africa has been reduced to a powerless partner in international affairs, is there any reason to believe that this position can be changed?

It is this challenge which Rodney takes up in *How Europe Underdeveloped Africa*. Rodney is a radical optimist; radical in his condemnation of capitalism, optimistic in his hope that, if Africans can be persuaded that their underdevelopment is not their fault, they will be encouraged to go straight on to socialism, wherein lies their only chance of real independence from the West. "If we can determine when underdevelopment came about", he proposes, "it would dismiss the lingering suspicion that it is racially or otherwise predetermined and that we can do little about it".[61]

It would be quite possible to show how underdevelopment came about without constructing opposing African and European sides (as Rodney himself begins to do in *A History of the Upper Guinea Coast*). Rodney states his aim, however, within the familiar framework of an exercise to disprove a racial slur, and the construction of sides follows naturally, it not necessarily, from this. Once the sides are established, it becomes impossible fully to show how underdevelopment came about, because of a reluctance to detail the extent of participation of the African side; and we find, in fact, that Rodney does not carry through with his stated aim. His book does not adequately explain underdevelopment in Africa, because he dwells on what European capitalists did to Africans, without sufficiently elucidating the African response. He gives many reasons for continuing poverty in Africa, but this is not the only feature of underdevelopment. The successful farmer, the African businessman or woman, anybody who is neither victim nor puppet, has no place in Rodney's analysis. He does not, therefore, deal with the internal constraints upon change which have developed as a result of the relationship with Europe. His concern is all with the contradiction between European and African development, and, in order to emphasise this, he keeps to the simplicity of two antagonistic sides, European aggressors, mindlessly providing what "Capital required", and African victims.

Thus, while Rodney draws very widespread attention to the relevance of dependency theory to Africa (and this is the great merit of his book), in the event he uses it only to explain *lack* of change in Africa. He does not analyse changes in the same way, for fear that evidence of African participation in the process which led to underdevelopment might dilute the case against Europe. His theme is not the illumination of African society in the situation of imperialism, but simply the refutation of any and all claims that imperialism brought benefits of any kind to Africa. This limited aim was well suited to the context of African studies in the sixties; and it perpetuated, rather than challenged, the idea of a European and an African side in history.

The difficulty was that if all the complexities were allowed in, the clear delineation of sides would necessarily be lost. Once established, capitalism is not something which is done to people, but a system which involves them.[62] This was what urgently needed to be analysed, but the framework of *How Europe Underdeveloped Africa* could not do it. It is important to point this out, not because dependency theory has nothing to offer, but because, as explained earlier on, it has a great deal to offer. For those whose acquaintance with it is mainly through Rodney's book, therefore (and this must include a large number of students), it is worth pointing out that while he used it as an approach to an indictment of Europe, he did not suggest any new insights into African society in his period. As we know from reading his other work that he could have done so, we must conclude that he refrained from elaborating any analysis which would seriously challenge the nationalist orientation of his readers.

Before leaving the subject, however, we should perhaps also consider the possibility that dependency theory lends itself to writing about the nature of society in the dependency in oversimplified terms. The focus on relations of exchange, rather than relations of production,[63] may produce the impression that we are looking at a class struggle in which Europeans comprise the capitalist class and Africans the working class; this is certainly the impression given by Rodney's book. This is rather like the idea that women are a class: it has the advantage of a striking metaphor, and inspires solidarity, but it is uninformative, and creates mystifications of its own which a stricter adherence to materialism would help to avoid.

Is it possible, however, to analyse Europe's contribution to Africa's lack of development without reducing Africans to one-dimensional victims? Hopkins's *Economic History of West Africa*, contemporary with Rodney's book, succeeds in this.[64]

He analyses the pre-colonial economy, the slave trade, the "legitimate" trade, the Partition, the colonial economy, and the economic bases of nationalism, in a way which illuminates both the possibilities of, and constraints on, economic growth and change created by the structures of European and African economies and the relationships between them. He spends little time on what might have, would have, or should have been, but in writing about what actually took place, he satisfies us that the thrust of European involvement was not to develop Africa, but to develop Europe. At the same time, he shows Africans mobilising themselves to gain, and to increase, whatever advantage came to them from the relationship. That there *was* advantage to be gained does not in any way contradict the idea that Europeans tried to create wealth in order to repatriate it; what it does do is to bring Africans back to life, so that history is continuous, rather than interrupted.

This does not mean that a non-Marxist must write a better economic history of Africa than a Marxist; far from it. It means that a non-Marxist did what a Marxist might have been expected to do and, indeed, what Marxists have done increasingly as the identification with nationalism has worn off. At first, there was the feeling that any form of independence was a necessary and useful step. In addition, a good deal was hoped for from those nationalisms which professed socialist ideologies of various kinds, while nobody thought that the implementation of such ideologies was likely to go smoothly. It seemed right, therefore, to support the new regimes through the totalitarian phase which was not unexpected in the establishment of a socialist order. This phase of support, and its eventual withdrawal, are described by Roger Murray in a review of *Ghana: The End of an Illusion*:

It may now be admitted that the image of Ghana (or Indonesia, or Algeria?) conventionally sustained and expounded by wide segments of the left was markedly discrepant from reality. Was this merely a matter of "mistaken" analysis, explicable perhaps in terms of distance, paucity of information, and the like? I do not think we can be content with this, plausible as it may seem. The "mistaken" analysis is connected to a larger political and organisational problem.

For it is simply not the case that the "damaging" facts only came to light with the dredging operations conducted by the National Liberation Council in its pursuit of legitimation: the truth is that these facts were, at least in general outline, *profane but unspoken knowledge* on the left. The corruption, the grotesquerie, the complicities, the cult of the leader, the absence of genuine party life, the systematic elimination of all autonomous or critical groups, left as well as right, the sedimenting of new and gross class and power dispositions centring upon the state—none of this was news to anyone who lived and worked *in situ*, or who took the trouble to study the situation at all closely. What was involved was not absence of local evidence; it was a misinterpreted application of revolutionary responsibility and commitment.[65]

With this realisation, it became less important to be positive about the African past, and attention could be focussed on areas which embarrassed nationalist historians. One of these is the question of slavery in African societies. The "positive" view has been that there was little of it, that it was not onerous, that slaves were rapidly incorporated into their new community, that they had opportunities to become rich and important in their own right, etc. As we have seen, Africans themselves were the least embarrassed by African slavery, and for the most part did not bother with such justifications, but in Western writing they formed a hedge around a subject which ought to have been studied far more fully, and approached as an economic institution. This is now being done by Marxist historians, as they begin to take a greater interest in pre-colonial African society.

While it is beyond the scope of this work to undertake a detailed survey of recent Marxist scholarship, it is appropriate to consider the effect it has had on African history generally. There has been a shift of emphasis throughout African studies in the seventies, a shift, broadly speaking, from a political focus to an economic one. While this involves both Marxists and non-Marxists, it must be attributed in part to the growing number of Marxist historians, as well as to the growing appeal of their radical pessimism as disillusionment with African independence increases. History is no longer seen as a story of cumulative successes brought about by one set of leaders after another. Rather, it is a series of problems leading to one conflict after another.

Throughout the sixties and seventies, historians have been trying to formulate a view of the place of African history in world history. Historians in the sixties, interested in trying to lay foundations for nation-building, focussed on the idea that African leadership was comparable with the leadership of more successful places; here was the thought behind drum-and-trumpet history, and the race for progress. More recently, the idea has come to the fore that the problems of the African masses are comparable with those of people in other relatively unsuccessful places. One aspect of this change is that there are fewer nationalist, and more Marxist, historians, but it is also evident in the changing orientations of historians who fall into neither category.[66] The issues, sources, kinds of evidence, emphases, and flavour of writing are all affected, and one way of looking at what is involved may be to compare the issues which received most attention in the sixties with those which have been of more interest recently.

There is increasing interest in differentiation as well as in centralisation, and in the organisation of production as a factor in state-building. The conditions of material life are receiving more attention,[67] and ecological factors are coming more to the fore: climate, disease, demography, and diet. The focus on kings, conquests, diplomacy, and militarisation is shifting to peasants and slaves. While the politics of protest have been studied throughout the sixties and seventies, earlier writers were interested in them as manifestations of nationalism, while later writers looked for economic issues and the beginnings of class formation. Finally, the trend towards isolating Africa as the proper unit of study has begun to reverse itself, and historians are thinking about Africa more in the context of the whole Third World.

## NOTES

1. There are a number of different positions within Marxist thought on Africa, and debates among writers. A useful discussion of this can be found in Waterman's introduction to *African Social Studies*, an anthology of radical writings on Africa edited by himself and Gutkind, and in Copans' chapter in the same volume, "African Studies: A Periodisation". See eds. P. Gutkind and P. Waterman, *African Social Studies: A Radical Reader* (London, Hei-

nemann, 1977). This also contains an excellent bibliographical article by Christopher Allen, listing references in all the social sciences. Allen has a complementary article, "A Bibliographical Guide to the Study of the Political Economy of Africa" in eds. P. Gutkind and I. Wallerstein, *The Political Economy of Contemporary Africa* (London and Beverly Hills, Sage, 1976). For more (and more detail) on different Marxist approaches, see Robin Law's review article, "In Search of a Marxist Perspective on Precolonial Tropical Africa", *Journal of African History*, vol. 19, no. 3 (1978). As soon as we compare Marxist writers with others, a parallel problem arises: among the latter, too, there is a wide spectrum of assumptions and approaches. It would be convenient if a descriptive label could be found to cover the whole spectrum of writing which is not Marxist, but of course one can not. "Liberal" and "bourgeois" are both too narrow; the latter is too pejorative. For the most part, I have simply used the term "non-Marxist", except where I wished specifically to contrast Marxist with nationalist viewpoints. This usage is *not* intended to imply that non-Marxists comprise one homogeneous school of thought.

2. Especially W. Rodney, *How Europe Underdeveloped Africa* (London, Bogle L'Ouverture, 1972), which is discussed below. The inspiration for African dependency theory comes from the work of A.G. Frank on Latin America; see his *Capitalism and Underdevelopment in Latin America: Historical Studies of Chile and Brazil* (London, Monthly Review Press, 1967).

3. J. Saul, "Nationalism, Socialism and Tanzanian History" in Gutkind and Waterman, *African Social Studies*, p. 149.

4. E.g., J. Saul, "The State in Postcolonial Societies: Tanzania"; eds. R. Miliband and J. Saville, *Socialist Register* 1974 (London, Merlin Press, 1974); C. Leys, "The 'Overdeveloped' Postcolonial State: A Re-evaluation", *Review of African Political Economy*, no. 5 (1976); B.J. Berman and J. Lonsdale, "Crises of Accumulation, Coercion and the Colonial State: The Development of the Labor Control System in Kenya, 1919–1929", *Canadian Journal of African Studies*, vol. 14, no. 1 (1980).

5. C. Meillassoux, *Anthropologie économique des Gouro de Côte d'Ivoire* (Paris, Mouton, 1964); "From Reproduction to Production: A Marxist Approach to Economic Anthropology", *Economy and Society*, vol. 1, no. 1 (1972); "On the Mode of Production of the Hunting Band" in ed. P. Alexandre, *French Perspectives in African Studies* (London, Oxford University Press, 1973); E. Terray, *Marxism and "Primitive" Societies: Two Studies* (New York, Monthly Review Press, 1972); "Long-distance Exchange and the Formation of the State", *Economy and Society*, vol. 3, no. 3 (August 1974); C. Coquery-Vidrovitch, "Research on an African Mode of Production", trans. Susan Sherwin, in eds. M.A. Klein and E.W. Johnson, *Perspectives on the African Past* (Boston, Little, Brown, 1972); reprinted from *La Pensée*, no. 144 (1969), p. 39 (this article can also be found in eds. Gutkind and Waterman, *African Social Studies*);

"The Political Economy of the African Peasantry and Modes of Production" in Gutkind and Wallerstein, *Political Economy*; eds. D. Crummey and C.C. Stewart, *Modes of Production in Africa: The Precolonial Era* (London and Beverly Hills, Sage, 1981).

6. L. Cliffe, "Rural Class Formation in East Africa", *Journal of Peasant Studies*, vol. 4 (1977); I. Wallerstein, "The Three Stages of African Involvement in the World Economy", in Gutkind and Wallerstein, *Political Economy*; D. Crummey and C.C. Stewart, "The Poverty of Precolonial African Historiography" in Crummey and Stewart, *Modes of Production*; ed. M. Klein, *Peasants in Africa: Historical and Contemporary Perspectives* (London and Beverly Hills, Sage, 1980).

7. M. Legassick, "Perspectives on African 'Underdevelopment' ", *Journal of African History*, vol. 17, no. 3 (1976); R. Law, "Marxist Perspective"; A.G. Hopkins, "On Importing André Gunder Frank into Africa", *African Economic History Review*, vol. 2, no. 1 (1975).

8. E.A. Brett, *Colonialism and Underdevelopment in East Africa* (London, Heinemann, 1973); C. Leys, *Underdevelopment in Kenya: The Political Economy of Neo-Colonialism, 1964–1971* (Berkeley, University of California Press, 1975); "Underdevelopment and Dependency: Critical Notes", *Journal of Contemporary Asia*, vol. 7 (1977); S. Amin, *Accumulation on a World Scale* (2 vols.) (New York, Monthly Review Press, 1974); G. Kay, *Development and Underdevelopment* (London, Macmillan, 1975); contributions to Gutkind and Wallerstein, *Political Economy*, especially I. Wallerstein, "Three Stages", and P. Ehrensaft, "Polarised Accumulation and the Theory of Economic Dependence: The Implications of South African Semi-Industrial Capitalism"; and ed. R. Cruise O'Brien, *The Political Economy of Underdevelopment: Dependence in Senegal* (London and Beverly Hills, Sage, 1979).

9. M. Klein, "Introduction" in Klein, *Peasants*; L. Cliffe, "Rural Political Economy of Africa" in Gutkind and Wallerstein, *Political Economy*; J. Samoff, "Underdevelopment and Its Grass Roots in Africa", *Canadian Journal of African Studies*, vol. 14, no. 1, 1980.

10. R.M.A. van Zwanenberg, *Colonial Capitalism and Labour in Kenya 1919–1939* (Kampala, East African Literature Bureau, 1975) (see Introduction and Chapter 9); B. Magubane, "The Evolution of the Class Structure in Africa" in Gutkind and Wallerstein, *Political Economy*.

11. B. Hindess and P. Hirst, *Pre-Capitalist Modes of Production* (London, Routledge and Kegan Paul, 1975); H. Bernstein and J. Depelchin, "The Object of African History: A Materialist Perspective", *History in Africa*, vol. 5 (1978), pp. 1–19, and vol. 6 (1979), pp. 17–43. Bernstein does, however, outline a programme for writing history in "Marxism and African History: Endre Sik and His Critics", *Kenya Historical Review*, vol. 5 (1977). For a critique of this position, setting out a different view on the relation between theory and

fact, see R. Law, "For Marx, but with Reservations about Althusser: A Comment on Bernstein and Depelchin", *Africa*, vol. 8 (1981).

12. See G.S. Jones, "History: The Poverty of Empiricism" in ed. R. Blackburn, *Ideology in the Social Sciences* (London, 1978), p. 113.

13. Ibid., p. 96.

14. E.g., J. Samoff, "Grass Roots", and the Sage "Series on African Modernisation and Development".

15. A. Temu and B. Swai, *Historians and Africanist History: A Critique* (London, Zed Press, 1981), p. 7.

16. Ibid., pp. 5–6.

17. Saul feels that I. Kimambo and A. Temu's *A History of Tanzania* does not live up to its avowedly socialist approach, for just this reason: its contributors gloss over the divisions within society at every stage of pre-independence history, in the interests of representing a unity on which the Tanzanian nation could be based. "Whatever may be the popular mythology encouraged by contemporary leaders", he writes, "Africa has moved some way from the communalism of the traditional past, and the serious historian must look for the first seeds of class formation as assiduously as he traces the initial sparks of nationalist consciousness!"—J. Saul, "Nationalism, Socialism and Tanzanian History", in P. Gutkind and P. Waterman, *African Social Studies*, p. 149.

18. F. Engels, *The Origin of the Family, Private Property and the State*, trans. Alec West (London, Lawrence and Wishart, 1972), pp. 235–36.

19. See, for example, Jeff Holden's outline of the kind of oral research possible for the Samorian period in the Sudan, especially pp. 103–05, "Possibilities of Economic Analysis" in J. Holden, "The Samorian Impact on Buna: An Essay in Methodology", in eds. C. Allen and R.W. Johnson, *African Perspectives* (Cambridge, Cambridge University Press, 1970). He obtained information on the ownership, uses, and production of farming villages worked by slaves; the organisation of work by kinship; and the mode of inheritance.

20. For a brief and accessible explanation of the basic concepts of Marxism which are relevant here (mode, forces, and relations of production) see Crummey and Stewart, *Precolonial Historiography*, pp. 22–26.

21. Different viewpoints on African slavery, and some reasons for them, are discussed by Martin Klein in a review article in the *Journal of African History*, vol. 19, no. 4 (1978), pp. 599–609. Entitled "The Study of Slavery in Africa", this reviews eds. S. Miers and I. Kopytoff, *Slavery in Africa: Historical and Anthropological Perspectives* (Madison, University of Wisconsin Press, 1977) and C. Meillasoux, *L'esclavage en Afrique précoloniale* (Paris, Maspero, 1975), and also provides a wealth of other references on the subject. See, e.g., F. Cooper, *Plantation Slavery on the East Coast of Africa* (New Haven, Yale University Press, 1977); R. Harms, "Slave Systems in Africa", *History in Africa*, vol. 5 (1978); P. Lovejoy, "Indigenous African Slavery",

*Roots and Branches, Current Directions in Slave Studies* (Toronto, 1979) with comments by Kopytoff and Cooper; "Plantations in the Economy of the Sokoto Caliphate", *Journal of African History*, vol. 19 (1978); ed. P. Lovejoy, *The Ideology of Slavery in Africa* (London and Beverly Hills, Sage, 1981).

22. M.G.S. Narayanan, "Modern Indian Historical Writing on Ancient India: Some Problems of Conceptualisation", paper presented to the Institute of Commonwealth Studies, University of London, Postgraduate Seminar in "The Writing of History in New Nations", 17 Feb. 1975, p. 4.

23. This bias obviously serves the present rulers, and a growing interest in scholarship which undermines it has coincided with scholarly disillusionment with current African regimes. On this subject, see Colin Ley's review of ed. M. Lofchie, *The State of the Nations: Constraints on Development in Independent Africa* (Los Angeles, University of California Press, 1971), pp. 315–17, in *Journal of Modern African Studies*, vol. 11, no. 2 (1973). See also Bernstein and Depelchin, "Object", part 2, p. 27. A contributing factor to this bias, of course, is the nature of anthropological research, which comprises a major source for African political history. Anthropologists were often most closely associated with the ruling strata of the societies they studied, and found their informants among these people.

24. E.J. Hobsbawn, "Karl Marx's Contribution to Historiography" in ed. R. Blackburn, *Ideology in Social Science: Readings in Critical Social Theory* (London, Fontana/Collins, 1972), p. 277. This article was first published in *Diogenes*, no. 64 (Winter 1968).

25. S. Amin, *The Class Struggle in Africa*, Reprint 2 of the Africa Research Group from *Revolution*, vol. 1, no. 9 (1964); I. Cox, *Socialist Ideas in Africa* (London, Lawrence and Wishart, 1966); I.I. Potekhin, "On African Socialism: A Soviet View" in eds. W.H. Friedland and C.E. Rosberg, *African Socialism* (Palo Alto, Stanford University Press, 1964), pp. 97–116.

26. See, e.g., Rodney, *Underdeveloped Africa*, pp. 40–41.

27. Waterman's introduction, "On Radicalism in African Studies", in Gutkind and Waterman, *African Social Studies*, p. 3.

28. Ibid., p. 7.

29. See Milton Morris, "The Soviet Africa Institute and the Development of African Studies", *Journal of Modern African Studies*, vol. 11, no. 2 (1973), p. 258.

30. Waterman, "Radicalism", p. 7. The works he refers to are:

1. L. Kubbel, "On the History of Social Relations in the Western Sudan in the 8th to the 16th Centuries", *Africa in Soviet Studies 1968* (Moscow, "Nauka", 1969)

2. M. Malowist, "The Social and Economic Stability of the Western Sudan in the Middle Ages", *Past and Present*, vol. 33 (1966)

3. D. Olderogge, "Feudalism in the Western Sudan in the 16th to 19th Centuries" (in Russian), *Sovietskaya Etnografiya* (Moscow, 1959)

4. J. Suret-Canale, *Les Societés traditionelles d'Afrique et le mode de production asiatique* (Paris, Centre d'Etudes et des Recherches Marxistes, 1969)

31. E. Sik, *The History of Black Africa*, trans. Sándor Simon (Budapest, Akadémai Kiadó, 1966), vol. 1, p. 19.

32. See, for example, Sik, *Black Africa*, p. 17.

33. See R. Law, "Marxist Perspective", p. 449. A number of writers address the question of flexibility in the succession of stages of development: see, e.g., K. Botchwey, "Marxism and the Analysis of the African Reality", *Africa Development*, vol. 2 (1977), pp. 11–12; E. Hobsbawn, "Marx's Contribution", p. 279; H. Bernstein, "Marxism and African History"; Gutkind and Wallerstein, *Political Economy*, p. 10. Crummey and Stewart, *Precolonial Historiography*, p. 26: "Historical materialism shares with other historiography of the second half of the 19th century a belief in progress . . . [but not that] progress was universal or unilineal, without retreat. The African data confirm that there are numerous variations in the form and sequence of actual modes of production".

34. Crummey and Stewart, *Precolonial Historiography*, p. 12.

35. Rodney, *Underdeveloped Africa*, p. 64.

36. Cox, *Socialist Ideas*, p. 33.

37. J. Suret-Canale, *Afrique Noire, Occidentale et Central: 1: Géographie—Civilisations—Histoire* (Paris, Editions Sociales, 1958), pp. 169–70, quoted in E. Alpers, "Rethinking African Economic History: A Contribution to the Discussion of the Roots of Underdevelopment", *Ufahamu*, vol. 3, no. 3 (Winter 1973), p. 110.

38. Rodney, *Underdeveloped Africa*, p. 143.

39. Ibid., p. 145.

40. Ibid., p. 144.

41. Ibid., p. 74.

42. Ibid., pp. 73–74.

43. I.I. Potekhin, *African Problems* (Moscow, "Nauka", 1968), p. 137.

44. O. Onoge, "Revolutionary Imperatives in African Sociology" in Gutkind and Waterman, *African Social Studies*, p. 41.

45. Saul criticises Kimambo and Temu's *A History of Tanzania* on these grounds also. "Socialism is . . . assimilated (even reduced) to nationalism", he writes, and "All 'opposition' is reduced to its lowest common denominator, and a relatively undifferentiated effort by all Tanzanians to reclaim their liberty becomes the sum total of relevant occurrence".—Saul, "Tanzanian History", p. 149. See also my discussion of the same book in Chapter 4 of this book.

46. See Saul, "Tanzanian History", pp. 147–50; Nyerere's introduction to his *Freedom and Socialism—Uhuru na Ujamaa* (Dar es Salaam, Oxford University Press, 1968); and a report entitled "Be Honest, Nyerere Tells Histo-

rians" in *The Standard*, Tanzania (11 Nov. 1969). For this reason, Kwesi Botchwey writes, "contrary to the imaginings of petty-bourgeois academics, there is nothing patriotic about the denial, a priori, of the existence of class differentiation, (and therefore of exploitation) or backwardness (in terms of the development of productive forces and knowledge of the workings of nature generally) in Africa before its contact with nascent capitalism" ("African Reality", p. 14).

47. E. Genovese, *In Red and Black: Marxian Explorations in Southern and Afro-American History* (New York, Vintage Books, Random House, 1968), p. 8.

48. Ibid., p. 4.

49. Bernstein and Depelchin, "Object", part 2, pp. 25–26. See also J. Depelchin, "African History and the Ideological Reproduction of Exploitative Relations of Production", *Africa Development*, vol. 2 (1977) on the use of ideology to mystify political practice in Africa.

50. The works with which it is contrasted here are: W. Rodney, "*Jihad* and the Social Revolution in Futa Djalon in the Eighteenth Century", *Journal of the Historical Society of Nigeria*, vol. 4 (1968); *A History of the Upper Guinea Coast, 1545 to 1800* (London, Oxford University Press, 1969); and "The Guinea Coast" in ed. R. Gray, *The Cambridge History of Africa* (Cambridge University Press, 1975), vol. 4. Rodney's article, "African Slavery and Other Forms of Social Oppression on the Upper Guinea Coast in the Context of the Atlantic Slave Trade", *Journal of African History*, vol. 7, no. 3 (1966), is not substantially different from his presentation of the same material in *Upper Guinea Coast*.

51. The opposed views of how development is achieved are discussed at greater length in S.J. Hildebrand, "A New Paradigm in African Studies", *Ufahamu*, vol. 5, no. 2 (1974).

52. A.G. Frank, *Capitalism and Underdevelopment; Latin America: Underdevelopment or Revolution* (London, Monthly Review Press, 1969); *Lumpenbourgeoisie: Lumpendevelopment—Dependence, Class and Politics in Latin America* (London, Monthly Review Press, 1972).

53. J. Fage, "Slavery and the Slave Trade in the Context of West African History", *Journal of African History*, vol. 10, no. 3 (1969), p. 402.

54. For example, Fage writes in *A History of West Africa* (Cambridge, Cambridge University Press, 1969, an updated edition of his book first published in 1955), pp. 218–19:

Political independence by itself could not make West Africa richer. Its peoples were still faced with the same problems of poorer soils, less—or less developed—natural resources of minerals and of energy, and poorer facilities to improve their standards of health and education and their general living standards than were possessed by more favoured nations in Europe and North America. Independence made them better off in that they now had freedom to concentrate on programmes of economic and social betterment, and freedom to choose what policies seemed best adapted towards this end, but they now had to work out for themselves how best to secure from the richer nations the aid—the capital and the skills—needed to get such programmes going.

Some of the difficulties in applying this model to development in the post-independence period are interestingly discussed by Colin Leys in his review of ed. M. Lofchie, *The State of the Nations: Constraints on Development in Independent Africa* (see note 23).

55. C.f. Saul, "Tanzanian History", pp. 147, 150–51.

56. African history, for so long merely a part of the history of Europe, became Africa-centred in the sixties. The new approach rightly sought to put Africans back into African history, but in doing so it took Africa out of world history; and only this isolation, Marxists say, makes African economic activity look promising. Saul, in the article referred to above, criticises the "Africa-centred" approach on these grounds, as does Alpers in an article in *Ufahamu* 1973, with reference to work which focusses on African entrepreneurship and trading activity in an effort to show that Africans were not mere passive recipients of foreign trade as colonial historians supposed:

Africanists will need to integrate their particular findings within the much larger and more clearly articulated setting of the radical pessimists. Otherwise, the assumptions of Western scholarship will lead them, often unwillingly, into the comforting belief that the precolonial economic specialisation arising from this trade was in some vague sense leading to "progress" or "development". And here . . . the only way to resolve this conviction with the realities of Africa's underdevelopment in the twentieth century is to lay the blame exclusively upon the impact of the brief period of formal colonial rule as Davidson and many others did not so many years ago. With colonial rule thus treated like the Atlantic slave trade as something of an aberration in the process of developing Africa along capitalist lines through mutually beneficial trade, it becomes possible again to see African entrepreneurs in the twelfth century as harbingers of "progress" towards "development". Nowhere is this tendency more clearly exposed than in Cohen's essay and in Gray and Birmingham's introduction.

(E. Alpers, "Rethinking African Economic History", *Ufahamu* [1973], p. 104.) The last sentence refers to D.W. Cohen, "Agenda for African Economic History", *Journal of Economic History*, vol. 31, no. 1 (1971), p. 217; and R. Gray and D. Birmingham, *Precolonial African Trade* (London, Oxford University Press, 1970). A quite recent example of the kind of thing he describes here is found in Basil Davidson's article, "Questions about Nationalism", *African Affairs*, vol. 75, no. 302 (Jan. 1977), p. 42: "Catching Africa in mid-point of adjustment to the outside world—one sees this adjustment most easily, perhaps, in the huge rise of raw material exports after the decline in the export of captives for enslavement—the colonial enclosure sharply forced the pace".

57. The phrase is Ranger's, used in T.O. Ranger, *The Recovery of African Initiative in Tanzanian History* (The University College, Dar es Salaam, Inaugural Lecture Series, No. 2, Dar es Salaam, March 1969). It is fair to add that in his introduction to *Emerging Themes* (p. xiv) he writes that "it is important to realise that the Africanisation of African history is not a matter of ignoring European activities in Africa".

58. Ranger, *Emerging Themes*, p. xxi.

59. Rodney, *Underdeveloped Africa*, p. 153. The period he refers to is 1805–1849.

60. As Rodney does, indeed, in *A History of the Upper Guinea Coast*.

61. Rodney, *Underdeveloped Africa*, p. 30.

62. See M. Legassick, "Perspectives", p. 439.

63. See Law, "Marxist Perspective", p. 441, footnote 3.

64. A.G. Hopkins, *An Economic History of West Africa* (London, Longman, 1973).

65. R. Murray, "Second Thoughts on Ghana", *New Left Review*, no. 42 (March/April 1967), p. 26. The review is of B. Fitch and M. Oppenheimer, *Ghana: The End of an Illusion* (New York, Monthly Review Press, 1966).

66. For example, many of the contributors to the Sage series on African Modernisation and Development would not describe themselves as Marxists, while others would; broadly speaking, however, they share an interest in the same sorts of problems, and a similar perspective. As Gutkind and Wallerstein say in their introduction to *Political Economy*, all the contributors address the question, "Why is Africa poor"? and all are informed by Marxist ideas to some degree. Ranger puts the same question in his article "Towards a Usable Past" in ed. C. Fyfe, *African Studies since 1945* (London, Longman, 1976), asserting that it is the one with which African studies will be chiefly concerned for the foreseeable future.

67. In this connection one must mention J. Vansina's recent book, *The Children of Woot: A History of the Kuba Peoples* (Madison, University of Wisconsin Press, 1978). The picture of material life several centuries ago, which Vansina obtains largely by linguistic study, is quite remarkable.

# 7

# THE HAIRY BRIDEGROOM

Africa's colonial rulers and mentors began the process of intellectual colonisation by telling Africans what they had to be ashamed of. I have argued that nationalist historians unwittingly perpetuated it by telling them what they had to be proud of. That this process failed to put forward any uniquely African point of view has been argued at length; in conclusion, I should like to suggest that it actually ran counter to a more realistic spirit discernible in much of the traditional history of Africa, in which efforts to establish pride in the past are frequently tempered by statements about the insoluble conflicts endemic to every society.

Any discussion of this must be tentative, for there are countless ways of thinking about past and present in Africa as elsewhere, and I do not expect them all to be the same, or even consistent within themselves. Nor do I think that the oral traditions I have looked at are exhaustive of African historical thinking. The most I can say is that they suggest certain generalisable contrasts with the Western historical tradition.

The investigation of oral traditions by anthropologists and historians has certainly given grounds, more often than not, for thinking that they are designed to justify the status quo: to confer prestige and authority on the ruling group, to suppress the memory of defeat, humiliation, or failure, and to pacify dissenting opinion if necessary.[1] In these respects, they would seem no different from the sources of history in the West, which an objective historian tries to balance against one another in order to get closer to the truth. Techniques for recognising the ways in which tradition acts as a charter for the community that preserves it have become part of the Africanist's stock in trade.[2]

What is less frequently recognised, however, is a counter-tendency of oral tradition stubbornly to preserve material which does *not* reflect well on the ruling strata, a tendency, indeed, to express dissent simultaneously with support. We are less likely to see this because in Western history it cannot be done. Points of view have owners, and their relationship is dialectical. In oral traditions, on the other hand, they may simply coexist. Another reason for their low visibility is that, while the supportive message of the tradition tends to be expressed in something like chronological narrative, the critical messages are often embodied in symbols and clichés, the kind of thing which historians tend to dismiss as extraneous or fanciful, and winnow out in the course of processing the tradition. It is the student of myth who, treating the tradition as a whole, comes to understand the relationship between what is told in the language of symbols and what appears to lie in the realm of fact (and often, in so doing, he discovers that the "facts" are also symbols!).[3]

Traditions have increasingly revealed themselves to be not so much (as historians used to hope) histories told in the language of myth, but rather myths of which history comprises one element (since it is after all what has happened to the community), but only one element among many which they consider equally important in their representation of their affairs. Structural analysis has been taking over from spatial and chronological reconstruction in recent years, and some of its insights have a bearing on the relevance of Western history to traditional African concerns. Myth exists in Western societies too, of course, both in its ancient forms and restated in our religious observances and in our fiction. Unlike African traditional historians, however, we distinguish between myth and history, either on the basis that one is fiction and the other fact, or by saying that they express different kinds of truth, the universal and the particular. What is odd, perhaps, is that we see particular truth as different from the universals we perceive about the human condition; people in history struggle to improve the lot with which their humanity has saddled them, and this is the basis of our evolutionist set of mind.

What a structuralist historian discovers in oral tradition, on the other hand, is a unity of "mythical" with "historical" truth. Traditions frequently set out the characters, the oppositions, the conflicts, the patterns of thought and of behaviour which the storytellers feel are characteristic of their world; and the very features of traditions which irritate historians—the clichés, the tales of magic, the reappearance of characters and events, the arrangement of material according to some dramatic rather than chronological logic—make sense in the context of an effort to state, again and again, not only what has happened but the *ways* in which things are felt to happen in history. It may seem odd that oral memory should burden itself with such repetition, if it is merely stating eternal verities; but Lévi-Strauss suggests that the problems with which it is concerned are often insoluble, and thence their treatment is circular. While Beidelman writes that "ideologies . . . serve to resolve, in the sphere of ideas and symbols, social features which cannot be resolved in the sphere of social activities",[4] Lévi-Strauss would take this a step further and say that these features cannot be resolved in the sphere of ideas and symbols either; they appear, superficially, to be resolved, but in fact they continue to be restated, over and over again.[5] I suspect, in fact, that structural analysis may hold a clue to an important difference between Western and African historical thinking (and again, I wish to encourage investigation rather than to overgeneralise about a *pensée Africaine!*). It seems to me that part of the evolutionist nature of Western history is the expectation that conflict can be resolved. It is not my purpose here to argue that it can be, or that it can't, but to treat the idea as a cultural artifact. Behind the belief in progress is a feeling that nothing is necessarily intractable. Is it too much to suggest that such a belief could be engendered by the brief and peculiar historical circumstances of those who hold it, instead of thinking that progress is a fact from which those circumstances of necessity follow? (It is suggestive to compare the eschatological Christian religion of the West, in which a dramatic resolution to problems is expected in the chronological future [both personal and historical] with African traditional religions in which death is not the end of social problems.) Thus while Western history is tracing the success or failure of attempts to solve particular problems, perhaps African traditions are setting them up as a depiction of the human condition. In such a depiction, no purpose could be served by refusing to recognise conflict or failure.

Even at the level of narrative, indeed, historians have often been surprised by the amount of embarrassing material which traditions preserve, and the criticism of rulers they express.

There is some evidence that this occurs more in polities where the government involves a balance of power: between priests and kings, for example, or societies of office-holders, or immigrants from different localities.[6]

Even in strongly authoritarian states, however, where memory-shredding might be supposed to be comparatively easy, it has sometimes been resisted to an extent which must challenge our expectations of oral tradition. Oliver expressed surprise in 1955 "that the Ganda did not try to produce a history which was consonant with the dominant position they held in the early twentieth century". Their rise to preeminence in the lakes region

is a story of sparkling success, but what is especially striking about it is that the Ganda do not try to invent a remote historical justification for their recent acquisitions. On the contrary, they make no attempt to conceal their modest beginnings and they frankly record serious defeats during the early reigns of the dynasty at the hands of their Nyoro enemies.

Similarly, of the codification of Nkole tradition in 1950, published by the East African Literature Bureau, he wrote, "It would be difficult to imagine more suspicious circumstances for the codification of history. Yet if one examines the content, all the opportunities for creating a really good national mythology seem to have been missed".[7]

This in itself must raise questions about the use of oral tradition as a justificatory charter. And if we add to it the kind of insight which structural analysis provides, into symbolic levels of expression, we find that explanation becomes even more prominent, justification less and less so.

Let us take, for example, the relationships between myth and history in the case of the Hairy Bridegroom, alias the Hunter King. This is a familiar figure in the traditions of East and Central Africa, the savage stranger who comes out of the forests or rivers to take a wife from among the villages, and often to become their king.[8] As an historical figure, he can be interpreted as a leader of a lineage segment leaving a crowded community in search of new lands, his aura of savagery explicable in terms of the natural fear of strangers. As a figure of myth he suggests the image of the young initiate, passing from the comparatively unsocialised stage of childhood to the moral responsibilities of adult men.[9] To adopt either of these explanations, however, is to put too much strain either on the historical phenomenon of piecemeal migration or on the universality of the symbolism of rites of passage. Both may well contribute to the widespread territory of the hairy hunter, but his significance for different communities varies according to what they consider important in their historical experience. It is in the context of culture and history, therefore, that the symbols of tradition must be examined, and we shall look at the significance of this symbol in two East African situations. What is common to both of them is the role of the hairy bridegroom in embodying the community's reservations about its power structure, and this is the point of taking him as an example of the capacity of oral tradition to express dissent as well as justification.

The traditions we shall look at are those of Bunyoro, which I have analysed in greater depth elsewhere, and of Shambaai, which are discussed by Feierman in *The Shambaa Kingdom*.[10] In Bunyoro, the significance of the Hairy Bridegroom lies in the relationships he contracts with his in-laws, whereas in Shambaai it is the sexual relationship between man and woman which is crucial. Neither of these would appear to have much to do with history, at first glance. But each is a metaphor for the power relationship between government and people, incorporating the attitude of subjects into what is, on the face of it, the rulers' tradition.

The traditions of Bunyoro run from the Creation of the world to the coming of the Europeans.[11] The gods retreated to heaven when evil appeared on earth, leaving a generation of immortals, the Cwezi, to rule over men. The next change of dynasty, when the mortal Bito rulers took over from the Cwezi, was the last, and it is on this change of dynasty that scholarly attention has mainly focussed. The traditions tell of the departure of the Cwezi, discouraged by their inability to stop quarrelling among themselves, and by a prophecy that their position was soon to be usurped by a barbarian whose rule would bring chaos to the land. On their way out of the country, the Cwezi passed a hunting party, to whom they casually bequeathed their rule; and then they disappeared. One of the hunters, Rukidi, proved to be the barbarian of the prophecy, for he was a foreigner, ignorant of manners and of the pastoralist life of the country he came to rule, and was received at first without enthusiasm, if also without resistance. It turned out, however, that he was related to the Cwezi, one of whom had begotten the child on a trip abroad. After learning etiquette and proper grooming, therefore, he was able to establish the legitimacy of his succession by beating the royal drum, when the people accepted his rule and that of his line.

Historians have interpreted this story as an attempt by the Bito dynasty to confer upon itself the authority of the rulers it displaced.[12] These are assumed to have been Hima pastoralists who ruled over the local Bantu until a Lwo invasion forced them to flee south, where states with Hima rulers were indeed found by Europeans at the end of the nineteenth century. The story of Rukidi, therefore, is taken to be an attempt to paper over this conquest by a barbarian people, giving Rukidi a fictitious kinship connection with the Cwezi and representing the conquest as a peaceful transition. This interpretation is consistent with the idea that oral traditions seek to justify the group which preserves them, even if, as in this case, its bona fides are not very impressive.

This reading of the tradition, however, leaves historians with a difficult problem. If the traditions are designed to make the Bito dynasty more acceptable, why do they go out of their way to stress the unsuitability of its founder? Is it, as Beattie and Oliver think, because the Bito were really so inferior there could be no hiding the fact? Or is it, as Wrigley and Needham argue, not a rather fumbling attempt to whitewash history (the necessity for which, after four hundred years of Bito rule, is rather doubtful), but a symbolic tale about anarchy and authority, and about the transition from nature to culture? "It seems necessary", Wrigley suggests, "to consider the possibility that the Nyoro kingship was deemed to have authority, not in spite of the savage origins of its mythical founder, but because of them".[13] And here, he picks up a crucial point: it is not Rukidi's people who are portrayed as savages, but Rukidi himself.

If we look now more closely at the figure of Rukidi, we see that he is not merely somewhat uncouth, as a Lwo warrior might have appeared to the Bantu people of Bunyoro. He is a *wild* man, a hunter, covered with long, unkempt hair. He is everything, in fact, that the Lwo—cultivators and herdsmen and careful hair-stylists—were not.[14]

His blood relationship with the Cwezi does not so much link his people with an ethnic group of vastly superior culture as connect him personally with a line of hairy bridegrooms, for he is not the first of these in the tradition. His father was a wandering hunter who had been born in hell, a stigma which barred him from taking power in the world above but did not prevent him from begetting sons in clandestine liaisons with its women. His grandfather, in turn, was a king who appeared before his father-in-law for the first time naked, dishevelled, and deeply embarrassed. As Wrigley points out, this is not the Nyoro image of a Lwo; but it *was* the Nyoro image of a bridegroom, in common currency as well as in the traditions. The bridegroom is awkward, unkempt, and unworthy to receive his host's daughter.[15] But there is another side to him as well, a context in which he is a deeply threatening figure, and this, I think, is the point of representing Rukidi *and* the much-admired Cwezi kings who preceded him as bridegrooms. Marriage sets up a web of relationships which Bunyoro feel to be fraught with difficulties (a view echoed in much of the mythology of the surrounding culture area).[16] Perhaps the most dangerous of these is the relationship between a man and his sister's sons.[17] The significance of the hairy bridegroom, I suspect, is that he puts his descendants in the position of sister's sons to the population into which he marries; and it is significant in this connection that Nyoro princesses were not allowed to have children because if they did, the royal clan would have sister's sons who might threaten them.[18]

While a son-in-law is "ruled" by his father-in-law, and owes him a number of duties, the tables are turned in the next generation: a sister's son "rules" his mother's brothers. These relationships are sanctioned by *mahano*, a mystical danger which attaches to various aspects of Nyoro life. It is rather an unfair relationship, for in case of any default in the mutual obligations of sister's son and mother's brother, it is the latter who is punished by *mahano*. In the context of death, this hostile domination is dramatised. Beattie tells us that when a Nyoro man died, if he had been a household head his sister's son had to perform rites symbolising the destruction of the household, with which he was ritually identified, breaking up the house, the hearth, and the eating utensils, and appropriating anything he might want for himself.[19]

There are in fact various overt suggestions of a conquest in the traditions, and I have enumerated these elsewhere;[20] even at a fairly obvious level, the traditions tell two contradictory stories at once, thus working in the point of view of the original population as well as that of their Lwo rulers. I draw attention to the symbolism of kinship and marriage here, however, because it is an additional way of expressing "underground" themes, and one that is far more likely to be missed.

The message here seems to be that the rule of kings is unwelcome at the best of times, not only in the event of conquest by the Bito, but even from the beginning, when the kings were gods. It is contained not in the language of royal politics but in the language of family politics, which do not seem very important to us but are of great concern to Banyoro. Just as kings rule subjects and chiefs rule villagers, some kinsmen and some in-laws are said to "rule" others, and this is not merely an idiom but a relationship sanctioned by mystical danger. Wrigley has remarked that the stories about the Cwezi are merely stories about an extended family, not about an extensive kingdom, and at one time he wondered whether this indicated that the Cwezi were not really kings.[21] It may be the other way round, however, that the language of family relationships is used to express wider political realities.

In fact, Beattie tells us that Nyoro are well aware of the negative side of their attitudes, and draw a distinction between the state and the community. The word for government, *bulemi*, implies "ruling" but is also associated with "weight" (*bulemezi*) and the idea of "something difficult, even oppressive. "Banyoro think of political authority as something heavy and burdensome, superimposed on and external to the multifarious and mostly face-to-face relationships which subsist between neighbours and kin who live in the same community and share the same background, interests, and values".[22] This is not surprising, of course. I should think it is more common than not where there is any distance between community and government. What *is* surprising is that this ambivalence is expressed in what is after all the royal tradition; and this means that it is not the partisan document we expect from traditional historians glorifying the kings and suppressing any dissenting points of view.

A very similar use of the language of symbols is found in the Shambaa traditions analysed by Feierman. Here is another hairy bridegroom, Mbegha, a dangerous and unruly person who is cast out by his own people and travels through the forest hunting, until he reaches Shambaai. Here he is welcomed for his skill at hunting pigs, which damage the farms, and the people give him starchy food to eat in return for this service and for meat. He travels round the country hunting, and stories are told of his activities in the various villages, including the settlement of disputes which Shambaa bring before him. As well as food, they give him a wife. Then he kills a lion, the people ask him to be their king forthwith, and he settles down, bringing the politically diffuse parts of Shambaai under his rule by force, persuasion, and marriage, and founding the dynasty which continued into German colonial times.

Here again is a story which appears to be a charter for the rule of Mbegha's line, and which celebrates his prowess and judgement. And yet, like the Nyoro tradition, this one also emphasises the dangerous and unpleasant attributes of the founder. According to Feierman's analysis, one set of symbols identifies him with sorcerers, wild beasts and the threatening forest: he is incestuous, unlucky, hairy, and anti-social, eating meat without starch like a Shambaa witch or an animal. Indeed, as his most important role as king is to ensure fertility by making rain, he has to be a sorcerer, with magical powers that can be used for good or evil. Another set identifies him with an older figure of myth who established the rule of patriarchy, subduing female communities by sexual fascination and physical force. A third set of symbols confirms the portrayal of Mbegha in Shambaai as a man among women, when he does the male work of killing farm pests and the men of Shambaai farm for him. Through these symbolic associations, Feierman believes, the Shambaa express their reservations about power, simultaneously identifying it with the sinister power of the sorcerer and the brutal force with which, in their view, men sustain their power over women.

The superficial intention of the teller of the Mbegha myth is to describe the wonderful qualities of the first king. But there is a serious problem. . . . What is the purpose of demonstrating the opposed qualities of Mbegha in [his place of origin]? . . . I interpret this as meaning that kingship necessarily is power, and power can be used either for great good or for great evil. . . .

Mbegha, in other words, encompassed within his person opposed but related possibilities of kingship in Shambaai. Mbegha as king was the embodiment of all the ideal virtues of a Shambaa ruler. Yet each aspect of his beneficial power had a complementary opposite—the same power used to bring death and destruction. In fact, in the course of Shambaa history there were kings who were given wives, and others who stole wives, kings who dealt death through the countryside, and those who brought life. There were kings who brought famine, and others who created plenty. But when the kingdom was truest to its good principles it was based on a relationship between king and subject for which Mbegha's relationship with the Shambaa was the paradigm. Thus the story of Mbegha is both an intellectual and a moralist's model of the

Shambaa kingdom. For it told how the kingdom should work, and at the same time how the kingdom, in evil times, does work.[23]

In Western governments, there is commonly a pretence that the rulers are, or should be, good men, and that their rule should be intended and received as beneficial. Most of us do not believe this, of course, but it is the idiom we expect to hear in official bulletins. Even this brief examination of African traditions is enough to suggest that some at least employ a different, more ambiguous idiom, and that further structural analyses might be expected to reveal more of the same.

Atkinson puts this very well when discussing how the traditions of Buganda, like those of Bunyoro, appear to be trying, but failing, altogether to conceal what was probably a conquest resulting in a change of dynasty.

This historical problem has been blurred by the structure of the traditions we have investigated . . . but . . . scholars have "discovered" what the myth attempts to "conceal". How is this possible? It is not primarily because the events that we have in retrospect considered historically important are structurally anomalous and therefore obviously out of place in their structured context and easily spotted. On the contrary, the elements of the traditions which provide the historical clues educed by Kiwanuka and others have been kept as part of the traditions precisely because they have been incorporated *into* the structure. If they had not been so incorporated, they would not be present at all.[24]

It is, in other words, the storyteller's *intention* to make the ambiguities of their historical experience available to his listeners.

I have argued against the equation of success with worthiness throughout this book, and conclude with one more argument derived from these traditions. To write a partisan history of *any* party is to invite contradiction, as I have said. But to pretend that power is representative of the common will seems particularly unflattering to the perceptiveness of people who tell, in their royal traditions, this story about the first principle of power.

The Creator's brother asked why the two of them had stomachs, so Ruhanga the Creator gave him food. Then Ruhanga said, "Now I have supplied all your requirements, but it would have been better for mankind had you not heeded the stomach; for it will be your master, it will cause pain, labour, and theft". But Nkya replied, "Nay my brother, but it is only hunger that has ears; apart from it, there would be no submission among men, for man will only obey him who provides him with food".[25]

## NOTES

1. For examples of this, see E. Meyerowitz, *Akan Traditions of Origin* (London, Faber and Faber Ltd., 1952), p. 21; S.O. Biobaku, "The Problem of Traditional History with Special Reference to Yoruba Traditions", *Journal of the Historical Society of Nigeria*, vol. 1, no. 1 (Dec. 1956); L. Barnes, "History in a Changing Society", *Rhodes-Livingstone Institute Journal*, no. 11 (1965); I.A. Akinjogbin, "The Expansion of Oyo and the Rise of Dahomey 1600–1800" in eds. J.F.A. Ajayi and M. Crowder, *History of West Africa* (London, Longman, 1971) vol. 1, p. 326. See also J. Vansina, "The Use of Oral Tradition in African Culture History", in eds. C. Gabel and N.R. Bennet, *Reconstructing African Culture History* (Boston, Boston University Press, 1967), p. 42. There is an interesting suggestion in M. Priestly and I. Wilks, "The Ashanti Kings in the XVIIIth Century: A Revised Chronology", *Journal of African History*, vol. 1 (1960), which is relevant to this. A king, Osei, who succeeded Osei Tutu, is actually omitted from Ashanti history, and the writers speculate that this may be because he was killed in the only major defeat suffered by the Ashanti in the eighteenth century (p. 42).

2. The pioneering guide in this area was J. Vansina, *Oral Tradition*, trans. H.M. Wright (London, Routledge and Kegan Paul, 1965). See also Vansina, "Culture History". More recently there is eds. K. Brown and M. Roberts, *Using Oral Sources: Vansina and Beyond: Special Issue of Social Analysis*, no. 4, 1980.

3. For excellent illustrations and discussion of this point, see W. MacGaffey, "African History, Anthropology, and the Rationality of Natives", *History in Africa*, vol. 5 (1978).

4. T.O. Beidelman, "Myth, Legend, and Oral History: A Kaguru Traditional Text", *Anthropos*, vol. 65 (1970), p. 96.

5. C. Lévi-Strauss, "The Story of Asdiwal" in ed. E. Leach, *The Structural Study of Myth and Totemism* (London, Tavistock Publications, 1967) and C. Lévi-Strauss, *The Raw and the Cooked: Introduction to a Science of Mythology*, vol. 1, trans. J. and D. Weightman (London, Jonathan Cape, 1970).

6. A. Roberts, *History of the Bemba* (London, Longman, 1973); R.G. Willis, "Traditional History and Social Structure in Ufipa", *Africa*, vol. 34, no. 4 (Oct. 1964); and "The Head and the Loins—Levi-Strauss and Beyond", *Man* N.S., vol. 2, no. 4 (Dec. 1967).

7. R. Oliver, "The Traditional Histories of Buganda, Bunyoro and An-

kole", *Journal of the Royal Anthropological Institute*, vol. 85 (1955), pp. 111–12.

8. C.C. Wrigley, "The Story of Rukidi", *Africa*, vol. 43, no. 3 (1973), p. 223.

9. Ibid.

10. See C. Neale, *Pride and Prejudice in African History: The Idea of Progress in the Revision of African History, 1960–1970* (unpublished D. Phil. thesis, University of Sussex) and S. Feierman, *The Shambaa Kingdom: A History* (Madison, University of Wisconsin Press, 1974).

11. I used R. Fisher, *Twilight Tales of the Black Baganda* (London, Marshall, 1911) as my core text in analysing these traditions. The relevant material from Fisher is reproduced in full in my thesis, which also contains references to other relevant literature of the culture area.

12. J. Beattie, *The Nyoro State* (Oxford, Clarendon Press, 1971); R. Oliver, "A Question About the Bachwezi", *Uganda Journal*, vol. 17, no. 2 (1953).

13. Wrigley, "Rukidi", p. 222; see also R. Needham, "Right and Left in Nyoro Symbolic Classification", *Africa*, vol. 37 (1967) and "Nyoro Symbolism: the Ethnographic Record", *Africa*, vol. 46.

14. Wrigley, "Rukidi", p. 223.

15. J. Beattie, "Nyoro Marriage and Affinity", *Africa*, vol. 28, no. 1 (1958), p. 7.

16. G. Leinhardt, "Nilotic Kings and their Mothers' Kin", *Africa*, vol. 25, no. 1 (1955).

17. Beattie, "Nyoro Marriage", p. 10.

18. Beattie, *Nyoro State*, p. 101.

19. Beattie, "Nyoro Mortuary Rites", *Uganda Journal*, vol. 25, no. 2 (1961), p. 172.

20. Neale, *Pride and Prejudice*, Chapter 7.

21. C. Wrigley, "Some Thoughts on the Bachwezi", *Uganda Journal*, vol. 22, no. 1 (1958).

22. Beattie, *Nyoro State*, p. 6.

23. Feierman, *Shambaa Kingdom*, pp. 63–64.

24. R.R. Atkinson, "The Traditions of the Early Kings of Buganda: Myth, History and Structural Analysis", *History in Africa*, vol. 2 (1975), p. 44.

25. Fisher, *Twilight Tales*.

# FURTHER READING

In a work of historiography, everything is grist to the mill. A bibliography encompassing most of the writing which has stimulated the argument of this work is precluded by considerations of space, and one must, regretfully, choose only those which will be of most use to the general reader who wishes to go into the matter further. I have selected for this list, therefore,

1. collections in which a number of approaches are represented, giving a feel for the state of the art at the time of writing;
2. works whose contents and/or bibliographies comprise an economical introduction to a special area;
3. and (the great majority), the most cogent comments on the state of African historiography in my period.

A.K. Armah, "A Mystification: African Independence Revalued", *Pan-African Journal*, vol. 2, no. 2 (Spring 1969).

H. Bernstein and J. Depelchin, "The Object of African History: A Materialist Perspective", part 2, *History in Africa*, vol. 6 (1979).

M. Chanock, "Development and Change in the History of Malawi", in ed. B. Pachai, *The Early History of Malawi* (London, Longman, 1972).

Eds. D. Crummey and C.C. Stewart, *Modes of Production in Africa: The Precolonial Era* (London and Beverly Hills, Sage, 1981).

D. Denoon and A. Kuper, "Nationalist Historians in Search of a Nation", *African Affairs*, vol. 69, no. 277 (1970).

M.S. Dipoko, "Cultural Diplomacy in African Writing", *Africa Today*, vol. 15, no. 4 (Aug./Sept. 1968).

S. Feierman, *The Shambaa Kingdom: A History* (Madison, University of Wisconsin Press, 1974).

Ed. C. Fyfe, *African Studies since 1945* (London, Longman, 1976).

Eds. P. Gutkind and I. Wallerstein, *The Political Economy of Contemporary Africa* (London and Beverly Hills, Sage, 1976).

Eds. P. Gutkind and P. Waterman, *African Social Studies: A Radical Reader* (London, Heinemann, 1977), especially the introduction and the bibliographical essay by C. Allen.

S.J. Hildebrand, "A New Paradigm in African Studies", *Ufahamu*, vol. 5, no. 2 (1974).

Eds. B. Jewsiewicki and D. Newbury, *African Historiography* (Beverly Hills, Sage, forthcoming).

M. Klein, "The Study of Slavery in Africa", *Journal of African History*, vol. 19, no. 4 (1978).

R. Law, "In Search of a Marxist Perspective on Pre-colonial Tropical Africa", *Journal of African History*, vol. 19, no. 3 (1978).

J. Lonsdale, "States and Social Processes in Africa: A Historiographical Survey", *African Studies Review*, vol. 24, nos. 2/3 (June/Sept. 1981).

W. MacGaffey, "African History, Anthropology, and the Rationality of Natives", *History in Africa*, vol. 5 (1978).

————, "African Ideology and Belief: A Survey", *African Studies Review*, vol. 24, nos. 2/3 (June/Sept. 1981).

G.C.M. Mutiso, *Socio-Political Thought in African Literature* (London, Macmillan, 1974). This contains a good bibliography.

C. Neale, *Pride and Prejudice in African History: The Idea of Progress in the Revision of African History, 1960–1970* (unpublished D. Phil. thesis, University of Sussex).

Ngugi wa Thiong'o, *Petals of Blood* (London, Heinemann, 1977).

B. Ogot, "Some Approaches to African History", in ed. B. Ogot, *Hadith I* (Proceedings of the Annual Conference of the Historical Association of Kenya, 1967, Nairobi, East African Publishing House, 1968).

————, "Three Decades of Historical Studies in East Africa, 1949–1977", *Kenya Historical Review*, vol. 6, nos. 1/2 (1978).

D. Parkin, "Medicines and Men of Influence", *Man* N.S., vol. 3 (1968).

O. Patterson, "Rethinking Black History", *Harvard Educational Review*, vol. 41, no. 3 (1971).

C. Pieterse and D. Munro, *Protest and Conflict in African Literature* (London, Heinemann, 1964).

Ed. T.O. Ranger, *Emerging Themes of African History* (Nairobi, East African Publishing House, 1968).

————, "The 'New Historiography' in Dar es Salaam: An Answer", *African Affairs*, vol. 70, no. 280 (1971).

Eds. R. Rotberg and A. Mazrui, *Protest and Power in Black Africa* (London, Oxford University Press, 1970).

T.N. Tamuno, *History and History-Makers in Modern Nigeria* (an inaugural lecture delivered at the University of Ibadan, 25 Oct. 1973, Ibadan University Press, 1973).

A. Temu and B. Swai, *Historians and Africanist History: A Critique* (London, Zed Press, 1981).

I. Wallerstein, ''The Evolving Role of the Africa Scholar in African Studies'', *Canadian Journal of African Studies*, vol. 17, no. 2 (1983).

C.C. Wrigley, ''Historicism in Africa: Slavery and State Formation'', *African Affairs*, vol. 70, no. 279 (1971).

# INDEX

## About the Author

CAROLINE NEALE, formerly a teacher of history and English in Tanzania, now resides in Australia. She is the author of *Show Me English* and has contributed to *African Historiography*.